Conjectures &
Confrontations

Other Books by Robin Fox

The Keresan Bridge:
A Problem in Pueblo Ethnology

Kinship and Marriage:
An Anthropological Perspective

The Imperial Animal (with Lionel Tiger)

Encounter with Anthropology

Biosocial Anthropology (editor)

The Tory Islanders:
A People of the Celtic Fringe

The Red Lamp of Incest:
A Study in the Origins of Mind and Society

Neonate Cognition:
Beyond the Blooming Buzzing Confusion
(editor with Jacques Mehler)

The Violent Imagination

The Search for Society:
Quest for a Biosocial Science and Morality

Reproduction and Succession:
Studies in Anthropology, Law and Society

The Challenge of Anthropology:
Old Encounters and New Excursions

Conjectures & Confrontations

SCIENCE, EVOLUTION, SOCIAL CONCERN

ROBIN FOX

Routledge
Taylor & Francis Group

LONDON AND NEW YORK

First published 1997 by Transaction Publishers

Published 2017 by Routledge
2 Park Square, Milton Park, Abingdon, Oxon OX14 4RN
711 Third Avenue, New York, NY 10017

First issued in paperback 2017

Routledge is an imprint of the Taylor and Francis Group, an informa business

Copyright © 1997 by Taylor & Francis

Library of Congress Catalog Number: 96-47505

Library of Congress Cataloging-in-Publication Data

Fox, Robin, 1934–
    Conjectures and confrontations : science, evolution, social concern / Robin Fox.
        p. cm.
    Includes bibliographical references and index.
    ISBN 1-56000-286-7 (cloth : alk. paper)
    1. Anthropology—Philosophy. 2. Social sciences—Philosophy. 3. Social evolution—Philosophy. I. Title.
GN468.F69   1996
301'.01—dc20   96-47505
                                                                        CIP

ISBN 13: 978-1-138-50847-7 (pbk)
ISBN 13: 978-1-56000-286-4 (hbk)

To

Sir Raymond Firth

Sir Karl Popper

and all those teachers, colleagues,
and fellow students, who made the
old London School of Economics
such a transforming influence for
me and so many of my generation.

Contents

Preface

This is the third of a trilogy of books of essays that I rashly promised Irving Louis Horowitz of Transaction Publishers. (It is in fact the fourth of a series that began with *The Seach for Society,* [Rutgers University Press], 1989, and the fifth if we count the original *Encounter with Anthropology,* 1973, now reissued with Transaction, 1991.) The previous two, *Reproduction and Succession* (1993) and *The Challenge of Anthropology* (1994) contained both published and unpublished pieces, the latter often being items resurrected from the graveyard of abandoned *Festschriften.* As a consequence they ranged in time of writing from the late sixties to the near present. This volume is different: these are all published or commissioned pieces and they are no older than 1990. This is not to say they represent the very latest in what I *want* to write. I will probably only get around to that when I retire. No. They represent something more interesting perhaps because they were all pieces I was *asked* to write. Thus they are like a collection of term papers: I was in effect given a series of essay topics and asked to demonstrate how I would deal with them from my particular biosocial science perspective. "Discuss the apparent paradox that the more efficient bureaucracies become in meeting human needs the more effectively they frustrate those needs." Also, I am asked, presumably as a result of achieving near senescence, to write encyclopaedia entries and "state of the art" pieces more often than I would like. "Discuss the present state of the social sciences. To what extent do they reflect the state of society itself?" Particularly in an age when our students, and hence younger colleagues, seem not to be educated in the history of their subject, or in very much else for that matter, I suppose such obligations cannot be dodged. It is not altogether their fault. It is part of the general fragmentation and ideologization (may one say that?) of the social sciences about which I have already complained at length and to little effect. But it is also no secret that I have always tried to insist that an evolutionary perspective is ultimately the

ix

only one that will hold the fragments together, and the essays included herein are an attempt to show what that continues to mean to me.

Those in the first part are largely concerned with the first set of exam questions to do with the evolutionary perspective, and those in the second part are largely "state of the art" exercises. Since I have also expressed a number of ideas on both subjects and some others in various interviews, I have included two of these, in the French tradition of *entretiens avec*...These are more by way of oral examinations, and I guess are interesting if only because they show how someone with my orientation thinks on his feet when presented with a question. Of course, what you get here is several times removed editorially from the original, and a good deal was left on the cutting floor. Also, particularly with visual interviews, so much that could be conveyed by attitude, gesture, and body language, is not representable in print, so sometimes adjustments have to be made to clarify the meaning. (How do you *write* an expressive shrug accompanied by an ironic smile?) But the result is true to the original, even if it does make one sound more eloquent and coherent than one actually is. (But when faced with raw transcripts the editing is definitely necessary. I once had a talk transcribed in which I frequently used the phrase "the hammer drives the booms" and it was only the context which reminded me that what I was talking about were the hamadryas baboons.)

Also, ever since *Encounter with Anthropology*, I have included autobiographical comment along with the theoretical stuff, to give it some context and to illustrate how at least one social scientist has clung onto the roller coaster of current ideas. This has always been well received, somewhat to my surprise, perhaps because it gives some life to dem dry bones of social theory, as well as some comic relief. So the interviews here continue the tradition in another form. Purists may argue that these personal musings and opinions should be kept distinct from the real stuff. But the real stuff is always embedded in a real life and is both influenced by and influences it. The major issues of policy and living are also the major issues of the social sciences, and one cannot divorce one's own social existence from one's theories about it. This is not to say one cannot be objective, but that the subjective motives strongly influence one's decisions concerning what to be objective about (if you follow). I have framed the book between two halves of the interview from *Current Anthropology*, to show, symbolically, how a book (indeed all one's books) is enfolded in a life, and how it (they) should be read as an integral part of that life.

It may well be that those of us who buck the mainstream of a consensual paradigm have to be a particular kind of person. Future sociologists of knowledge and historians of ideas (should they still be interested in the real world) will therefore find some of the spade work done for them in my various books, including this one, since I have always sought to situate myself, as it appears we must inelegantly say these days. Also, the "confrontations" of the title are emanations and refractions of the "personal stuff." You cannot have a view of life and the world like mine and avoid them. My opposition to "political correctness" does, I think, have a direct connection with this *Weltanschauung*. I don't spell the connection out, but the reader can easily make it.

I make absolutely no apologies for being white, European, male, bourgeois, protestant (in a general sense), and heterosexual (in the same sense.) Fairly soon I will be a dead white male, and I see no point in apologizing for that either. So how come someone who so nicely fits the current mold of situated disapprobation has indeed bucked the mainstream for so many years, even though he has produced enough within it to show that he can, and to keep them listening? Somewhere I said that some people just have different drummers banging away in their cradles. But God forbid I should be accused of genetic determinism! Actually as far back as, I think, 1928, Robert Park insisted that the innovator was a "marginal man"—one who was a member of at least two cultures but committed wholly to neither. My own type was ruthlessly satirized by Tom Wolfe as his "transatlantic man"—but I have straddled more than national cultures, although I was born an Anglo-Irish mixture. I was brought up, don't forget, in the world of Lord Snow's famous "Two Cultures" and I have always had a foot in both the humanistic and the scientific camps. At the same time I have, starting from the social sciences, hitched onto various of the natural sciences with perhaps unbecoming enthusiasm. Anthropology itself is a strange "two culture" world, and those few like myself who still consider it a unified discipline, have to do their own balancing act. Thus, without asking for the distinction, one is forced to become a "marginal man." But, as I argue concerning bureaucracy, the real work is done anyway "in the interstices of the system" where we marginal types belong.

The rest is in the books and I will not belabor it here. Enough for the moment to say that the title is obviously a take on Karl Popper's *Conjectures and Refutations*, (1963) which had its deep influence on me as did all his works. His words to me as a student echo down the years: "Think what evidence there might be that would prove you wrong. If you cannot think of anything, then be highly suspicious of your theory!" All my attempts to remain true to science have been in fact a long Popperian echo, so it seemed a good thing to echo in my title, the title of his lively opus. It is meant as homage, not as hubris. But as the Greeks understood, we can know no man's virtue until he is dead. So I will refrain from further premature comment on my own coy professional modesty. Popper is included in my dedication, along with Raymond Firth and the "old" London School of Economics. People have queried that. I guess we all believe the alma mater of our youth was special and has gone downhill since. But if nothing else, the present LSE is six times bigger than its ancestor of the forties, fifties, and sixties, and the whole ambience of the place has changed from the little exclusive family that it was to yet another very good, but very big college. The "old" LSE was truly special, and it took a lot of raw youths like myself and made them feel special in turn, and thus have some intellectual courage and sense of confidence that we might never have gained elsewhere. Lord Dahrendorf in his magnificent history of the school calls the fifties "The Golden Age of Students." And indeed it was. There was a closeness of students and faculty (and what a faculty!) that would have been hard to duplicate elsewhere. The very scruffiness of the place in a curious way added to our sense of being different and being better: we were at the same time above worldly things and right in there mixing it in with the world. The world came to us, and we did our best for it. I think some of this spirit shines through what follows here.

So, although he will perhaps be surprised to hear it, does the influence of my other dedicatee, Sir Raymond Firth. His influence is more pervasive and more subtle. What he passed on to me was a respect for "Malinowskian" anthropology in the broadest sense: an anthropology dedicated to a wide and tolerant view of social science and its goals and methods. Firth, in the thirties, had actually asked Julian Huxley to his weekly seminar to discuss the ethological version of "ritualization," and when I was teaching at the LSE he helped me to involve people like John Napier in my classes to teach primatology and human evolution. He made a place in his graduate program for other people like David (now Sir David) Attenborough, who was—somewhat to my amazement as I look back on it—actually my supervisee for a year before he took off to run BBC 2. (I think I remember telling him he would regret this decision.)

Firth's concept of "social organization" as opposed to "social structure" was also congenial to my ethological approach. "Social structure" according to Firth was the model according to which we conceived our societies, "social organization" was the reality by which we lived them, with all its inconsistencies and compromises. My own notion of "living according to rules" as opposed to "living according to strategies" (as exemplified in my essay on "Principles and Pragmatics on Tory Island" for example—chapter 9 of *The Challenge of Anthropology*) is pure Firth. His "Principles of Social Organization" are in fact not only compatible with an ethological view of behavior, but have much to offer ethologists if they would pay attention to them. Behind all this however was the example of the man: his firm dedication to high standards that was tempered by a decency and humanity that I have always tried, not always successfully, to emulate. He is, in the true and good sense of the word, a gentleman. I here thank him for his ideas, and his example.

I have ended—and not just as a gesture to humanistic anthropology—with a "philosophical poem" dedicated to the memory of, and I hope in the style and spirit of, Matthew Arnold. It used to be that poets tackled the big issues, from Lucretius in his *De Rerum Natura* through Mandeville's *Fable of the Bees* and Pope's *Essay on Man* to Erasmus Darwin in his *Zoonomia*, and, yes, Matthew Arnold in, among others, *Empedocles on Etna*, and certainly Hardy in *The Dynasts*. And we mustn't forget Tennyson's *In Memoriam* since it did give us "Nature, red in tooth and claw," and continues to move Stephen Jay Gould to tears. (Personally, my own favorite lines of his on Nature are: "How careful of the type she seems,/ How careless of the single life." Tennyson was not to know that 99 percent of all species that ever existed have disappeared, so that in the long run She is pretty careless of types as well!) Of late, poets have largely eschewed this role, thus helping to widen the gap between the two cultures. And indeed most poets are so poorly informed these days that it is as well they leave it alone. But poetic commentary, insofar as it is poetic and is making a point and not just expressing emotions in irregular prose, is as much serious argument as prose opinion. It can be wrong. The world may not be as my shaman's vision sees it (and he is a successor to the Palaeolithic hunter with his vision of the Neolithic revolution—"What the Hunter Saw" in *The Violent Imagination*.) So dispute him, refute him; he is there, he will listen.

Acknowledgements

The people to thank here are mostly those who set me the exam topics and who offered me honest and useful criticism of my answers. In no particular order they are: Andrew Marshall, Michael Lind, Owen Harries, Irving Kristol, Joseph Carroll, Jane Lancaster, Larry Arnhart, Jonathan Benthall, Peter Ucko, Albert Sommers (RIP), Edie Turner, Norman Leavitt, Paul Gross, Alex Walter, Adam Kuper, and Richard Heffner. Among the many who gave me input were Lionel Tiger (and the members of the Department of Defense seminars, especially Stuart Kauffman), Donald Elliott, Peter Berger (and the other members of The Conference Board seminar), Barbara Ehrenreich, Frederick Turner, James Q. Wilson, Ashley Montagu, Susan Cashel, Robert Trivers, Howard Bloom, Robert Layton, Edwin Hartman, and Felix Browder. As always, Irving Louis Horowitz and Mary Curtis were the inspiration and support for the whole venture (their's once again is the title with its deliberate Popperian echo). The whole staff of Transaction Publishers made it all seem more like a family party than a business venture. Above all, deepest thanks to my editor, Laurence Mintz, not only for his dedicated work, but for his genuine love of the British composers which warmed my heart and stirred a gentle nostalgia for a time when they were everything to me. I dedicated *Reproduction and Succession* to my (then three) wonderful grandsons, Michael, Julian and John. Now I am delighted to add Christopher. It says something when a scholar becomes more interested in his grandsons than his work: something his theory can explain, perhaps, but nothing it can compete with.

The following journals and their editors, and associations and their officers, are thanked for their permission to reprint various previously published material: *Current Anthropology*, (The Wenner-Gren Foundation/University of Chicago Press); *Human Nature* (Aldine de Gruyter); The Conference Board; *Criminal Justice Ethics*, (John Jay College of Criminal Justice); *Anthropology Today*, (The Royal Anthropological

Insitute); The New York Academy of Sciences; *Anthropology and Humanism Quarterly*, (American Anthropological Association); *The National Interest*. I also thank Richard Heffner for permission to reprint the interview with him from "The Open Mind" (PBS).

Introduction: The Biosocial Orientation

> "Such an enquiry naturally involves consider-
> able risk. The person who ventures to follow his
> problem where it leads, regardless of the
> boundaries set by specialties, may well stumble
> into unfamiliar terrain. If our social-scientific
> studies, however, are to lead to a significant
> conception of man, more scholars must
> undertake this kind of risk."
>
> —Lewis S. Feuer, *The Scientific Intellectual*

Feuer was not talking about biosocial science as such—he was concerned that as a sociologist of knowledge he was having to delve into history and natural science—but his words directly apply. If you take a problem
like the incest taboo, as I did as far back as being an undergraduate in the
early 1950s, and "follow it where it leads," to use Feuer's words, then you
end up not only in sociology, anthropology, and psychology (where perhaps you belong by right of training), but in ethology, primatology,
palaeontology, history, epistemology, neurosciences, endocrinology, genetics
(Mendelian and population), zoology, and even jurisprudence. A more than
passing knowledge of classical literature doesn't hurt.

Most social scientists, like their other academic colleagues, are perhaps
naturally hesitant to go off on such an ambitious intellectual treasure hunt,
and one can hardly blame them. A good deal of the "theory" they indulge
in is in fact an elaborate rationalization for not doing so: a reaffirmation of
the "autonomy" of their subject. Also, it is truly hard mental work, and
there are easier ways to get promotions and merit raises. I remember when
I decided that I must learn genetics (in England in the mid-sixties), the only
efficient way to do it was through "programmed learning texts." These
were large volumes that took one through from the basic to the advanced
level by means of text followed by quizzes. If you passed the quiz you
could go on to the next piece of text; if not, you had start all over again. I

could of course have just read a textbook, but I wanted to be sure I had really learned it and the programmed learning route kept one honest. I did several examples going up to London on the suburban electric train in the morning, and several coming back at night, consuming a pipeful of Balkan Sobranie on each trip. (I worked through the Australian Aboriginal kinship systems in the same way. I think I mention this in one of the interviews.) I did this for two years: one year for each volume.

Multiply this kind of effort by several powers, and you have the sheer hard work of mastering knowledge in a variety of non-social science subjects. I don't mean to be hard on my colleagues, but most of them were simply appalled at the idea of all this effort. They thought me quite mad and told me firmly that I didn't "need" to do all this frenetic downloading of what to them was extraneous information. But if I was to follow the genetic arguments about inbreeding so essential to understanding the famous taboo, then what was I to do? My colleagues couldn't understand why I just didn't stand pat with Durkheim and deny the relevance of such stuff to the explanation of "social facts" (which can only be explained by other social facts, as we all know.) I tried to point out that in the natural sciences such a stance had long ago become untenable. All biology was based on chemistry, all chemistry on physics, and all physics on mathematics. Most of the work now was precicsely in the areas of overlap that were "disciplines" in themselves: biochemistry, physical chemistry, mathematical physics, and so on. Insofar as we were biological creatures it was idiotic—to me at least—to put up these barriers between the social and biological. The social *was* biological—what else could it be? From where else could our sociality have been derived but its origins in biological evolution? And what sense did it make to shut ourselves off from the most powerful theory existing for the "explanation" of "social facts?" or any other facts that were the property of living creatures: the Darwinian theory of evolution by means of natural selection (with its modern modifications of course.)

Back then I was told that it was because Man (we still said that, and with a capital letter) had "culture" and that this made him totally different from the all other living things. Well, I quickly disposed of *that* creationist argument (with Lionel Tiger in "The Zoological Perspective in Social Science" in 1966, and in my own "The Cultural Animal" written in 1968), and am no more enamoured of the latest version which has surfaced as "social constructionism." Why, I keep nagging, do we construct the worlds we do and not some others? There are, if the premise is correct, infinite possibilities. So where are they? Only in the realms of science fiction it seems, and even there, alien societies have to be "constructed" always with reference to human models or we would not be able to understand them.

Language, cognition, categories, dispositions, and motives are everywhere recognizably "human." The details of course differ, but all those years ago I suggested that to become obsessed with the differences as opposed to the basic forms (or central tendencies if we want to be less Platonic) was to suffer from "ethnographic dazzle." I have dealt at length, for example, with the many differences between kinship systems. Indeed my book published in 1967 *Kinship and Marriage* is still in print in many languages and still the basic text on these differences. But find me a society *without* a kinship system, and without one that operates on the six basic parameters I outlined in "Kinship Systems as Natural Systems" in 1979. Such societies do not exist. Even the most daring of science fiction writers have not figured out how to "construct" them, and some of the best, like Frank Herbert, positively revel in the implications of them. This being so the question becomes not whether or not we "socially construct" the kinship systems we have, but why we construct the limited number of types we do out of all the possible types. And one cannot ignore the possibility that such construction is one of our adapted cognitive predispositions. At least, to be good Popperians, we have to treat it as a hypothesis that must be open to serious test, and search for its possible refutability. And as good scientists in the Western tradition we might have to invoke Occam's razor and not multiply our explanatory concepts beyond the least necessary—especially when we find, as I did my "Primate Kin and Human Kinship" (1975) that all the ingredients of human kinship systems (except the linguistic) were there in the kinship behavior of our primate relatives.

But one faces a curious reluctance in the social sciences to accept simple explanations. They seem suspect—too easy; they must be "reductionist" (which, incidentally, any natural scientist would applaud). There is a strong tendency towards what the medieval logicians would have called *ignotum per ignotius*—the use of explanations that are more obscure than the thing to be explained.

The history of "explanations" of the incest taboo is replete with such, and I had to cut through them to some simple basics as early as 1962

("Sibling Incest") with a "law" as elemental as "The intensity of hetero-sexual attraction between co-socialized adults after puberty will be in-versely proportionate to the intensity of physical contact between them before puberty." It is true that to *get to* the simple explanation one has often to take elaborate detours through a lot of material, as in *The Red Lamp of Incest* (1980), but in the end, if we are indeed dealing with adaptative behavior, then the resultant formulation will be simple and indeed a "reduction" to a basic algorithm, as we have learned to call them by computer analogy. "Programed learning" (the program having lost its French -me suffix) has taken on a meaning far deeper than I could have envisaged in that stuffy, damp, smoke-filled railway carriage, ply-ing between Waterloo Station and Kingston-upon-Thames some thirty long years ago.

All this has been hashed and rehashed many times, and it is not my intention here to give a full history of the "biosocial movement" in the social sciences but simply to set the scene for these essays, especially for those younger readers (and, alas, a lot of their older colleagues) who either take its present establishment for granted, or more likely, are scarcely aware that it is there except when some ideological cause célèbre brings it to their passing attention. Ideally they should have read all my previ-ous books, or for that matter any one of them, in which case this intro-duction would be unnecessary. But there are now, post-baby boom, so many books and so many audiences that it is no longer possible, as it was in my younger days, to assume anyone has read anything. So this is a welcome to the world of the unread.

These unlettered colleagues may well be a bit confused because they have come to know the field as "sociobiology" after the word coined by E. O. Wilson in his famous text of that name (1975). Indeed many of them, if they comment at all, confidently date the movement from Wilson's book. But Wilson was a product of a distinct strain in evolutionary popu-lation genetics and was working within that paradigm, and although he addressed himself, at the very end of his book, to a few topics of human social behavior (drawing, incidentally, on a lot of my own previous work), he was not a social scientist addressing social scientists; indeed he had very little idea of the concerns of social scientists, which was part of the problem with their largely adverse reaction to his work.

The "biosocial movement" proper, on the other hand, can perhaps be dated to the paper by Tiger and me already cited (1966). (For a fuller account see my entry "Sociobiology" in A. and J. Kuper, eds., *The Social Science Encyclopedia*, 2nd. ed., London: Routledge, 1996.) We, and those who shared our concern to return the social sciences to the evolutionary fold, were not working with any specific theory of, for example, evolutionary genetics, although we were happy to assimilate the insights of these scientists. I invited their leading theorist, William Hamilton, to contribute to the 1974 symposium that led to my *Biosocial Anthropology*, which also came out in 1975. We were if anything more influenced by the work of the European "ethologists"—Lorenz, Tinbergen, etc., and the burgeoning subdiscipline of primatology (Washburn, Hall, etc.) itself drawing workers from both anthropology and zoology proper, and by the rise of transformational grammar under Chomsky. We were primarily concerned, not with pushing any one theory, but with a general reorientation of the social sciences in the direction of considering *all* theories about the evolution of social behavior. That is why I have called this introduction "The Biosocial Orientation."

Those of us who grew up in the social sciences of the fifties, were all much influenced by the great Robert Merton. However much we might eventually come to disagree with his version of Functionalism, we were all spurred on to think deeply about the issues about which he wrote so elegantly in, for example, *Social Theory and Social Structure*. (We loved his insistence, directed at his sociological colleagues and perhaps especially those from Harvard, that "no scientific virtue inheres in bad writing.") One of his most telling criticisms of contemporary social science was that most of what it paraded as "theory" was nothing of the kind: it did not measure up in any way to what science demanded of a theory for example. It was, in fact, he said, not "social theory" but "social orientation." A lot of this consisted of arguments for the autonomy of sociology that I have already mentioned, but in general it concerned itself with setting out programs for what sociologists "ought" to be doing and how they ought to be doing it. It was thus closer to moral prescriptions than scientific theory. We took the point, but chose to make a virtue of what he thought a fault. We saw ourselves indeed as engaged in a preliminary exercise: the reorientation of the social sciences in the direction of a paradigm (as we learned to call it) of the evolution of social behavior. Our major efforts, therefore, were directed at showing that there were plausible evolutionary explanations—of various kinds—for social facts like incest avoidance, or male bonding. We looked at the work of the population geneticists like Hamilton and were intrigued by the idea that there could be an explanation for things that Darwin could not explain, like "altruistic" behavior, including the sacrifice of their immediate reproductive fitness by various "castes" in insect societies. But we were equally impressed by, for example, the discovery of various physiological correlates with behavior as in aggression and testosterone, or dominance and serotonin, or pleasure and endorphins. (In pursuit of these endocrinological bases of social behavior—plus a heavy dose of neurosciences—I spent an academic year of intense learning at Stanford Medical School. I have a diploma to prove it.)

We moved all over the biological landscape in looking for clues to the evolution of behavior. Our major concern was simply to get them looked at, to erect hypotheses, and to figure out how to test these. At this stage we had little notion how to achieve this end except by, to use the jargon of the time, "accounting for more of the variance" than purely cultural (or constructionist) theories could do, plus, of course, our perennial appeal to Brother Occam. We spent a lot of time fighting off accusations of "genetic determinism" or "Social Darwinism" and the like, which were in turn mostly politically or ideologically inspired rather than seriously scientific. I wish I had the time back that was wasted on that silly issue.

At the same time, to be totally honest, a lot of the speculation that went on in the name of evolution was itself pretty wild and woolly—and continues to be. This goes with the territory. I can only say that it is no wilder than most of the stuff emanating from the present denizens of constructionism and deconstruction and the like. And it at least has the potential of giving rise to testable hypotheses. I am therefore prepared to give it the benefit of the doubt, even when I am very doubtful: just look at the plethora of "explanations" of the female orgasm. Where will it end? If they are all true, it is inconceivable that nature would go to such extraordinary lengths to ensure the reproductive job gets done that gets done very well *without* orgasm in all other sexually reproducing creatures, or why the net reproductive rate seems to be highest in those societies where female orgasms are least likely to occur! But let them roll out the scenarios and the correlations. As I have insisted, what we wanted to achieve was an *orientation*: we wanted these kinds of questions at least to be *asked*. Don't forget, when we started, the social scientists were mostly not asking them at all. They had in the past, certainly, but that kind of retrograde thinking had been unceremoniously dumped by the enlightened ones.

Again, I do not want to re-walk the well-trodden paths of this history. I am trying to explain where these essays are "coming from." And they are not coming from "sociobiology" *sensu strictu*, but only in its much broader meaning as the general science of social behavior. The "biosocial movement" (and Tiger coined "biosociology" before Wilson's neologism swept the board) was always eclectic in its dealings with the natural sciences, and never assumed that all social behavior could be subsumed under the formulae of evolutionary genetics per se, however much it valued this contribution to the study of ultimate mechanisms. It was just as concerned with the demonstration of proximate mechanisms even if their ultimate explanation (i.e., the original reason for their selective success) was lost in the proverbial mists of time. They would not be there (the physiological correlates for example—as in Tiger's relation of endorphins to optimism and all its social consequences) if they had not been selected at some point.

Our social behavior is, strangely, the record of its own evolution: it is what it is because it is the end process of that evolution, and one of our mantras was "the best evidence for the evolution of human behavior is human behavior." I, taking my cue from Freud, converted this into "we constantly reproduce that which produced us." In the same way that our anatomy and physiology are the record of our physical evolution, our behavior is the record of our behavioral evolution, and our social behavioral evolution at that. This was the "message" of Tiger and Fox in *The Imperial Animal* in 1971. Much has been learned since then, but the basics have not changed. We originally were going to call the book "The Evolution of Human Social Behavior" but our publishers saw the potential audience disappearing behind a collective yawn and insisted on a snappier title. We should perhaps have used the original as a subtitle, but that was not how it was done in those days. But the evolution of behavior was the focus and is the focus if behavior is interpreted in its widest sense (which would include linguistic and cognitive "behavior" for instance.)

Behavior, according to the Nobel Prize-winning geneticist, Jacques Monod, even when acquired through experience, is "acquired according to a programme," and that programme (we have regained the -me) "will follow a certain preestablished pattern defined in the species' genetic patrimony." (*Chance and Necessity*). We were, and have been, looking for any clues to that programme, and for its relation to the environmental input necessary for its realization. For one of the great things ethology taught us was that there is a defined behavioral "output" exquisitely timed to the life cycle, but this output assumes a defined "input" from the environment. These inputs were usually called "releasers" by the ethologists: they elicited the necessary behavior at the necessary time. Thus the output of the infant (complicated and rich and far from a blooming, buzzing confusion, as Jacques Mehler and I tried to show in *Neonate Cognition*, 1985) assumes the environment of "maternal care"—the basis of Bowlby's synthesis of ethology and psychoanalysis, and the startling outcome of the famous Harlow experiments with maternal deprivation in monkeys. This all led me to redefine "instinct" (that much abused word) as "the organism's demand for appropriate environmental input." This is why we were so impressed by the "ease of learning" hypothesis that also hailed from the ethologists: the major clue to those features of behavior that were "hard wired" was the relative ease with which they were learned—language very easy: toilet training very hard. So much for the bugaboo of genetic determinism! And yet to this day I am still picking up articles from unreconstructed behaviorists who are still insisting on the simpleminded dichotomy that has ruined so much decent debate: that it is "learning" and not "genes" that determines behavior. Also, after thirty years of evidence and argument to the contrary, this still seems to be the "either/or" thinking of the ordinary citizen and especially the editors and talk-show hosts. "Are we the slaves of our genes?" thundered a recent front cover of a magazine issue that featured an interview with Tiger and Fox. "Is prejudice hereditary?" clamored a headline of a review of one of my books in the *New York Times*. Well, as they say in Ireland, there seems to be no help for it.

But as the classic deprivation experiments in ethology showed, behavior was selected for in a particular environment, and that environment was indeed "assumed" by the organism. This assumed context for behavior later came to be known as the "environment of evolutionary adaptedness" or EEA. In other words, the environment in which evolved any particular behavioral pattern whose output was recorded in the genome. But this raised the possibility of another interesting approach to recent social behavior (that is, behavior over the past 12,000 years or so of the present interglacial period): to what extent were the environments that our species "constructed" over this period compatible with the EEA of the species? The major adaptations that produced modern man, excluding those he inherited from his primate ancestry (binocular color vision, for example) occurred during the Pleistocene, and particularly the Upper Palaeolithic. From *Homo erectus* on (since about two million years ago that is), we made our major strides forward into the form we have—physically and behaviorally—today. And the social environment—the behavioral EEA—was that of the small nomadic hunting and gathering band.

The bewildering swiftness, in evolutionary terms, of the changes over the past few thousand years, have all but obliterated that environment and replaced it with a series of contexts, largely derived from huge population numbers, which are, to put it neutrally, at least very different from those in which our behavioral, cognitive, and emotional predispositions evolved. To what extent then can we still "construct" social worlds that are designed as templates for the "species' genetic patrimony?" Or are we suffering from what I chose to call "Consciousness out of Context" (1989)? This matters for social science because of the assumption of "social pathology" in so much of our behavior.

This assumption of pathology depends of course on what one first establishes as "normal." Too much of this is simply taken for granted. Thus the "nuclear family" is assumed to be "normal" and its "breakdown" a "pathology." (Forgive the flurry of scare quotes; it goes with the uncertain territory.) But why do we assume it to be normal? What if evolutionary science can show that it is not part of the EEA? Then what we may be witnessing is not a pathology at all, but a struggle of the "normal" EEA context of extended kinship groups to reassert itself in new forms. Think of other so-called pathologies—teenage pregnancy "epidemics" for example, or the retreat from literacy, or the formation of inner-city gangs. Are these pathologies or again are they more like a social antibody system that is in fact seeking to repair the pathological situation brought about by modern industrial society? A lot of what follows in this book will be concerned with issues of this kind, including the search for genuine pathologies: for those items of social structure totally inimical to the Upper Palaeolithic animal that we are. (I have put the essay on bureaucracy first since it jumps right into this issue.)

Invoking "behavioral plasticity" will not save us. Total behavioral plasticity is a chimera and would never have evolved in competition with "domain specific algorithms" as any evolutionary geneticist can elegantly demonstrate if you are willing to follow the math. A totally "plastic" animal would simply not have known what to do, and could not be guaranteed to learn what was necessary either in time or at the right time (language is the supreme example, incest avoidance is another good one.) It would have been in a state of flip-flop helplessness most of the time and gone down in the reproductive struggle to those organisms more definitively programmed. I paraphrase the stricter demonstration, but that is the sum of it.

A recent trend in the movement (we love to give ourselves names—now where did that come from?) calling itself "Evolutionary Psychology" is in the process of amassing evidence on the specificity of our mental functions and their relation to the EEA context—something I too argued for in "The Evolution of Mind" in the early 1970s. In the early days of ethological influences we were largely concerned with the emotions, their evolution and function (hence our excitement over the discoveries of the properties of the limbic system in the brain.) But now the field has properly shifted to human cognitive abilities—so long regarded by the special creationists of the social sciences as the ultimate mark of our irreducable uniqueness. And this shift helps us to raise the same question with mental functions as with emotional ones: to what extent are we providing "appropriate" input? The results are going to be an embarrassment to those who are convinced that we can provide any environment we choose to "construct"—which would be funny if it were not also so potentially tragic.

But here I am overstepping the Popperian bounds and becoming assertive rather than hypothetical and conjectural purely. Yes, it *is* all conjectural. And a good deal of what follows in this rather freewheeling book is frankly speculative and on the edge. Writing largely for a general audience I have not felt too constrained by conventions of academic caution and have allowed myself a greater latitutde in the speculative direction. But what the master taught us was that conjecture was the very soul of science. Without it there would be no science. What matters is how we *test* the conjectures and above all whether they are open to refutation. "Think what evidence there might be that would prove you wrong." Well, I'm happy to say, I could be wrong about everything that follows! For the sake of keeping the reader awake, I write more assertively than I should. If we constantly harp on the conjectural nature of the hypothesis, then the reader is likely to get nervous and give up. So it must be assumed in all that is written here. If these are my answers to the exam questions (those that concern substance and not state of the art) and you think they are the wrong ones, then come up with the evidence that will refute them in their specificity and show how it does so. I will be happy to go back to the drawing board with you. But it is no longer any use to hurl insults, or to be loftily dismissive, or mutter Durkheimian (or Derridarian) incantations. There is just too much reality out there, and it won't let us ignore it.

Interview

An Accidental Life I

with Alex Walter

When Adam Kuper—professor of anthropology at Brunel University (U.K.)—was still editor of the international journal Current Anthropology, *he instituted a series of interviews with some of the elder statesmen of the discipline—Claude Lévi-Strauss, Clifford Geertz, Ernest Gellner, and so on. His idea was to get them to talk freely about their "life and times" and he was particularly interested in the people and ideas that had influenced them. Kuper is one of our better historians of the subject, and these fascinating dialogues will remain one of his better ideas for preserving "contemporary history." In his very last issue as editor, he reserved space for an interview with me, which was surprising since I am one of the younger elder statesmen and had not thought I was quite ready to summarize my own "life and times." But since I had been the anthropologist most actively involved for the longest time with the "biosocial movement" he reckoned I should have my place. Alex Walter is one of the very best graduate students I have ever had (and is consequently finding it difficult to get a job), and he kindly undertook to be the straight man. But the questions are entirely his, and I took them as they came.* Current Anthropology *requested a picture of me "in the field", and since I had studied the* corrida *in Colombia, I sent one of me (taken by Lionel Tiger) doing some cape work with a bull. I thought it would be a bit more lively than the usual "anthropologist outside his tent" stuff. The editorial staff panicked however, and suffered visions of picketing from the animal rights activists and the like. So I sent them a picture of me with a shotgun—ready actually to do nothing worse than blast skeets out of the sky—which they published, but with misgivings. I only tell this story in anticipation of the "PC" interview later on.*

WALTER: How did you come to be interested in anthropology in the first place?

FOX: As is usual with everything that has happened in my life, it occurred quite by accident. In retrospect, one's life might appear as a nice plan, but in fact I've more or less backed into or stumbled into everything I've done professionally and personally. Anthropology was no different. It was a series of accidents, really.

WALTER: Was there anything in your family background that led you to anthropology?

FOX: Initially I had a very settled and happy childhood in the Pennines of West Yorkshire in the 1930s. My father had been in the Indian army since he was a young man, serving on the Northwest Frontier. He loved that life and regaled me with detailed stories of it. He left India in 1932 to marry my mother. She was from a mixed Catholic-Protestant Irish family that had settled in South Yorkshire. So I started with this mixed inheritance, and it led to a curiosity for all things Indian and Irish. I could count up to ten in both Hindi and Urdu. I was simultaneously fascinated by our local celebrities, the Brontës, who were, of course, the children of an Irish immigrant themselves. I guess this was my introduction to the comparative method.

WALTER: Did anything you learned in school during this time influence you later to become an anthropologist?

FOX: I wasn't in school for most of the war; the schools were closed or being used for other purposes. I learned by reading—the libraries were open—and by listening to the BBC. School was something new that I had to cope with after the war. It was another tribe with strange customs, as was the city in which I lived. I was a country boy. So I was very early sensitized to quite marked cultural differences, and this aroused my curiosity about them .

WALTER: Did anything in your studies further this interest?

FOX: I got interested in Frazer (1911–15) through reading T. S. Eliot, and when I went on to reading Frazer himself I became fascinated by the descriptions of exotic customs and such, but I frankly did not think too much of taking it up at the time. Before that, when doing classics, that is, Latin and Greek, I had been very interested in archaeology and ancient civilizations, and my mother had given me H. G. Wells's *Outline of History* (1951) as a present. I remember being astonished with a history that started with the origins of life on earth—but none of it prompted me to want to do anthropology or archaeology specifically later at the university.

WALTER: Did you first become interested in anthropology at the London School of Economics?

Fox: Actually, I went to the LSE to do economics, initially because I was interested in politics—I was a card-carrying young conservative—and I wanted to get ammunition to use against socialism, but during my first year, in 1953, I got tired of economics. I did not think it had the answers to very much. I was interested in general questions about human behavior, and economics wasn't telling me anything. I still think its vision of man is dry and restrictive, almost a caricature, and this is why economists can't predict a damn thing or tell us anything sensible about the economy. So I read through the LSE catalog and decided I wanted to do sociology instead. I went to see T. H. Marshall, who with Morris Ginsberg was in charge of sociology then. You had to pick a special subject within sociology to major in, and looking down the list, criminology and social psychology and social statistics looked kind of forbidding, but there was social anthropology sitting there, and I thought, "Social anthropology. Ah, Frazer! Strange customs, weird people, and distant lands, that sort of fun stuff." So I decided I would change to sociology and do the social anthropology specialization. Marshall sent me across to see Maurice Freedman, who was then at the LSE, before he moved to Oxford, and Freedman said to me, "Why do you want to do social anthropology?", and I said, "I read the abridged edition of *The Golden Bough,*" and he laughed heartily and said, "Well, don't imagine you're going to be doing any of *that* kind of thing," and he thrust a copy of Radcliffe-Brown's *Structure and Function in Primitive Society* (1952) at me and said, "Go learn that by heart. That's what you are going to be doing. You're not going to be doing anything about Sir James Frazer." This upset me considerably, but I stuck to it, and that's how I got into social anthropology.

WALTER: Did you have a thorough grounding in anthropology as an undergraduate?

Fox: It actually was only a small part of the sociology degree. I think out of eleven papers it was three that you did in anthropology, including one special ethnographic area.

WALTER: Did you pick North America as your special area? Eventually you did research on the Pueblo Indians there.

Fox: No. I picked South Africa because it was taught by Isaac Shapera, who was easily the most systematic lecturer. It wasn't picked out of any particular interest in things African or South African (although I liked the Zulu and the Lovedu) but for the purely pragmatic reason that he was such a well-organized lecturer, and it was well known that his examinations consisted in your giving well-organized answers to his well-organized questions. As long as you did the work, it was a fail-safe kind of area. It was easily the most popular for that reason with students.

WALTER: But you did choose to pursue anthropology at the graduate level?

FOX: I never intended to go on into anthropology at the graduate level at all. In fact, Ginsberg saw sociology as a branch of social philosophy, and social philosophy and moral philosophy were two of the most important papers in the sociology degree, and these were the two that I enjoyed the most and did the most work at.

WALTER: At this time you were actually leaning towards philosophy more than anthropology?

FOX: Yes. Ernest Gellner came with his assault on Wittgenstein and began teaching ethics, and, of course, the LSE had such fantastic people as Popper and Oakeshott and then Ayer was at University College. I was fascinated and read through most of the major philosophers, certainly all the British empiricists and utilitarians, as well as Spinoza, Descartes, Kant, and Leibniz and the Greek philosophers, and hence got a sound philosophical education. Also, Donald Macrae taught social philosophy and did everything from Plato to Toynbee, and Tom Bottomore gave us basic Marx.

WALTER: What kind of lasting influence did the philosophers at the LSE leave on your thinking?

FOX: From Gellner I picked up a stern antirelativism which stuck. I obviously liked the "piecemeal social engineering" concept of Popper, and I also liked the conservative organicism of Oakeshott, and Ginsberg's ideal of a rational ethic. But Ayer had the most initial influence, I think. I read *Language, Truth, and Logic* (1954) and the world changed for me virtually overnight. Between the logical positivists and their "principle of verification" and Popper and his "principle of refutation," I think I managed to pick up a devotion to the idea of science and scientific method as the one road to truth. That has stuck—at least in principle. Bertrand Russell was another big influence, and although he was not a teacher he was the honorary president of the LSE Rationalist Society, of which I was secretary. We had time to talk a few times, and I added him to my list of culture heroes.

WALTER: Why didn't you stay in England and study philosophy?

FOX: I wanted to, but I came to an awkward moment, because at that time in Britain they still had the draft: "national service" as it was called. Now, I was not a pacifist; I had no particular moral objections to being in the army (it was my father's profession, after all), but it was highly inconvenient at that point. I didn't particularly want to go and get shot in Suez or Cyprus. It seemed a sort of pointless way to end one's existence, since we were going to have to give these places up anyway. It just seemed to me to be ridiculous. But at that time you could get (as you could in America later) deferments for higher education, and I decided to get my deferment at a large distance from the draft boards in England and go to America.

WALTER: Did you at that time decide to go to Harvard to study at the Department of Social Relations?

FOX: Not quite. I had been put on to this idea by various American professors, of whom there were plenty at the LSE. Dave Schneider was one. Norman Birnbaum, in sociology, was another, and they both said, "Go to Harvard and do sociology or anthropology," but I really was dead keen on becoming a philosopher. So I applied to Cornell, and indeed had been accepted and promised a teaching assistantship with Max Black and Norman Malcolm, to do a thesis on the freedom of the will. (I had already actually started it!) But to please these other people, and Raymond Firth also, who had contacts with Harvard, I also applied to Harvard as a kind of backup, and eventually, literally at the last moment, as I was about to board the *Queen Mary* or whatever it was, one of those big ships with three funnels, Cornell reneged. I got a telegram saying, "Please come to our graduate school, but we have no more funds for assistantships." I was left high and dry, whereas Harvard had promised me two nice fat little scholarships in the Department of Social Relations. I just changed all my tickets from Ithaca, New York, to Cambridge, Mass., and again, entirely as plan B, I ended up at Harvard.

WALTER: Did you know what you wanted to do when you got there?

FOX: People such as Talcott Parsons, George Homans, Clyde Kluckhohn, and Gordon Allport were there, to say nothing of Skinner in psychology, so I thought it wouldn't be a bad place to be, but I hadn't paid much attention to how they were organized or what they wanted. It came as a great shock to me, in fact, when I got there. I had rather the British idea of graduate studies on my mind. The joke in England is that the ideal Ph.D. student is the one who comes in twice: once with his proposal and then three years later with his thesis. I wasn't at all used to doing courses all the time, constantly having exams for which you learned everything and learned nothing at the same time because you were too damn busy to take in very much. Also, the Department of Social Relations was a very weird affair. It was created under the inspiration of Parsons's theory of action, and it was divided up into the four areas that corresponded roughly to his quadripartite division of the social sciences: sociology, social anthropology, social psychology, and clinical psychology. You had to pass exams in all four areas, which included everything from the theory of social action to interpreting Rorschach tests, to culture and personality, to pushing buttons in small-group experimental sessions, and so on. But they also had a real problem, because no other university in America had followed Parsons's model; this was a purely Harvard thing. So the people coming out with Ph.D.'s in social relations had to go and teach as either clinical psychologists or social anthropologists or whatever. People who just had degrees in social relations had a hard time getting jobs. You not only had to do the four divisions, then, but you had to do all the other material that went along with making you a fully qualified, say, anthropologist. It was consequently hair-raising; it was a bombardment of material. I learned an enormous amount about an awful lot of things, some of which I've forgotten, some of which I've retained. I audited Skinner's courses on pigeons, I did Whiting's courses on socialization and personality, I ran rats, I interpreted Rorschach tests, and I sat with Bales in his little booth and pushed buttons in his small-group interaction process analysis sessions. You name it, we did it. We did complicated nonparametric-statistics courses. All these things were being done at the same time, and it was really bewildering.

WALTER: Did you ever think of quitting?

FOX: Now I don't know what I might have done. Again the decision was taken for me, because I think I might just have stayed there another year or so and then decided I'd had enough of it and gone home, as it were, or tried to go to Cornell and become a real philosopher. But because I had elected to do the social anthropology option as my specialization, I had to do at least nine months' fieldwork. Since I was only on a Fulbright travel visa to the United States, I tried to fit this in on vacations. I was very lucky in having a very kind advisor in Evon Vogt, who introduced me to Charles Lange, who was working in New Mexico on the Cochiti tribe. He agreed to get me into the Pueblo, so I spent as much time as possible reading everything I could find on Cochiti and the Pueblos—which wasn't difficult in the Peabody Museum library; it had everything, Boas's Keresan texts, and so on. I spent a lot of time with those texts.

WALTER: Was there any reason for concentrating on the texts ?

Fox: I had become very interested in linguistics, at first through Kluckhohn's work on Navaho and then through Paul Friedrich and Dell Hymes, who had both come in as lowly instructors and were therefore thrown in with the graduate students. Linguistics was the only thing out of all of this maelstrom of activity that really fired my imagination. I decided I wanted to do linguistics, so I thought I could easily go for three summers to Cochiti and do something on morphophonemes or the things that we were all hot on then, particularly the Sapir-Whorf hypothesis and Kenneth Pike's integrative approach. Actually, they wanted me to join the now-forgotten Values Study, but I regarded this as largely a semantic exercise, and eventually the idea was dropped.

WALTER: You weren't interested in culture-and-personality studies at the time?

Fox: Not at that point. It was after the first year when this interest arose, and during the first year I was too busy doing all their required courses in clinical and social psychology. I hadn't done much on culture and personality at that point, except a little with Kluckhohn.

WALTER: So you were all set to become a Southwest Amerindian specialist with an emphasis in linguistics?

Fox: Yes. I went off to Cochiti and spent three months there. This was straight out of D. H. Lawrence for me; I was plunged down among the mesas and the pine trees and the desert Southwest, and these marvelous Indians, living in their pueblos doing their dances, and suddenly things that had just been abstractions to me, such as matrilineal clans, became real living things that mattered desperately to people. I actually saw exogamy in action! Kluckhohn took me around the Navaho reservation. I was fascinated. I saw, in the Rio Grande Pueblos, people who organized society in moieties. These had been simply terms in textbooks. Here I was living amongst them and learning the language as best I could. I actually fell in love with the culture and desperately wanted to go back again. So when I went back to Harvard for the second year, 1958, I was hooked. I wanted very much to go back to Cochiti, so I really had to define myself as an anthropologist and give up the renegade philosopher act.

WALTER: Then your decision to become an anthropologist was the result of your hands-on experience with fieldwork?

FOX: Not entirely. I also had to live, and the only place that would give me money for the second year was the Laboratory of Human Development. This was run by John Whiting, who was then in the School of Education. He wanted some students essentially to read ethnographic monographs and code them for his cross-cultural stuff. Now, that seemed to me to be very good, because it was a way of reading a hell of a lot of anthropology and getting paid to do it. You sat there and read through these ancient ethnographies, "Behind Mud Walls," and so on, and you coded according to whether toilet training was severe or not-so-severe or nonexistent or whatever, and all these codings eventually ended up in cross-cultural comparisons. I wasn't interested in the cross-cultural comparisons; I was interested in the ethnographic stuff, but I became fascinated with what was being done in the lab and in fact spent most of that second year with Whiting reading Freud and the behaviorists and that curious attempt to synthesize the two that came out of Yale with Miller and Dollard.

WALTER: Was it when you were working with Whiting during that second year that you became interested in the incest issue and did the research for your paper "Sibling Incest" (1962)?

FOX: It was during that year that I actually really developed it, but it started as an undergraduate essay for Maurice Freedman, who was a marvelous, marvelous teacher, much underestimated. People thought that he was very rigid, but when you got behind that you found he was immensely fair, very kind, and very interesting. He had thrown out a lot of ideas to me about a lot of things, including incest. I had written a standard essay on the incest taboo my first year as an undergraduate. In a subsequent year he gave me Jack Goody's paper on incest, and I first began to pick up on this conflict between Westermarck and Freud and also, of course, the whole Malinowski-Jones debate over the Oedipus complex and the Trobriand Islanders, but I hadn't got the ideas very well formulated yet. Strangely enough, the idea actually got formulated in a paper I did for a sociology course with Robert Bales. This incest stuff wasn't small-group sociology, but I told him about these things, and he suggested that I see if I could come up with some sort of law of interaction that would explain all this. Whiting also became absolutely fascinated with this and had notions of his own. That is when I put it together as a paper and first invented terms like the "Westermarck effect" and the "Freud effect," trying to show why these two were not incompatible but were talking about complementary conditions and situations. I formulated my law in terms of secondary reinforcement, since that was the big cry of the day. If you couldn't find secondary reinforcement you hadn't found a cause for the behavior in question, so I had to look for one, and it was phrased in that interactionist language which I had learned from Bales.

WALTER: But you didn't utilize any of Whiting's cross-cultural statistical method?

FOX: In fact I did. There was a whole second part of that paper which eventually got lost. I went through all this cross-cultural data from the Human Relations Area Files on whether incest taboos were stricter in herders and pastoralists or people on small islands and whether brother-sister taboos were stronger in some places and circumstances than in others, and so on. I got some very interesting correlations. I took these back with me to England, and Donald Macrae, who was then editor of the *British Journal of Sociology,* got very interested in this and asked for the theoretical part for the *BJS.* Of course, I wanted him to include my cross-cultural data as the second part, but he didn't want to do that. He was only interested in the theoretical stuff, which did, of course, have ethnographic examples. Macrae enjoyed ethnographic examples, but he was very, very skeptical of the whole HRAF thing. As far as he was concerned, it was based on deep methodological and philosophical errors which everybody who had read Galton's critique of Tylor's original paper should know. In his opinion, Murdock had done us all a great disservice by reviving it, so he was not really interested, and somewhere along the way the whole second half of the paper got lost along with all the original little file cards which had all the information. But the first part *was* published, and it drew two people into my network, Arthur Wolf and Joseph Shepher, who were both to make significant contributions to the study of inbreeding avoidance later on.

WALTER: Was it out of this research on incest that you developed an interest in ethology?

FOX: Yes. I hadn't been interested in it at all at Harvard. I remember that there had been one character from Oxford who spent a year there who was a student of Tinbergen and was therefore scornfully referred to by all my peers and associates as "one of those neo-instinctivists from Oxford." I more or less parroted the orthodoxy on this at the time.

WALTER: You never finished your studies at Harvard. You went back to England. Why?

FOX: I was caught in a visa trap. I either had to stay on and complete my Ph.D. or clear out then and there. The University of Exeter in England offered me a job, and a job was a job, so I took it and went back to England without finishing. I finished everything for the Ph.D. at Harvard except for submitting the thesis, but I didn't have time to do that.

WALTER: When at last, then, did you become interested in ethology?

FOX: It was even after Exeter; it was when I went to the LSE four years later. Burton Benedict, who was at the LSE then, was a fellow of the Zoological Society, and took me along to the London Zoo, and I began talking about these incest ideas to people like Desmond Morris. He had a bunch of very bright young ethologists around him in a seminar, and I joined in and put my ideas to them, and they began throwing ideas back. They hadn't thought of it systematically either, but they threw lots of things out to me about animal behavior which seemed absolutely relevant. The more I thought of this, the more I got pulled into animal behavior, not just on the subject of inbreeding and outbreeding but more generally on the idea of ritualization. The big thing in ethology then was ritualization. I also met John Bowlby at this time, and we discussed his work on the mother-child bond and his synthesis of psychoanalysis and ethology.

WALTER: Was this also when you met Lionel Tiger? Did you actually meet at the London Zoo?

FOX: Yes. Everybody thinks it is a joke, but it isn't. It was, in fact, at a very famous symposium of the Zoological Society. Tinbergen, Lorenz, and Huxley were there. Even Edmund Leach and Victor Turner from anthropology were there. Anthony Forge asked me whether I had met Lionel Tiger, and I said, "Surely you jest," but he didn't, and so I did meet Tiger. I think it was outside the gibbon cage, even though he may remember it differently, but we met there and began to swap ideas. He said he was working on this idea of male bonding, and he suggested that it had to do with the evolution of hunting in man, and I said that it went farther back than that, to the primates, and we both got very excited and went to look at male bonding in baboons and in other primates. Michael Chance was talking about this very thing and giving lectures on male hierarchies in primate societies. We attended these, and that is how that whole thing started.

WALTER: How did your colleagues react to the first paper you wrote with Tiger, "The Zoological Perspective in Social Science" (1966)?

FOX: The reaction was remarkably mild. We thought we were being incredibly daring in proposing that the social sciences should reintegrate themselves with Darwinism, but I think our elders and betters and even our peers regarded this as sort of a mild fling. There is a saying in Ireland that no man is responsible for what he says in his cups, and when he is sober the next day he's forgotten what he said when he was drunk the night before. I think they regarded this as something we wrote when we were drunk the night before and we weren't to be held responsible for it. Clearly, we didn't mean it in the sense that it was anything more than just a little idea we were throwing out. They expected us to come to our senses and like good cobblers stick to our lasts, whatever these were—matrilineal kinship in my case and the Ghanaian civil service in Tiger's.

WALTER: Was it also at about this time that you wrote *Kinship and Marriage* (1967a)?

FOX: Sort of. I wasn't interested in kinship very much—I wanted to teach linguistics—but Firth told me that I was to teach a course called "Advanced Kinship." "No way," I thought. At Cochiti, I had taken genealogies and done all the standard things you are supposed to do, and I also became interested in this somewhat on Tory Island in regard to land tenure, boat crews, and things of that kind. But I was not prepared or equipped to teach it theoretically, as a class. But I was low man on the totem pole, and this is one of the things I was required to do. So, again, I was pushed into it. It was not something I wanted.

WALTER: How, then, did you come to write one of the most popular books ever written on kinship?

FOX: The book came directly out of my kinship lectures. I had to find a way of making a simple and straightforward logic out of kinship, as much for myself as for my students, since I couldn't go in there claiming massive knowledge because I didn't have it. I decided to treat it as a logical problem. I decided to ask what the premises are from which you can derive kinship systems, and this caught on with students; I apparently found a good way to do it. I also sat down and taught myself the Australian systems. I did this mostly on the train commuting in and out of London, with a pad on my lap, enjoying the mystification of my fellow passengers. I think they thought I was doing electrical wiring diagrams. (I got these comments a few times from them.) I never imagined the thing would ever become a book. In fact, the only reason it became a book is that some of the students had been practicing shorthand taking down the lectures and had then taken these home and typed them. One of them showed the lectures to a friend who was a Penguin editor. Next thing I knew I had Penguin coming around asking me to make this into a book. They wrote out a contract for a sum that seemed to me astronomical. I now realize the sum was utterly pitiful, but it was more than I was earning in a year! They knew what they were doing. There was indeed a gap here to fill. They wanted to get their claws into this, but it was really through the efforts of the students that the thing came to be a book at all. For me, the best by-product of this effort was my rereading of Lévi-Strauss. I had read him first as an undergraduate but without close attention.

WALTER: What kind of relationship did you have with Raymond Firth at this time?

FOX: Raymond, to whom I owe more than almost anyone and to whom I have paid less tribute than ever I should but whose kindness to me and generous tolerance of me were outstanding, considering what a pain in the neck I must have been, seemed to have taken a liking to me as an undergraduate. Also, I think he had a kind of pride in me, since I think no one else had ever gone through the sociology/social anthropology degree as an undergraduate and come out the other end as a fully fledged teaching anthropologist. I was a first for him, and I was proof that their undergraduate teachings paid off. I think that is why he hired me in the first place, since I did not have an awful lot to my name. He hired me on promise more than anything else.

WALTER: Isn't it true that Raymond Firth was quite upset with you for writing *Kinship and Marriage?*

FOX: This is true. Here I was with one or two years of experience, teaching kinship really as a penance and then threatening to bring out a book. He thought this was the prerogative of a more mature hand, a job for somebody who had been at it for years. However, as I said, it was never my intention to write a book on kinship. What I was trying to do was write a Ph.D. thesis, and I was torn between writing something on the Cochiti and writing something on Tory Island. I almost wrote it on Tory Island because that was the more recent experience, but it was also the experience I had digested the least; therefore I did not feel I was ready to write it up, whereas the Cochiti stuff was all laid out, and I also had begun to see that my account of the Cochiti did not jibe with Eggan's classic account of the Western Pueblos, a great book, but one that just sat and gathered dust in reverence. I realized that there was a thesis in using what I had found to do a kind of massive critique of that whole acculturation hypothesis. Acculturation was the big buzzword of the thirties and forties in American Indian anthropology, and as far as I could see it was being misapplied to the Pueblos. So I ended up writing two things: the kinship lectures which turned into a book and the thesis which eventually became *The Keresan Bridge* (1967b).

WALTER: Your experiences at the London Zoo didn't make much impact on either of these works. Did you see any connection at this point between your kinship studies and ethology?

FOX: Neither work had very much to do with ethology. The ethology at this point didn't bother anybody. People saw it as a kind of hobby. Well, that is how it looked, but it wasn't necessarily how I felt. My real interests had switched almost completely to evolution. For example, I was still interested in kinship systems, but I was interested in how humans came to evolve kinship systems. I got interested in primate kinship systems for this reason. I was curious as to how human kinship systems could have arisen out of primate social organization. For example, we knew about the evolution of the skeleton and of musculature, but the idea that the ritualized signaling of the fiddler crab was somewhere there in the central nervous system and had evolved just like its huge right claw, that was novel. That the ritual fighting of deer was somehow as much in their genes as their antlers themselves was something that completely fascinated me because I began to wonder how much of human behavior is like that. How many of the cultural universals that anthropologists go on about are really biological universals? In other words, is there an ethogram of human behavior, as there is an ethogram for each animal species? The reading I was doing, therefore, was mostly on evolution and ethology, but the teaching and writing I was doing was mostly on social anthropology. They did let me teach a course called "Man, Race, and Culture," which was an old course that Maurice Freedman used to teach. I inherited the title, so we did not have to invent a new one, and I used it as an excuse to talk about all these things to students, and it was really out of that set of concerns that the *Imperial Animal* (Tiger and Fox 1971) arose when I joined this to what Lionel Tiger was doing over at the University of British Columbia.

1

Why Bureaucracy Fails

This chapter began as a talk to an audience of military and nonmilitary personnel from the Department of Defense, and some invited academics. The topic intially was military bureaucracies and the possibility of making them into innovative institutions. This was one in a series of remarkable seminars organized over the years by Andrew Marshall, the director of net assessment for the DOD, who never asked for anything but a freewheeling intellectual discussion from us. But the military men were truly interested, being dedicated bureaucrats constantly, and often dangerously, threatened by their own bureaucracies. They perhaps better than anyone understand the fatal weakness, and yet the indispensibility, of such institutions, a situation that is our contemporary Catch 22. And so they were properly fascinated with the idea that the drive to make their bureaucracies more efficient might—indeed must—backfire. Death from friendly fire is something they know all about.

We are all either bureaucrats now or so enmeshed in bureaucracies that we might as well be. I have just completed some eighteen hours of work acting as an unpaid accountant for the federal and state governments in the preparation of my income tax returns; returns based on records accumulated with many other hours of effort over the tax year. This I have in common with us all—honorary government bureaucrats. I like to think that as a university teacher and scholar I am not really a bureaucrat, but really I am. I hold an office by appointment and merit, not by hereditary title or family connections. I hold it because I fulfill certain conditions and meet certain qualifications. When I leave it it will be filled by someone else with the appropriate qualifications. I receive a regular salary, not payment in kind or occasional payments, and have a career structure through which I can rise, achieving tenure for life and eventually a pension. I have to meet a host of bureaucratic requirements to keep this position, and I stand somewhere (although often it is not clear just where) in a hierarchy of decision makers in my institution. The institution itself is a complex of hierarchies of office holders like myself, most of them as baffled by it as I am. Someone once said of the University of London (to which I also once belonged) that an intelligent man with a certain amount of time and application should be able to understand how it worked, but that no intelligent man would dream of trying. However (the university bureaucrat's favorite word) we must try, if only because, by a weird recursion, it is part of the bureaucratic job description of a social scientist that he try to understand such things. But as my title suggests I intend to beg the question, since most studies of bureaucracy are premised on the assumption that they should indeed study "how it works" when it is blatantly obvious to those of us who belong to them or tangle with them that they do not work. They are indeed self-perpetuating and can bumble along for quite some time, and we must examine why. But they do not work in the sense of fulfilling their purposes, aims, or goals, which are, after all, usually quite rationally and explicitly set out in their charters. Even if in their own terms they achieve "efficiency" (another favorite bureaucratic word)—that is, they rationally adapt means to ends—they do this at the expense of those they are supposed to serve and those who serve them. Show me a happy bureaucrat and I'll show you a warped human being. Oh, they exist all right, and that is another part of the problem.

Bureaucracies fail because of what Marx might have called their "internal contradictions." This is not news to social scientists, I suppose. What may be news is that these contradictions are inevitable. Behind most social science attempts to analyze the failures of bureaucracy lies the implicit assumption that with enough rational and scientific enquiry we will be able to pinpoint the trouble and cure it. Indeed, if there were not such an assumption no one would be willing to fund the research in the first place. It is assumed, not unreasonably, by the world at large, that it is the business of social science to come up with ways to patch and mend our torn social fabric. They do not pay us to say "whatever you do won't work" anymore than they pay medical researchers to say "there is absolutely no hope ever of curing this disease, sorry about that." Again, the funds would dry up. So the social scientists plug away with studies of conflict resolution, management style, recruitment strategies, motivational problems, work satisfaction, informal organization, information flow, and all the familiar list. A lot of this is quite interesting from my point of view since it helps to show why bureaucracies can never work, but my colleagues are uniformly horrified when I offer such a justification for their efforts. They are infected with the basic rational utopianism of the social science agenda: give us enough time and enough grants and we will cure this chronic case of social malfunction. For one thing is obvious to both of us: there is no way that we can do without bureaucracies; modern society is utterly dependent on them for its existence. To say that they are hopelessly flawed by their very natures is like saying that modern medicine simply cannot cure the diseases we fear most (as is indeed the case, but we won't go into that one.) The thought is unbearable. Something we are utterly dependent on simply must be made workable. It is that simple. The alternative is a kind of death sentence, or at least a sentence to a life of almost unendurable pain.

Fortunately no one is giving me a grant to do this research, which is not really research anyway but simply informed observation. So having no utopian agenda, and no masters to please, I can tell it like it is. The "internal contradictions" of bureaucracy are indeed chronic; they are incurable. No amount of social science tinkering is going to do more than cover the patient with bandaids. But like the Fisher King with his suppurating wound, the patient will not easily die; it may equally suffer eternally unless there is some catastrophic intervention. We are dealing then with a chronic invalid who is absolutely necessary to our continued existence in society as we know it.

Despite all the social and psychological studies then, why do we not seem able to determine why bureaucracy fails *as a matter of principle*? The short answer is the time-frame in which we pose the question. If we do not look at this, or any other institutional problem, in an evolutionary time-frame we are bound only to get partial answers. Most sociologists of bureaucracy are unwilling to look even at a deep historical time-frame, much less an evolutionary one. It was not always so. One of the great fathers of sociology, Herbert Spencer, who invented the idea of looking at social facts in an evolutionary time-frame—quite independently of Darwin in fact—gives a brilliant account of how state bureaucracies emerged from the organization of royal households. The titles of various officers in the English government still reflect this origin: Lord Privy Seal; Lord Chamberlain; First Lord of the Treasury; Chancellor of the

Exchequer. All these are "ministers" because originally they were royal servants: they "ministered" to the king and met in his "cabinet" or antechamber. But while this gives us some sense of historical depth, we have to plunge much deeper into history to get an answer to our question. We have to plunge in fact into that period of history when serious genetic changes were still taking place and our present anatomy and mentality was being formed. Normally we do not think of this as "history" and even condemn it officially to being "prehistory" and this is the origin of our error. Evolution is simply history over long periods of time during which genetic change and adaptation occurred. (These can occur over relatively short periods of time as well, but usually such changes are minor, as with, for example, the evolution of the overbite in modern man.) If we think in these terms then we have to understand the history of bureaucracy as encompassing a huge period of time when it did not exist. The fact of that nonexistence is crucial. During that period of several million years we were formed as a species. Bureaucratic institutions were only invented a few thousand years ago, and only became totally pervasive in recent times. We have then to ask the crucial question whether or not they are compatible with the kind of creature that we evolved to be.

This is not such a strange question once one gets used to it. It is no different in principle from asking whether one should keep animals in cages and train them to do tricks for our amusement. There is no question that this can be done, but is it good for the animals? Equally obviously we can invent vast bureaucratic structures and train people to live in them, but is it good for the people? The question is only strange to those who have been reared in a cultural orthodoxy that says that any animal, including the human animal, can be trained to do anything so no problem exists except the problem of adequate training. To such a mentality, if bureaucracy keeps failing it can only be because we are failing in our training methods, and the answer is to find out why and improve them. The DSMIII, the official diagnostic manual of the psychiatric profession, used to list as one of its accepted "emotional illnesses" (those that qualified for medical insurance), "job dissatisfaction," thus reflecting exactly this thinking. People who hated their dull, repetitive, inhuman work, were "suffering" from "emotional illness." The answer was to change their attitudes until they accepted their lot. You can look this up; I didn't invent it. I don't know if this is still listed, but it used to be. Needless to say, my approach is to treat this as problematic rather than settled. If people in general are persistently unhappy with something despite all efforts to improve their attitudes, then I suggest we at least look at the possibility that the thing in question might be inimical to their basic needs, and their misery might not stem from their personal inadequacies. If caged animals sometimes lash out and attack their trainers, should we put the blame on the animals or on the cages and the trainers where the animals were not supposed to be in the first place?

What then I am going to argue, and what Tiger and I stated baldly in *The Imperial Animal* in 1971, is that bureaucracies fail because they are, in some sense, inhuman. In some sense they are human because they are human inventions. But it is one of the paradoxes of an animal endowed with intelligence, foresight, and language, that it can become its own animal trainer: it can invent conditions for itself that it cannot then handle because it was not evolved to handle them. It has always been my point, when faced with any so-called breakdowns in modern society, to ask whether or not these are really breakdowns or whether or not they are in fact endogenous healing processes. The idea that they are breakdowns (as with teen gangs, teen pregnancies, strikes and industrial unrest, high divorce rates, illiteracy, declining educational standards, collapse of nuclear family values, terrorism, and the like) has to assume that they were somehow in a "normal" state to start with. This again begs the question. We do not ever really ask what the normal state of these institutions is. Indeed the social sciences do not know how to ask it. The normal state for them is the state we have created. It can be no other. It is again as if we are assuming that the cages and trainers are "normal" for the animals, so that their rebellions against this state are a kind of pathology.

For Max Weber, the great analyst of bureaucratic systems, it was modern capitalism and mass democracy that brought to fruition the "pure" form of the institution. Historically it had existed in various proto-forms, but only in industrial society were its full virtues developed and realized. This was part and parcel of the march of society towards a *rational* form of organization, away from the traditional, sacerdotal, and hereditary forms of the preindustrial age. Hear Weber: "The decisive reason for the advance of bureaucratic organization has always been its pure technical superiority over any other form of organization. The fully developed bureaucratic mechanism compares with other organizations exactly as does the machine with the non-mechanical modes of production." Exactly. He lists the virtues succinctly: "Precision, speed, unambiguity, knowledge of the files, continuity, discretion, unity, strict subordination, reduction of friction and of material and personal costs..." It is interesting that in stressing these virtues perhaps he gets to the heart of the problem without realizing it. Thus, he stresses, that when fully developed, "Its specific nature...develops the more perfectly the more the bureaucracy is "dehumnanised," the more completely it succeeds in eliminating from official business love, hatred, and all purely personal, irrational, and emotional elements which escape calculation. This is the specific nature of bureaucracy and it is appraised as its special virtue." (I left out—marked by the ellipses—the words "which is welcomed by capitalism" since later experience has shown us that it is welcomed even more by socialism, even if it was a capitalistic invention.) It is indeed. But as we can see from the list, the things it eliminates are absolute necessesities of human existence even if they are irrational and beyond calculation. He continues: "The more complicated and specialized the modern culture becomes, the more its external supporting apparatus demands the personally detached and strictly "objective" *expert*, in lieu of the master of older social structures, who was moved by personal sympathy and favor, by grace and gratitude." In terms of the criteria of rationality and efficiency, these messy personalistic values of traditional society must succumb to the impersonal and universalistic virtues of bureaucracy. But Weber is concerned with what is right with bureaucracy—in the sense of what "fits" with modern society and its organizational needs. For those of us concerned with what is wrong with it, Weber's list of what has to be abandoned again reads like a nostalgic reminder of some of the things that make life worthwhile: "sympathy and favor, grace and gratitude."

We have to find somewhere to start in spelling out the basic flaws and their relation to the evolutionary context. So let us look at what I consider to be the main flaw: bureaucracy is a rational relationship between means and ends, but *the means of the bureaucracy tend to become the ends of the bureaucrats* to the point where the initial purpose of the enterprise gets totally lost. The examples are too numerous to cite and too well known to need elaboration. We all of us are either constantly faced with the frustrations this engenders, or are guilty of perpetuating this very behavior. We all have experienced hospitals, which ostensibly exist for the cure of the sick, where the preservation of the hospital hierarchy and the observation of its rules often take absolute precedence over the needs of patients. We are so disturbed by this obvious truth, since our lives and well-being are seriously at stake, that we need a whole industry of T.V. fantasy shows full of caring doctors and personally involved nurses and the like to bolster our morale and calm our worst fears. We are numb by now with examples from the world of crime where the police supposedly exist to see that justice is done but in fact are obsessed with "making convictions stick" at all costs including perjury and planted evidence. Without the convictions there cannot be promotions and pensions. University departments and university administrations, need I remind my most obvious audience, are riven with this problem. The purposes of universities might be a bit vague, but "teaching, research, and service" are usually high on the list of objective goals. But as we all know these ends become easily subservient to the means of promotion and control. University administrations are less interested in any of these than in expanding the control of the administration over the faculty. They will support research, for example, insofar as it makes them look good, not as an end in itself, and they will readily sacrifice teaching if there is a greater payoff for them in some other direction. Above all they seek a ceaseless expansion of the administration itself, and the patronage that goes with it.

The history of warfare is replete with examples of the means-ends confusion. One only has, to this audience, to mention "inter-service rivalry" to touch off a chain reaction of examples. Here, maintaining the distinctiveness of different units becomes more important than winning the wars (the ostensible purpose again of a military organization.) In fact, if we are to believe some of the things we hear round this table, winning the wars is merely incidental to maintaining the special interests of the various services and units within the services. Huge sums of taxpayers' money are yearly wasted on projects concerned with this maintenence of differential status. In that ultimate example of bureaucracy-for-its-own-sake, the United Nations, practically no one can tell you the provisions of the U.N. Charter. But each unit and sub-unit is fiercely aware of the competition for funds under the yearly budget scramble. All other functions are subordinated to the task of maintaining and increasing that share. This reaches its peak in the months before the budget presentations are due. Anyone who has dealt with this monster knows that it is impossible to get business done—the business for which the departments exist—during this part of the year. You will be told quite frankly, "No one is available since they are all in budget meetings."

As I said, we could produce endless examples, but you can do this exercise for yourselves. Or go down to the local motor vehicles office and try to get the simplest thing accomplished. But this is only one aspect of this particular flaw—the substitution of bureaucratic means for the ostensible ends of the organization. It is itself a result of a perhaps deeper flaw. All bureaucrats are obsessed with *rules*, and with the observation and enforcement of rules as an end in itself. They are rarely concerned with the purpose of the rules; it is enough that the rules exist and must be enforced. But people at large are not all that interested in rules except as means. People have *goals* and they employ *strategies* to achieve them. Rules are for them simply one set of aids or hindrances in the achievement of the goals. But for the bureaucrat (in his role as bureaucrat) the observance of the rules is the only goal. He is not interested in the personal goals and strategies of the ordinary citizen, but in that citizen's observation of the relevant rules. The possibilities then for a head-on clash and a tangle of misunderstandings are multitudinous, and again the examples are too numerous and even banal to need reciting. "We have our rules you know." "You can't have read the rules properly." "If only you'd followed the proper procedures." "There is a rule you know." It is all too dismally familiar. And this underlines the point that what I am talking about here is not some esoteric theoretical deduction from evolutionary or organizational or psychological theory, but the kind of observations obvious to our common sense. What is not obvious to our common sense is how things got into this state, and here we must make a brief detour through our evolutionary history, because if we do not then we are still left with the standard social science answer that what is wrong must lie in a failure of our socialization or training or adjustment, and that it can in principle be put right. George Orwell and Franz Kafka knew that it couldn't be put right, but they could only describe how it might achieve its ultimate awfulness. We will try to underpin their humanistic insights with a little dash of science.

We have heard bureaucracies described as "complex adaptive systems" by the complexity theorists. This is a happy turn of phrase because it allows me to introduce the concept of "complex mal-adaptive systems." We are not adapted to them, nor they to us. What can this mean? Adaptation, in the evolutionary sense, refers to the process whereby organisms become fitted to their environments. No organism can be "adapted" in an abstract sense; it is adapted to an environment. This is why the nature/nurture debate was always a silly one. The adaptations of any organism assume a specific environmental input. This is why I have defined "instincts" as "an organism's specific demands for specific environmental input." But here is the rub: environments can change, or in the human case can be changed, faster than the organism's genetic adaptations can keep up. Every organism has what evolutionary biologists call its "environment of evolutionary adaptedness" (EEA). This is the environment in which its distinctive characteristics as a species evolved, and hence the environment that it "expects." We must never lose sight of this: adaptation is a *relationship* between organism and environment. What is "in the genes" is there because of adpatations to this environment and "assumes" the input of this environment for the realization of its behavior over the life cycle. To use a crude example, it does not much matter what is in the genes of a fish if the fish is not in water. Adaptation has produced genes that "assume" the input of water (often specifically either fresh or salt water); a fish out of water, that is, an orgamism out of its environment of evolutionary adaptation, is either dead or severly disabled. It might survive if the novel environment can mimic enough of the EEA to fool the genes, as it were. But how long or how well it can survive is a moot point.

The EEA of *Homo sapiens sapiens* is variously described as the late Pleistocene, or the upper Palaeolithic; in layman's terms the old stone age. We entered this little differentiated from our ape cousins except for our upright stance and small teeth, and we ended it as modern humans, our brains having grown three times in size over less than two million years. This is the context of our history of adpatations—physical, emotional, cognitive, and social. The brain is the major organ of this adaptation, although it followed on such features as the upright stance and the opposable thumb.

It is often argued that one of the things we developed in the period was also "general intelligence" or "consciousness" or something that in essence frees us from any kind of obligations to specific adaptations. Apart, however, from the great difficulty of defining or locating these features, even their most avid proponents have to admit to a substrate of *domain specific modules* (or algorithms), which are cognitive and emotional adaptations of a specific and not a general purpose kind. It could be that so-called general purpose intelligence (or consciousness) only appeared after language itself appeared, and represents the fact that we can talk about our own motivations and needs in a way denied other animals. "General purpose intelligence" is a problem as a total explanation of what motivates us since it clearly provides no motivations, although it may help us to be endlessly malleable in trying to adjust our motivations to our environments. In the end we must recognize that we have a wide repertoire of specific needs that require an environmental response. These needs were sculpted in the upper Palaeolithic and require an environment that at least mimics that period in some major respects for us to feel "satisfied" and remain emotionally healthy. And the particular question for us is whether or not bureaucracies in any way meet these needs. Whether our bodies, our feelings, our satisfactions, our mental images, our cognitive maps, our social perceptions or any other of our Palaeolithic adaptations find a "template" here into which they can fit.

There is surely a prima facie case that they cannot. Take the social environment of our evolution. This was a tribal environment made up of small nomadic groups. It was an environment of kin, who were friendly, and non-kin who were hostile. Millenia of "kin selection" had prepared us to favor relatives, and to, for example, settle disputes by face-to-face encounters. It was a highly personal world—a world of persons, known and lived with daily. Leadership, for example, would be a highly personal matter. Our sentiments and cognitions are finely attuned to such a world. A special area of our brains does nothing but sort through faces in order to select the familiar. Our "general purpose intelligence" may be able to devise a world of impersonal encounters and general rules, but it must constantly be at war with the specifically personal and even kinship-oriented sentiments that motivate us. We can be pulled apart by this, because bureaucracy can tap into the sentiment of group loyality (it does this very effectively)—a definite part of the basic system of sentiments—and then set this against the equally strong sentiment of kin loyalty. This in fact sets up bureaucracy's most vital struggle: the war against nepotism. We are so used to seeing "nepotism" as a bad thing that it takes an effort of imagination to reverse our system of values even as a thought experiment. But if we rephrase it as I have consistently done to talk of the "war of bureaucracy against kinship" then perhaps we can see what is at issue. To achieve the virtues that Weber sees as the essense of bureaucratic efficiency, it is vital that offices and positions be filled by merit—by those qualified to fill them. This usually requires systems of training and objective examination, such as were first perfected by the Chinese. But as we know, the tendency for upper-level bureaucrats to fill these positions with kin or with loyal supporters rather than with the most qualified persons is a constant threat to bureaucratic systems. Virtually every study of the new bureaucracies of newly independent countries has come to the despairing conclusion that this is endemic, as it was in the early bureaucracies of the "advanced" countries. It is to the bureaucratic mind the worst example of "corruption" in the system, and it is our pride in the West that we have pretty much rooted it out, although cynics looking at the admissions policies of universities might doubt this.

In the days when immigrants dominated the ward politics of American cities, such "corruption" was rife, with family and ethnicity taking precedence over competence. It is still not totally absent by any means, and this gives "reformers" a more or less constant platform. I am not talking here of appointments that result solely from the outcome of the power struggle. The president can appoint his own cabinet for example, they do not have to pass competitive examinations. The boards of governors or regents of state universities are appointees, unlike the faculty-administration bureaucrats whom they control. The boss can make his incompetent nephew managing director. While people may regard this as unfair they do not quarrel with it in the way they would the nepotistic appointment of a civil servant. It is part of the spoils system of politics, in the broadest sense. Those with the power get to choose their henchmen. But the civil service and its imitators are supposed to be (and often are to a remarkable extent) free from nepotism. This, as I said, is seen as a triumph. But even here, the civil servants by means of special schooling and priviliged entrees will try to favor the chances of their own kin, and will largely succeed as long as the kin are minimally competent. When I explained, forty years ago, to one of my old English uncles that I was going to be a college lecturer he expostulated: "My God! Couldn't they do something better for you than that?!" The "they" of course was "the family," the connections, the old boy network, etc. It would be interesting, if we had the time, to look at the Japanese systems in some depth, because they seem to try to have the best of both worlds: kinship particularism and bureaucratic universalism. This not only infuriates (and intrigues) Westerners who have to deal with it, but it presents the Japanese themselves with some trying strains and problems, and it remains to be seen if they can continue this curious and for now effective balancing act. Personally I doubt it, for they are overweighting the system in the direction of loyalty to the pseudo-kin corporation. I wonder how long the Palaeolithic system of needs can be fooled by this imbalance? There are ominous signs of cracks in the system already.

The example of nepotism is the most obvious because the most public. But we can extract from it a general principle: that whatever the bureaucracy regards as the greatest crimes against its own perfect realization will turn out to be basic adaptations of the human EEA. Look again at Weber's list of what bureaucracy displaced and you will see what I mean. It will be argued that even hunting bands had to be "efficient" and that therefore the pursuit of rational organizational efficiency is not inimical to the human animal. In a limited sense this is true if we remember that the efficiency in question operated between kin or affines and at the expense of strangers. The idea that one should spend one's working life operating impartial rules for the benefit of perfect strangers even if this meant disadvantaging kin and friends would be incomprehensible to the most "rational" Palaeolithic hunter. The hunter's rational efficiency certainly can be harnessed to the bureaucratic task, but it will find its limits fairly quickly. The bureaucrat will be able to do it as long as he ceases in effect to care about the strangers he must service. Either that or he must treat them as pseudo-kin. It will depend on the nature of the service. Social workers, teachers, and probation officers easily convert their charges into pseudo-kin, and the strain of trying to operate on them in terms of general rules will become intolerable. Motor vehicle and immigration officers simply see lines of strangers about whom they do not and, for the sake of their sanity cannot, care. To this end they must totally suppress their Palaeolithic kinship sentiments and develop the unlovely "bureaucratic personality." In either case, for both the bureaucrat and the client, there is an inbuilt strain that can only be detrimental to both. Something there inside, cannot be denied—but it has to be. This is never more apparent than in the attempt of bureaucracies to do the ultimate in universalism and deny the reality of sexual differences in "the workplace." If merit is all that counts, then sex is irrelevant—or theoretically should be. Thus perfectly normal sexual interactions among a sexually reproducing species are outlawed from that place, and female soldiers and firemen are deemed identical with males. If they inconveniently fall in love or get pregnant this is seen not as perfectly natural but as some kind of system failure. The military opposed the open introduction of homosexuals into combat units, for example, because of the "tension" this would arouse; but in the same breath they propose to introduce females into the same units and insist that no such "tensions" need ensue. It would be a low blow to say "tell it to the Marines."

Let us look at this issue of bureaucratic "efficiency" since for Weber it was the raison d'être of successful bureaucratization. It produces another double-bind outcome. Let us risk another generalization (which like all generalizations is probably wrong, but might be useful): The more successful, in terms of efficiency, a bureaucracy is, the further it will depart from the basic pattern of EEA adaptations, and the less satisfactory it will be for its participants. In other words, the more it succeeds in efficiency the more it will fail in humanity. In either case it will fail. Let us take the obverse: The less efficient a bureaucracy is, the more chance it has to give free reign to basic motivations, but by the same token the less likely it is to succeed in its bureaucratic object. My youngest daughter spent some time in the pre-lapsarian USSR—at what was then Leningrad State University. What impressed her was not so much the oppressiveness of the state bureaucracy (although that was there) as its colossal inefficiency. It was so inefficient that, in her opinion it was only kept going by a tacit conspiracy between the cynical workers and the corrupt officials, summed up in the joke, "We pretend to work; they pretend to pay us." It would only, she figured, take a small push to send the whole edifice toppling. (We did not need a multibillion dollar arms effort or a Star Wars defense system to defeat the evil empire; all we needed, she said, was to fly in some thousands of strategic comrades to the USA and let them loose with credit cards for twenty-four hours in shopping malls. It would be infinitely cheaper and work much more effectively.) She was right. Gorbachev saw that the situation was hopeless and gave the necessary shove. What brought down communism (soi disant) was not the hatred of the super-efficient state bureaucracies but the opposite: their total inefficiency and failure to deliver even basic consumer goods. Ironically, it was also this inefficiency that allowed them to totter along for so long without a general uprising. These were things Weber could not have forseen in his linking of bureaucracy and capitalism. It took socialism to show us the limits of bureaucracy, but I doubt we have learned the lesson. We now assume that "communist" bureaucracies (for Marx a contradiction in terms) are fallible whereas "democratic" (i.e., capitalist) multinational bureaucracies are the salvation of the future. But a bureaucracy is a bureaucracy, and ethnicity is ethnicity, and never the twain shall meet. Multinational corporations are still in their historical infancy. We shall see. But I will venture another of my solid sociological predictions: they will fare no better than their socialist counterparts. We are already witnessing massive dislocations in human lives as these monsters drive rapidly towards greater "rationalization" and "restructuring" in the name of almightly efficiency in the pursuit of profit. This may well provoke a total disillusion with them as great as that experienced in the socialist bloc. And to those who cry scorn, I can only point to the once seeming inevitability of the continuance of their socialist totalitarian counterparts. As Weber saw, there are certain properties of bureaucracies that are independent of their function. It doesn't matter whether they are civil or ecclesiastical, mercantile or collegiate, capitalist or socialist, they are all driving towards the same goals; what we have added to Weber is that these goals are intrinsically unattainable. And to resort to our evolutionary jargon, they are unattainable because bureaucracies try to subordinate the domain specific adaptations of the human EEA to general purpose rules of too recent invention to correspond to most of these basic needs.

A brief note is needed on Weber's other major concern of "rationality." He saw this as a trend affecting everything in Western society, not only bureaucracy, but even religion and music. Weber was not so naive as to equate this with "progress" as such, but he did regard it as inevitable. The older systems of traditional, patrimonial, prebendary, feudal, and sacerdotal "domination" or "authority" were giving way inexorably to a "rational-legal" form of the same. This is all very familiar to social scientists, and commonly accepted. I do not dispute it. What I dispute is the inevitability of it. It is assumed that because we are capable of "rational" thought, and because this is in our value system the mode of thought to be preferred, if only again because of its efficiency, to mystical or customary or magical or any of the nonrational modes of operation, that there is indeed "progress" and that this progress is sustainable. But we have already seen that it is the most rational elements of bureaucracy that are most inimical to our basic EEA developed needs. How can this be if we are truly the "rational animal?" Well, the simple answer is that we are not. We are certainly *capable* of rational thought, but are we do not for most of the time operate on it. If certain of our contempary psychologists and philosophers are to be believed—and they are not making an evolutiionary argument it should be noted—we are not even operating on *conscious* thought for most of the time. Rational thought, in the sense of "logical" thinking ("if A equals B and B equals C then A equals C") or the causal linking of means and ends ("if A will get me B and B equals C then C will also get me A")—this form of thinking is rare and is not what we mostly operate on. Nor do we operate well, for example, in terms of the estimation of probabilities. We readily ditch rational probabilities in favor of intuition and hunches. Our minds are not a seamless, rational general-purpose computer. Only Mr. Spock or Data has one of those, and each of them, interestingly realized his own limitations in *not* being able to operate in terms of intuition, hunch and prejudice, since these often give a more realistic picture of the world—having been part of our history of adaptation to it—than a rational-logical mentality which, being totally disinterested and purely inductive, would treat everything on its own merits and prejudge nothing. The brain (and I fear I am again repeating an old refrain) did not evolve primarily to indulge in abstract and logical thought; it evolved to *act* in order to survive. That imperative of action ensured that it would be selected to operate in terms of prejudgment and intuition. These prejudgments would be constructed for the environment of survival—the EEA—and would not include routine induction but rather rapid decision making in terms of stereotypes, for example. As I have said before, the rational thinking we prize so highly might well have been the outcome of the origins of language—of the fact that we can talk about and hence appraise our own mental functions. And this may be a relatively late development in evolutionary terms. But it is what we *hear*: "I wonder why I did that; perhaps it was because…?" Hence, because of our dependence on language we come to prize the afterthought more than the action, and to rate it more highly, even if without the action the afterthought of conscious rationality would not have been possible in the first place.

Thus, the attribute that most distinguishes bureaucracy may be one that is a both a latecomer in evolutionary terms, and a an afterthought in motivational and cognitive terms. We struggle, as children struggle with math, to keep it uppermost and to act is if our actions are predicated on it, but it is a losing battle. We are attempting to build a castle of sand that the waves of emotion and sentiment easily wash away. "Reason" said David Hume "is and ought to be the slave of the passions." Reason does not motivate; it literally does not move us. It awaits orders from the passions and carries these out. It adapts means to ends. If we are full of cold fury and want to kill someone, we know to use a hard sharp object and not a soft or brittle one if we have the time to choose. Reason will adapt means to ends rationally, but it cannot choose those ends. When "rationality" therefore becomes and end in itself, as Weber saw it does with bureaucracies, we are inviting disaster. We are in effect asking our brains to operate like computers, but, despite the best efforts of the artificial intelligence crowd to persuade us that this is just what they are, they are not. If we must use the computer analogy, then we are best served by the one the evolutionary psychologists use when they insist that the mind (I prefer to stick with brain) is not a general-purpose computer, but rather a linked series of dedicated computers. And they are dedicated to specific areas of survival in the EEA—the old stone age. We do have some general-purpose abilities, but they are limited, and not dedicated to survival, and hence in the long run subordinate to those that are, however well we use them in certain delimited and privileged areas (mathematics, logic, science, etc.) When it comes to living in the real world, our directions come from the dedicated modules, and these are, I have argued, largely inimical to the imposition of rational, impersonal, universalistic rules. To go back to my earlier metaphor, we are trying to use the brain like a circus animal: yes, it can do these things in short bursts, but they are not part of its natural repertoire and it cannot sustain them as a normal, continuous, satisfying mode of existence.

This has been a somewhat abstract, even if very abbreviated, argument, but I felt it necessary to make it, if only because "reason" has been so much touted as the unique defining characteristic of our species (we are *Homo sapiens sapiens*—Man the doubly wise) and hence we should welcome its ultimate realization in the institutions of bureaucracy as much as Hegel welcomed the same in the institutions of the Prussian state. And you may well counter that this whole essay is an example of sustained, if perhaps perverse, reasoning. Absolutely true. But I cannot use it to combat a sabre-toothed tiger, or find a water hole, or charm a young bride, or discipline a child. And I do not need it, or the reasoning power that produced it (again I think a power of language) to do any of these things. I do not even need consciousness, but that is another and longer story.

We can go on listing the obvious areas of failure. At the national level, for example, state bureaucracies try to substitute "citizenship" for "tribal identity." It can only fool some of the people some of the time. We can create an entity like "Yugoslavia" with an effective and efficient bureaucracy, and we can give it a king or a dictator and a flag and a national anthem and, yes, a bureaucratic unity. But we have seen how totally fragile this is in the face of ethnic and religious hatred. It could only work with an Orwellian totalitarian party-run force-backed system, and when that faltered, it reverted to savagery. People ask, why, when bureaucracy fails, do we act like savages? The answer is because we *are* savages—Palaeolithic, stone-age, hunting and feuding savages. We have not changed in any genotypic way since that founding period. So we must face the fact that the feuding Serbs, Muslims, and Croats are more "human" than the Politburo or the Pentagon or NATO, or even the department of motor vehicles. At the same time we must remember that so are the Bushmen, the family party, and the boys' club. There is a violent face to humanity as well as an inhuman face to bureaucracy. But there is also a gentle and supportive face that bureaucracies can never match. Tiger and I pointed out how frantic and fraught the yearly office Christmas party can become. For one day of the year people are allowed to be human. The results can be alternatively hilarious or embarrassing depending on the viewpoint. But it is clear to everyone that what went on at the party must be forgotten and not carry over into the work year. It is what Victor Turner would call a "liminal" time: literally a "threshold" but one that must be stepped over only gingerly and infrequently. It shows up the cracks in the system too well.

Some commentators have thought the real problem is one of size: it is the massive bureaucracies that don't work. There is probably something to this; when it comes to scale small is, if not necessarily beautiful, at least more likely to be more human. But the massive ones are amalgamations of many smaller ones, and the small ones don't do much better. You have to get down to the *very* small ones to begin to hope for a human operation, and only then because in face-to-face groups, whatever the "rules and procedures" a good deal of literal "eyeballing" can go on which can convey far more than memos. (In his fascinating examination of industrial society from the evolutionary point of view, Lionel Tiger points out how much the bureaucrats prefer the memo to the message; how the written communication becomes the ideal—because impersonal—substitute for human interaction.) The more there is eye-to-eye contact, the more the organizational unit can mimic a primate or small tribal unit.

In the military it is obvious that a platoon can operate like a small tribe; a regiment with its rituals and symbols can operate like a large tribe. Get much bigger and the analogy breaks down. Platoons are "buddies" and we know that men don't die for their countries or for the free world but for their buddies (a corruption of "brothers" of course, probably from German *bruder*.) This buddy system works well in small combat units but precisely because it is the opposite of the bureaucratic principle. "I don't care what the rules say, I'm not leaving my buddy out there to die," has become a cliché of most war movies. "Helping buddies" can totally subvert the bureaucracy. The Pentagon is not a group of buddies, but these groups as we know, exist in the interstices of such vast systems, and either run them from behind the scenes, or bring them down.

Another major fault line can be phrased thus: *The egos of the bureaucrats tend to get identified with the means-become-ends of their bureaucratic enclave.* Thus the bureaucrat will often persist in a totally irrational (from the point of view of the system) defense of an institution or paradigm since his ego-identity is at stake. There is nothing intrinsically wrong with such an indentification; it is fine for members of totem clans who identify with the eponymous animal that is their legendary ancestor and symbolic focus. Defend it to the death. But it can be a disaster in say academic or military life. A scientific or scholarly paradigm that has totally outlived its usefulness can persist for years because its defenders have simply too much ego involvement in it to give it up. The goal of scientific advancement can be wholly sacrificed to the means of, say, Behaviorism, simply because the Behaviorist from his PhD onwards has so thoroughly identified with the theory that if it were to collapse so would he. A striking example in the military world is of course the strange (to outsiders) persistence of the cavalry and massed cavalry tactics right through the Second World War. If we think it was only the Poles who were guilty of this military anachronism we are wrong. Even after the need to convert to tanks for modern warfare had become apparent to every lance-corporal, General Sir R. G. Eggerton could write, in opposing the formation of a Royal Tank Corps (in 1925):

> If we turn to the introduction of mechanical transport into the Army to replace the horse, and look into the faces of individuals who deal with the horse and the faces of the men who deal with the machine, you will see in the latter what I might call almost a lack of intelligence...I consider that the horse has a humanising effect on men, and the longer we can keep horses for

artillery and cavalry the better, because thereby you keep up the high standard of intelligence in the man from his association with the horse.

My daughters as teenagers would have agreed wholeheartedly. And this business about retaing the cavalry fascinates me since I had an uncle who was in the 17th/21st Lancers (the "Death or Glory Boys"), who used to describe to me the "tactical" training they were receiving: knee locked behind that of the next rider to keep a perfect line, and lances at a sharp, choreographed downward angle at the bugle-sound of the charge etc. And this was in 1940! In fact, from the battles of Laupen (1339) and Crecy (1346) the lesson had been learned that cavalry were horribly vulnerable even to the longbow, never mind the cannon and eventually the machine gun. Yet the French, who lost more than ten thousand men at Crecy to the English hundred or so, were still piling up appalling cavalry losses at Verdun more than seven hundred years later. The English, as we have seen, despite their initiative with tanks, still carried on the identification with the totem-horse, and Field Marshal Sir Douglas Haig—who incidentally thought the machine gun a much overrated weapon—declared that airplanes and armored vehicles could never be more than mere adjuncts to men and horses. In 1925 he was predicting that "As time goes on, you will find just as much use for the horse—the well-bred horse—as you have ever done in the past." The German army of 1939, remembered for its Panzers and its blitzkriegs, in fact employed more horses than it had in 1914. I quote these examples partly for the amusement of the military in my audience, but they are beautiful illustrations of the chronic overidentification I am talking about. We laugh at them now, but I wonder if we might not come to see the present Navy's superaddiction to floating platforms with a pointy end at the front in much the same light in fifty years' time? Or the Air Force and Navy addiction to superfast fighter planes, which in fact have limited usefulness. The point is that whether it be animals, shapes, dogmas, or tactics, the bureaucrat responsible for them follows what I have called the natural totemic path and overidentifies until the thing identified with becomes his total raison d'être. The massive conservativsm and stagnation of bureaucracies lies in large part in this phenomenon.

The bureaucratic tactics of "defending the turf" and "justification at all costs" follow from the above, as does the "file and forget" ploy, the ultimate of bureaucratic stonewalling (along with the well-known "blame the predecessor" or "blame office reorganization" or the latest "the computer has been down.") Few go as far as the secret service "Never apologize, never explain, never complain" but this stone face of bureaucratic immovability is perhaps what dehumanizes its practitioners most and frustrates its clients to distraction.

The result is the truly Kafkaesque situation where the purpose of the institution or organization is obscured or distorted and in the end totally forgotten. The defense of procedures becomes, as we have said tirelessly, the goal of the operation. This is in turn boosted by that loyalty to primary units that we have already noted, and which is one of the mechanisms that can, for its practitioners, give bureaucracy a human face. But it can backfire for the clients of bureaucracy when this loyalty to the division or the office or the department becomes the goal of the practitioners, and not the servicing of the needs of the client as defined by the institutional goals and ideals. These ostensible purposes can be too far distant to stir the proximate motivations; they can even come to seem irrelevant, while the survival of the department is a life or death matter, or at least where the immediate rewards lie. The brilliant novels of John Le Carré are in fact some of the best contemporary explorations of the reality of this paradoxical phenomenon. But at a more humble level (and these personal illustrations are relevant because we are talking of how impersonal bureaucracy frustrates the ordinary person) my eighty-seven-year-old mother was due a certain sum for furnishings from the British social services when she changed residences from a nursing home to sheltered accomodation. This move was actually going to save the social services a lot of money. As a result of bank closings because of Christmas and bad weather, a certain amount of money, paid in by the social services themselves, had accumulated in her bank account, all of which was owed to the nursing home (where the social services had placed her to begin with) and none of which was capital. But the social services refused to give her the full sum due because her bank balance, on the day they made their calculation, was over the minimum allowed for such assistance to be given. All rational argument was ignored. The rule book said that this was how the calculation must be made—it did not ask about the nature of the income recorded but only the amount; and so it was. "Don't blame us, we just apply the rules." I am not saying that they misapplied the rules but that this is a typical example of the obsession with the rules—in fact the very generality of the rules themselves—that refuses to allow the most rational, not to say humane, treatment of a particular case. Weber may define this as "rationality," but one wonders where the rationality is in such a case? Is the blind following of inappropriate rules "rational?" The Scandinavian countries, recognizing this, try to get round it with the institution of the ombudsman. But this is to confess the very failure of the system's "efficiency." They have to reintroduce the "grace and favor" of prebureaucratic "masters" to try to redress the rational balance. I am sure that part of the popularity of the western as a genre lies in the cliché "shoot out" where someone who frustrates you can be called out at high noon and the matter settled with the "little equalizer."

> "I've got a little list...
> And they'll none of 'em be missed."

I cannot resist adding one last fault line in the form of Fox's Iron Law of Mediocrity. This states simply: *Bad departments can only get worse.* The reason is obvious: mediocre people will not appoint anyone smarter than themselves. This is why the selection committees of mediocre universities inevitably pick even more mediocre presidents who in turn appoint still more mediocre administrators and so on in a descending spiral. Good departments do not necessarily get better, but mediocre ones of necessity get worse. They have to be hit from the outside in order to change. This has something to do with dominance hierarchies, and ego identity again. It may in fact have not have mattered all that much in the personalized Palaeolithic, but it surely is the death of those bureaucratic systems where intellectual merit is supposed to be the criterion of advancement. Having ribbed the military however gently on the horse issue, I throw this one in to show that inbuilt faults are not foreign to academic bureaucracies either. In fact I have to rein myself in (if you will forgive the horsey metaphor) from producing even more gory examples (especially of ego inflation) from my own turf.

Bureaucracy reached its apogee among the Northern European industrial countries. And those countries are the first to deplore the state of bureaucratic "corruption" in the Southern, Slavic, African and Eastern worlds. Indeed, most of us have found ourselves at the receiving end of such "corruption." It is not confined to the these areas of course. In the days when I hobnobbed with barristers, I talked to one old clerk of Lincoln's Inn who told me of his starting days when he was green about accepted procedures. He was told by the senior clerk to take five pounds from petty cash to pass on to the judge's clerk with the aim of getting a brief moved up through the legal logjam. In his innocence, and wishing to account fully for his expenditures, he entered this as "to bribe, five pounds" in the expense book. He was severely reprimanded by his senior who told him that the "B word" must never, never appear in the accounts. It should have been recorded as "case expediting expenses."

Central and South America are of course notorious, and usually much less hypocritical about their corruption. A colleague of mine was trying, by phone calls from New Jersey, to get a cage for primates out of Mexico City airport to an island off the Mexican coast where the monkeys were kept. His efforts were futile and increasingly frustrating despite calls to the American consulate and the like. He was constantly being referred to different offices, departments and officials, eventually round in a circle to where he had started, where, naturally, they claimed not to know anything about the case. In typical puritanical Northern fashion he was all for calling the police and the lawyers. I pointed out that they would all be relatives of the bureaucrats giving him the run around. Did we not have a native contact in Mexico City? We did. I called him. Did he have a cousin at the airport? Of course. So I asked him to call the cousin to make discreet enquiries about how much and to whom. It was in fact a rather dismal sum by dollar standards. It disappeared into the system and the cage emerged with profuse apologies for "unfortunate misunderstandings"—none the worse for a few months' storage. In Colombia, taking a perilous bus ride around the cliff road between Baranquilla and Cartagena in an ancient vehicle filled with people, pigs and sacks of god knows what, we were stopped at an army check point. Without any excuses, a soldier came aboard holding his captain's hat and began to collect some small sum from each passenger. I was about (northern puritan style) to protest at this blatant extortion when my colleague stopped me. Half the people on the bus were, he explained, probably carrying something illegal, or were without papers or worse, and we had a plane to catch. If the army did its duty, the bus could be held up for hours. Simpler to pay up and move on, no questions asked. "In your case" he said "think of it as a kind of tourist tax." We paid, the *capitano* saluted smartly, and the bus moved on to everyone's relief. "They get paid very little," my colleague said. "In this way some money goes directly to their families and not to the government who will only waste it." Such bribes oil the machinery of bureaucracy and are indeed like a small tax that does go directly to the underpaid officials concerned. "Is it any different," asked my wise colleague (a Colombian of course) "than slipping a twenty to the head waiter to get the best seat in the place?" Governments and multinationals of course know all about this and special funds are regularly earmarked for "expediting expenses."

Anecdotes, you will say. But who said that the plural of anecdote is data? Multiply them by the hundreds of thousands, yea even millions, and you have the picture of "customary corruption" by which these systems run. Add to them the "nepotism" (I will spare you the anecdotes about that, although some of them, from Colombia to New Jersey to the White House, are telling enough) that so horrifies the purists, and the inefficiency of course, and you get the bulk of the complaint, the bulk of the sins against true, impartial, meritocratic, uncorruptible bureaucracy. But again, if we look closely, given that we must have bureaucracies at all, these can be seen not as faults, but, on the evolutionary scale, as mitigating factors that help to give the impersonal persona a more human personality. In a "pure" bureaucracy, the bureaucrat can give but cannot take. This is intrinsically inhuman. In the "corrupt" bureaucracy a little human exchange takes place: something is given and something taken by both sides. "Nepotism" means that one gets to aid relatives and they you. It is right at the root not only of human nature but of the evolutionary process itself (in the forms of "kin selection" and "inclusive fitness" popularized by the sociobiologists.)

Some civil services, like the British, pride themselves on their uncorruptibility, and they do mangage to be relatively so, at the bribery level, by dangling orders and knighthoods and even peerages as rewards for squeaky clean behavior, thus appealing to snobbery and hierarchy, both powerful motives for conformity. They also brilliantly blend "traditional" elements (the monarch's "grace and favor" in the bestowal of titles) with bureaucratic promotion, thus getting some of the best of both worlds. Of course, the problem here lies in the fact that they act as a tremendous brake on initiative and make "keeping one's nose clean" the major aim to be pursued regardless of the actual goals, timetables, needs of clients, and so on. Malcolm Bradbury starts his wonderful satirical novel about British university life, *Eating People is Wrong* with the vice chancellor walking home on a rainy night wondering desperately what else he needed to do to ensure a knighthood before he retired. For an even better satire in the immobility and caution this introduces to British bureaucracy, read David Nobbs' marvellous *The Cucumber Man*. Nobbs is convinced that a whole British generation was corrupted by National Service which taught the fundamental lesson of how to look busy and make a little go a long way. The results for the British economy were predictably disastrous. But while direct nepotism may be outlawed, the class of established bureaucrats itself manipulates entry into the priviliged ranks by offering its kin preferred education at the "right" schools, cultivation of the "received" accent, wearing of the correct school tie, membership in the accepted clubs, and so on. Of course if one's offspring is a moron one is a bit stuck, but a place can usually be found for him in a firm where competitive examinations are not a requirement, and in the last resort there is always the army, although now that commissions can no longer be bought that has become a less attractive option.

While we are on the role of "corruption" let me mention one example in the area of the law, that supposedly most rational of rational enterprises. American law guarantees defendants a trial by a jury of their peers. Continental rational jurists might question the rationality of this, and the behavior of juries often leaves one gasping. It was instituted, in Magna Carta, to prevent arbitrary abuse of justice by the monarch, but has come to be a sacred cow in which twelve utterly baffled ordinary citizens, often picked precisely because they know nothing whatsoever about the case, have to decide the most complex issues of DNA testing (for example) in the face of an adversary system of witness examination that only adds to their confusion. But the amazing fact is that, in the USA at least, 85 to 90 percent of criminal trials never reach even an ill-prepared jury. They are "plea bargained" which is to say the defendant agrees to plead guilty, thus saving the court the trouble of a trial, and in return he is given a lighter sentence than he would have recieved if found guilty by a jury—often substantially lighter. We all know that plea bargaining exists, but I certainly never knew the extent of it until I read Milton Heumann's excellent *Plea Bargaining: The Experiences of Prosecutors, Judges, and Defense Attorneys*, (Chicago University Press, 1978.) But what Heumann points out in this excellent "ethnography" of the court system in Connecticut, is that the system could not function without this mechanism, which on the surface at least appears to fly in the face of justice (the ostensible goal of the system.) The courts are so overloaded that if everyone had a jury trial, there would be delays of many years and the expense would bankrupt the state. In consequence therefore "fairness" and "justice" have to be abandoned, and criminals are rewarded for *not* going to trial. He hastens to point out that in most cases of plea bargaining the guilt of the party is fairly transparent, but even so, according to the theory, justice should be evenly dispensed, not bartered away to solve the bureaucratic logjam. In "tight" times serious offenders end up with mere probabtion. Heumann shows beautifully how young lawyers entering the system are at first appalled by it, but rapidly come to develop skills in haggling over pleas that end up being their major asset and using up most of their time. They were not taught this in law school, and have to learn it on the job from older hands. Purist critics again rave against the system, but can offer no alternatives that will at the same time see that "justice is done" and that defendants can get their right to a "speedy trial." The "corruption" of the plea bargaining system then is another example of how the rational ends of a bureaucracy simply cannot be achieved, and how supposedly corrupt practices have to re-adjust the system itself so that humans can pass through it and not be crushed by it.

But my point is simple. All the things—and we have by no means exhausted them—that are taken to be major blemishes on bureaucratic univeralism and efficiency, can also be viewed as necessary mitigations of its literally inhuman impersonality; for the thing that Weber saw as its supreme virtue, we have reason to believe is its Achilles heel. (And here we must add the usual academic cavil: Weber was *not* insensitive to the dehumanizing effects of bureaucracy, but he was also the clearest exponent of its supposed virtues at the same time, so he gets to be the fall guy.) The major paradox is that if bureaucracies achieve their goal of absolute efficiency, they inevitably lose their humanity, and if they use subversive devices to restore their humanity they compromise their efficiency. But yet again, what we have added to the usual catalogue of complaints against the institution, is the fact that the major "fault lines" lie where the rules of bureaucracy, a very recent invention that has no corresponding evolved motivational system, run up against the adapted motivational and cognitive systems firmly evolved and implanted during the crucial EEA. If you ask us (the bulk of us), in the name of impartial rules, to privilege strangers above children, particularly in the face of scarce resources, we can do it—elephants can dance for a while on their hind legs—but we will do it with a bad grace, and most of us will subvert the system given half a chance.

We asked earlier how bureaucratic systems, if they are so inimical to human nature, can persist for such long periods. The answer is that those that did (Roman, Chinese, Egyptian, Ottoman—Empires in general) were never "pure" or "rational" bureaucracies in Weber's sense at all. They contained heavy "traditional" content (as the British bureaucracy does to this day—Weber thought it very backward in fact: "rule by notables" he called it) and were "patrimonial and prebendary" rather than meritocratic. Some historians have argued that Rome, for example, did not have a truly bureaucratic system at all. The Senate and citizens ran things in a more or less pragmatic manner. This might have been, in fact, one of the major reasons for the collapse of the republican system—when it had to deal not just with a city state but with a huge empire—and the emergence of the imperial system after Caesar. (See Christian Meier's wonderful *Caesar: A Biography*, New York: Basic Books, 1982.) Bureaucratic systems, as Spencer noted, seem to emerge originally from feudal monarchies and royal households. The communist systems, initially dedicated to pure meritocracy, soon became the playgrounds of the party members and their families, who rapidly constituted a new ruling class. Because we are intelligent, imaginative, and manipulable creatures, bureaucracies can fool us for some time into thinking they are providing EEA satisfactions. And they are great institutional teases: they provide just enough to keep most us of fooled for some of the time. But they are like drugs that mimic our endogenous opiates: eventually they destroy us if we become totally dependent on them. In their "corruption" may well lie our salvation.

Michael Young (*The Rise of the Meritocracy*) pointed out the dangers of totally meritocratic systems. In the "corrupt" systems we operate in, those who fail or who end up at the bottom of the heap can always blame the corruption of the system: social class, the influence of money, rampant nepotism, favoritism, and so on. But if everyone is given equal opportunity and equal education, and promotion is indeed entirely by merit, then those who fail have no excuse. They are simply too stupid to keep up and fall by the wayside. They are at the bottom of the heap through no fault but their own. They lack either IQ or effort or the necessary combination that makes for merit and promotion. Such a social system would be truly efficient, but it would also be a vast breeding ground for resentment and even revolution. We are getting dangerously close to it, despite the uncertain attempts at "affirmative action" which in any case do nothing for the growing white underclass. The "underclass" today can still appeal to discrimination (or now "reverse discrimination") and the like to excuse its condition. But how long can this last? Strange twists occur. The high-IQ and even higher "effort" Asians are flooding those elite universities that decided to go for pure merit—to the extent that "reverse quotas" are having to be instituted. As one section of the community becomes more literate, and more importantly computer literate, more than a third falls further into functional illiteracy and computer failure, and the situation gets worse daily.

For a full consideration of bureaucracy we would have to go in some depth into this whole issue of literacy per se, since, as Weber recognized, the "keeping of records" is at the heart of the bureaucratic enterprise, and hence, once bureaucracy becomes ubiquitous it demands a high level of general literacy. What is happening today seems to be a return to more archaic forms of "elite literacy"—and especially computer literacy. Needless to say, literacy is no more a Palaeolithic characteristic than bureaucracy itself, and the resistance to it may well be yet another diagnostic of our departure from Stone Age norms.

We work desperately to shore up this leaky social vessel, but what is it but the basic principles of bureaucracy, initially intended to serve society, become the principles of society itself? The road back from bureaucracy to humanity is difficult if not impossible. If we cannot do without it, we must understand its nature better in order to live with it, and this must include an understanding of its failure to satisfy those basic needs that are as much a part of us as our anatomy. Making bureaucracies the servants of those needs and not their rivals may well be the most difficult and yet necessary act of social engineering in the very uncertain social future.

One slight, if perhaps paradoxical, hope is that computers may help. By encouraging the return to cottage industry (working at home) and elaborate, nonbureaucratic networking, they might help redress some of the balance. But only for the computer elite of course. It is perhaps a strange turn of events that the very electronic wizardry that Orwell saw as the basis for endless bureaucratic tyranny could in fact end up working in the opposite direction. Rather than state control of the electronic media ending up in total thought control, personal computers may end up giving us a remarkable new independence. The students with faxes, video cameras, and computers in Tienanmen Square, who kept the world informed, may be prophetic. This does not stop the flood of computerphobia as evidenced by numerous movies (*2001: A Space Odyssey, The Net, War Games,* etc.) and books intent on an Orwellian illustration of the potential evils of a world in which the control of information is the control of personal lives. But this is only half the story; there is perhaps a more hopeful half: the information highway in the hands of Palaeolithic savages may yet prove the most deadly enemy of bureaucracy yet. Telectronic Tricksters are already playing havoc with the internet. We officially deplore, but the savage in us secretly admires. The revenge of the nerds may well be the salvation of something human from the ravages of bureaucratic efficiency.

Notes

The classic treatment of bureaucracy, from which I quote, is Max Weber's "Bureaucracy"—part II of *From Max Weber: Essays in Sociology*), translated and edited by H. H. Gerth and C. Wright Mills (London: Routledge and Kegan Paul Ltd., 1948), this being a translation of chapter 6 (part III) of Weber's *Wirtschaft und Gesellschaft,* 1922. One of the best recent treatments is James Q. Wilson's *Bureaucracy: What Government Agencies Do and Why They Do It* (New York: Basic Books, 1989). Herbert Spencer's contribution can be found in his *Principles of Sociology, Part V., Political Institutions* (London: Williams and Norgate, 1882). One of the very best satirical treatments, which is nevertheless full of brilliant insights is C. Northcote Parkinson *Parkinson's Law, or, The Pursuit of Progress* (London: Murray, 1958). The quotations on cavalry were drawn from two articles in *The National Interest:* Andrew F. Krepenevich, "Cavalry to Computer" (Fall, 1994), and A. J. Bacevich, "Preserving the Well-Bred Horse" (Fall 1994). Lionel Tiger's observations on industrial society in general, which, not surprisingly, resemble my own on its bureaucratic component in particular, can be found in his *The Manufacture of Evil: Ethics, Evolution and the Industrial System* (New York: Harper and Row, 1987). One of the best discussions of mental adaptation in evolution is in J. Barkow, J. Tooby and L. Cosmides, *The Adapted Mind: Evolutionary Psychology and the Generation of Culture* (New York/Oxford: Oxford University Press, 1992). On the "rationality" issue see R. Fox "Prejudice and the Unfinished Mind" reprinted as chapter 14 of *The Challenge of Anthropology* (New Brunswick NJ: Transaction Publishers, 1995).

2

Nationalism: Hymns Ancient and Modern

This was written at the behest of Owen Harries, editor of The National Interest, *who wanted a follow-up to my previous article for him on war—which was reprinted as chapter 8 of* Challenge of Anthropology. *The two are indeed best read as one article in some ways, but have become spread over two books, victims of awkward timing. Also, the original of this chapter was severely cut to make way for several other articles on the same theme. So here I have restored the first half which is largely my own testy opinions on the Balkan situation and an insistence that the "new" nationalism is no such thing. Thus the title, which Harries chose, and which has a nice nostaligic echo of my Anglican childhood. I had called it "Uncle Sam no es mi tio"—for reasons you will find in the second half.*

From George Bernard Shaw's *Saint Joan:*

CAUCHON: You understand it wonderfully well my lord. Scratch and Englishman and find a Protestant.
WARWICK: I think you are not entirely void of sympathy with The Maid's secular heresy, my lord. I leave you to find a name for it.
CAUCHON: You mistake me, my lord. I have no sympathy with her political presumptions. But as a priest I have gained a knowledge of the minds of the common people; and there you will find yet another most dangerous idea. I can express it only by such phrases as France for the French, England for the English, Italy for the Italians, Spain for the Spanish, and so forth. It is sometimes so narrow and bitter in country folk that it surprises me that this country girl can rise above the idea of her village for its villagers. But she can. She does. When she threatens to drive the English from the soil of France she is undoubtedly thinking of the whole extent of country in which French is spoken. To her the

French-speaking people are what the Holy Scriptures describe as a nation. Call this side of her heresy Nationalism if you will: I can find you no better name for it...

WARWICK: Well, if you will burn the Protestant, I will burn the Nationalist, though perhaps I shall not carry Messire John with me there. England for the English will appeal to him.

THE CHAPLAIN: Certainly England for the English goes without saying; it is the simple law of nature...

* * *

A recent lengthy visit to Europe (1993) left me feeling that the patients were truly taking over the asylum. In the EEC the drive towards unity and harmonious federalism has dominated until recently, with France and Germany leading the chorus. This all now seems to be unravelling at an alarming rate, with governments unable to form coherent policies from day to day, but faut de mieux, trying to ramrod ratification of the incomprehensible Maastricht treaty through by hook or by crook, in the face of increasingly angry and bewildered public opinion. The Danes said a flat no, then under intense government pressure yielded a slender yes. The French, after a barrage of manipulative government-backed propaganda barely said yes. The Norwegians are threatening to dissent. The British, having been muzzled by the government on the question of a referendum, have been treated to parliamentary shennanigans of a Gilbertian absurdity in which rebel Tories voted for what they didn't want in order to get what they did want (no Maastricht), and then reversed themselves on a vote of confidence to save the government they had just defeated, which from a Maastricht point of view wouldn't matter since a Labour government would be in favor of it anyway—who's next?

There was an Alice in Wonderland scene in the House of Commons where a solemn Tony Benn (aristoplebe extraordinary) on a point of order invoked the 1688 Bill of Rights (Clause 1) to the effect that an underhand Tory cabinet was about to use the Royal Assent to a (future) vote of confidence to thwart the will of Parliament—very unconstitutional. Even his jubilant Labour colleagues, while cheering wildly, had the decency to look baffled on this one. But I swear I heard at least one shout "Off with his head!!" (Major's, that is, not Benn's.) It might have been Lady Thatcher of course, who often confuses herself with the Queen of Hearts these days.

In their growing bewilderment, the publics freely confess they don't know *what* they are voting for (no one understands Maastricht) but there is certainly evidence of a swelling volume of discontent with "Brussels"— the bête noir replacing Rome, Moscow, or Berlin of old, and a feeling that anything above a loose economic union (which they have anyway) is too much.

The embarrassing scramble to get out from under the European Exchange Rate Mechanism didn't help. Examples pour in through press and television every day of unworkable EEC rules being resisted and perfectly reasonable rules flouted, and above all of a general malaise and disillusionment at all levels. The "deeply committed" Brussels bureaucrats, and the various—if somewhat shaky—allies in the particular national parties, plough ahead with an almost religious fervor; but dispute is still more the order of the day than consensus, and the excuse of "growing pains" is growing thin now nearly fifty years on. There is something rotten in the (United) State of Europe.

On the other side of the great historical divide, in Eastern Europe, an even more virulent repudiation of "unity and federation" is proceeding apace. At least the EEC "unity" is one that, in principle, the parties would like to achieve; they squabble bitterly over the details and degree. The externally imposed "unity" of the old Communist bloc (and Yugoslavia) was not wanted, and no one is too surprised that once the heavy hand was lifted, the "nations of the East" should have demanded "freedom" however they construed it. What was perhaps surprising to the West, struggling with the painful birth of a supranational unity, was the virulence with which ancient nationalist "freedoms" should have come so rapidly to dominate.

Whatever the squabbles of the unwilling EEC bretheren, they are nothing compared to the Yugoslav mess. French farmers or fishermen dumping produce on the public highways to protest against the threats to their subsidized uneconomic way of life, do not compare even remotely with the slaughter in Bosnia, or the serious risk of it that the Estonians were willing to take—even seemed to invite, and that Chechnya has experienced. In at least one case it happened with relative good sense and tranquility when the Czechs and Slovaks went their separate ways, and historians in years to come are going to have to look carefully at this example of what went right for a change. But otherwise we have bloody chaos and potential chaos. And even where it stopped short of this (the

Baltic States won the face off with the USSR, itself too beset with its own troubles to intervene) the virulence of the "new-old nationalism" still startled the world's observers.

The embarrassment for the confused and incompetent EEC continues, as the "new nations" of Eastern Europe start the process of solicitation to join the Western bund, just as it seems on the point of retreating from its vaunted goals. The Eastern nations, of course, are really only interested in the free-trade benefits. The last thing they want is to join another supranational *political* unit. This should mean that those West Europeans who are lukewarm towards unity ought to encourage their membership which is bound to water down the more grandiose ambitions of the Eurocrats in Brusssels.

Yugoslavia (that was) is only the worst-case scenario of the "new nationalism" which is simply the very old Balkan nationalism (or tribalism—we'll come to that) kept under wraps by Tito as heir to the Hapsburg and Ottoman burden. And here the paradoxes continue. No one in the EEC, I imagine, is going to look very favorably on "Greater Serbia's" application for membership. Yet it was one of the leaders of the the EEC Federal Unity Movement, Germany, that helped provoke the Yugoslav mess. No one doubts, for example, that Slovenia will float easily into the EEC under German sponsorship (when the Bundesbank speaks, everybody listens). But the rest of the West can perhaps be forgiven for asking "what's a Slovenia?" The Germans, with unbecoming haste, and with dubious motives to do with their unholy alliance with the Croatian Nazis in World War II (never forgiven by the Serbs who had more than a million victims of this cozy pact) decided to "recognize" Croatia and Slovenia, until then two provinces of a sovereign nation—Yugoslavia, as sovereign nations themselves, and push for their membership in the EEC. Slovenia has Croatia between it and Serbia, so it escaped the worst effects of Serbian anger, and may well end up having its own merry Maastricht monkey-house revels pretty soon. But easy success went to the collective German head—this was the first time they had been able to throw their weight around other than economically since World War II after all. They decided there was no limit to their benevolent handing out of "national" status and "recognized" Bosnia! At least Slovenia and Croatia could make some shadowy claim to being "national" entities, but Bosnia was a congeries of ethnic, religious, political, and even territorial groups that never did constitute a "nation" in any meaningful sense of the term. (The "Herzegovina" bit simply means "where the German warlords—*Herzogen*—ruled.")

The reaction of Belgrade was utterly predictable: they were the central government of an internationally recognized nation—Yugoslavia—and they objected to both unilateral declarations of independence by provinces and even more to the generous German bestowal of "nationhood" on these provinces and the spineless acquiescence (by default largely) of the rest of the EEC. The central government fought to restore its authority over its territory, suddenly to find itself dubbed "the Serbs" and a new and easy object of hatred to the "good" nations of the world; nations that would never, of course, and never had in their history, put down rebellious provinces within their own borders! The rest is, very dismal, history. Local Serb militias turned vicious. The Croats became victims, then turned vicious themselves, throwing the moralizing West into further confusion. The Bosnian Muslims (the who?) became, for a while, a new kind of Palestinian; first allied to the Croats then their victims in turn—or vice-versa, depending on to whom you talk or where you turn up. (That they had Iranians fighting with them and sent their men to Iran for training and arms seems to have been strangely overlooked in the rush to "blame the Serbs.") The U.N. has scored another triumph of muddle, indecision, and bad judgment, and the Germans are now trying to keep a low profile and hope everyone forgets that they started the whole thing, or "ethnic cleansing" is going to come back and haunt them. Some of us, at least, remember who taught that little skill to the all-too-willing Croats. [Again since the first writing of this piece strange developments have taken place wherein, for the first time since World War II, German troops have been allowed to operate on foreign soil. And this has to be, of all places, in Yugoslavia, where memories of their vicious previous "occupation" are far from dead. Is this intended as a deliberate provocation of the Serbs? Or will the Germans be kept securely in the Croat areas along with their former allies? One wonders. Either way it will do nothing to bolster confidence in the NATO exercise.]

Why, we might ask, did not the EEC nations, together with the USA and U.N. take the same attitude as they had taken, say in Nigeria, or the Congo, or even towards Rhodesia, and firmly support the recognized central government and refuse aid and comfort to the rebel provinces? How did the Serbs living in the province of Bosnia-Herzegovina, loyal to their legitimate central government, suddenly become routinely "rebel Serbs" and disloyal to the nonexistent "nation" of Bosnia? Is Bosnia more worthy than Biafra or Chechnya? One can only suppose that the EEC and NATO (including the Serb-demonizing U.S.) are intoxicated with the "new nationalism" as it has swept over east Europe and the Russias, and, as part of a more general confusion, are confusing this somehow with the "triumph of democracy" and even the "end of history." Since the entities that are breaking up are "communist totalitarian" regimes, then *anything* that takes their place is ipso facto a good thing, even if it is vicious neofascism or rabid Muslim fundmentalism or tribal xenophobia. [Since this was written, NATO, led by a totally confused U.S., has bombed the now-retreating Serbs into submission, allowing the Croatians to complete their "ethnic cleansing" of the weternmost Serbs, and imposed a "peace" which is creating a deeply divided country of three ethnic enclaves only kept from each other's throats by a massive armed force due to leave in a year. What, in God's name, do they expect to happen then, aspecially as the U.S. is insisting on "rearming" the Iran-backed muslims while vilifying Iran as a terrorist state?]

This re-Balkanizing of the Balkans is not self-evidently a good thing. Even Woodrow Wilson realized that the "self" in "self-determination" had, in a world of nation states, to be something self-sustaining—at least economically and politically viable. Thus the Czechs and Slovaks and Serbs and Croats—only minimally distinguishable in any case, had to learn to live together and cooperate, and no bad thing. (Serbian and Croatian, for example, differ only in the pronunciation of one letter of the alphabet. But this one letter has spawned a whole industry of rhetoric on "essential" linguistic differences. And of course the Catholic Croats use the Latin, and the Orthodox Serbs the Cyrillic, alphabet to write the same language.) But Wilson had some sense of history and its lessons. Small "nations" for example do not mean less war. They mean more smaller wars. But the cumulative effect of these is perhaps less awful than world wars between huge nation-states and empires. Wilson sought a balance, and what was produced wasn't bad—looked at rationally. The Hapsburg empire was dismantled, and hence a massive source of stability in Central Europe was lost. But the "new nations" even though composites of different ethnic, religious, and linguistic groups, were somewhere between dangerously expansive empire and predatory tribe. And for twenty years or so they stumbled along. And after World War II the heavy hand of Moscow kept them together much as that of Vienna had done previously. Similarly the Russian hegemony in the East, established by the expansionist policies of the tsars, held sway over the Baltics and the "-stans" and the other minor Soviet republics.

Now all this has come unravelled, and the unity of the EEC seems to be unravelling. In Italy, the Lombard League, which seeks virtual autonomy for the North, has achieved huge electoral success. Spain cannot contain the Basque problem. In the Middle East "national" identity compounded by sectarian Islam asserts itself in wars that drag in the whole world. In Africa, the "nations" that were the legacy of arbitrary colonial boundaries are riven with tribal strife, and the constantly ingenuous West is shocked to find the Zulus killing their black "brothers" to retain their own distinct tribe/nation status, or the Hutus trying to exterminate their "fellow Rwandan" Tutsis by hand. In Sudan the southern Christian tribes are fighting for independence from the Islamic north, and across wide stretches of the central Sahara the Tuaregs are fighting a brave but probably hopeless battle for the same right. In the Far East, India, Sri Lanka, the Phillipines, and Indonesia are fighting "ethnic separatists," and China (including Tibet) only remains a nation through the brute force of central totalitarianism. The prosperous southeast of Brazil wants to break off from the rest of the country, and Canada seems unable to solve the problem of Quebec. And so the sorry tale—from the Western progressive liberal point of view—continues. Why can't the world seem to settle down into nice well-ordered democratic nation-states, and concentrate on television-driven consumerism, the empowerment of minorities, the abolition of sexist pronouns, and other good liberal democratic enterprises?

In all this the U.S. in particular affects pious spectator status. This is all happening "elsewhere." For the optimists—the end-of-history crowd included—the world is rapidly going to adopt our own form of perfectionism and all will be democratically/capitalistically well. For the pessimists, it is the same old story of the world failing to live up to our own high standards and making its usual un-American mess of things. For the isolationists we should leave them to it; for the internationalists we must be the world's policeman (with or without the U.N. as suits us); for the pragmatists we should intervene only when our national interests are at stake (Somalia?). But one finds very few people taking seriously the proposition that we are not some kind of utopian solution to the problem but very much part of the problem itself. The massive distrust of government and the growing power of separatist sentiments is as potentially destructive to us as it was to the USSR. It has happened once in our history with terrible costs, and we are not in any way immune. The coming dissolution may not be as blatantly territorial as in the Civil War (although the virtual secession of half of Dade County, Florida, and the creation of a Spanish-speaking Cuban nation there should give us pause), but it will be no less ideological, and ideology kills as surely as ever territory did. [Since this was written, the Federal building in Oklahoma City was ravaged by antigovernment bombers.] We have always, from our beginnings as a "contractual" nation, been a mish-mash of warring factions only loosely linked by "national" sentiment, however noisy that has been at times—and it has had to be noisy to drown out the dissent. Can any sociologist tell us how to measure how much more or less of a mish-mash we are now? The mish-mash has been held together by some very strong sense of being "American"—something that led even segregated black and Amerindian regiments in World War II to feel "proud" of what they were defending. Does this still exist? Since the sixties and the mounting of the "multicultural" crusade, nothing is certain.

But I shan't dwell on this issue. It is the subject of another debate, and a particularly frustrating debate because the criteria don't seem to have been established. When has a "nation" reached the limits of its integration? What are the sure signs that it's various ethnic, racial, territorial, religious, linguistic, and interest groups no longer feel a common bond or purpose? I might be inclined to say "when they refuse to speak a common language"—but there is always Switzerland to claim as an exception! No. That debate must wait, and we should perhaps try to get back to fundamentals. We should try because most of the modern debates on "nationalism" don't get anywhere near them. One opens a new, very large, and much-hyped book like Liah Greenfeld's *Nationalism: Five Roads to Modernity*, (Cambridge, MA: Harvard University Press) hoping for fresh insights, and finds only the same dreary catalogue of facts. Most books on the "nationalism" issue are written by political scientists, sociologists, historians, politicians, and other peddlers of ephemera. The psychologists occasionally have a crack at it, but they are prisoners of their schools and disagree as loudly as the nationalists themselves. Ever since Freud assured us that the Russians would never rebel against a tsar they regarded as a "little father" and whom they had incorporated into their superegos, we have learned to be wary of psychological advice in this field. It could be true, for example, that devotion to national causes may be one way we escape Erich Fromm's "fear of freedom"; but that doesn't tell us why nationalism should be chosen.

My own interest in nationalism (please take the quotes as read from now on) was early sparked by the internationalism with which I grew up from the thirties through the fifties. Its two forms—of international socialism on the one hand and the idealistic hope in the League of Nations or United Nations on the other—both seemed doomed. The workers of the world just flat did not unite, let's face it. On the contrary, they seemed very happy to get a chance to dish it out to the workers of other nations. And again, the sorry history of the U.N. (following on the League) showed that governments of the nations of the world would not unite either. The U.N. always seemed to me to be killed by its own premise: that world peace and good governance could come about by the cooperation of independent nation-states. United *Nations* was almost an oxymoron. Nations existed to be disunited from each other, only coming together in temporary alliances out of self-interest. Here it seemed that the utopian internationalists had the better idea in that they wanted to abolish nations and achieve a "brotherhood of man" that refused to recognize artificial national boundaries. Theoretically, that made more sense, except that the boundaries just were not artificial; they were very real. And the U.N. by adding to its councils ever more self-declared "nations" (even if they were islands smaller than most small towns) constantly compounded its problems.

Internationalism of all varieties then seemed to be an idealistic failure. People at large just didn't think globally. But nationalism itself had major problems, not least that many "nations" and especially (but not exclusively) "new nations" were indeed artificial entities: the creations of colonial map makers (Kuwait is a nation?) or, as we have discussed, the Versailles Treaty carvers-up of eastern Europe. Many of these "nations" cut across more ancient racial, religious, ethnic, and linguistic boundaries, especially in Africa where whole tribes were split in this way, or forcibly incorporated with traditional enemies. This raised the issue of the relation of "nation states" to these other units. For what seemed to be required of nation states was that they *behave* like homogeneous tribes, even if this was plainly a fiction. The problem continues to plague modern "new nationalisms." The Scottish nationalists, for example, have to plaster over the tremendous differences between the lowland (Presbyterian, mercantile, urban) Scots, and the highlanders: Gaelic, Catholic, of Irish origin and only recently emerged from territorial and kinship dominated tribalism. (There were more Scots fighting *against* Bonnie Prince

Charlie at Culloden than for him.) And the Republican Irish embarrassment over their northern Protestant bretheren needs no embellishment. One could go on multiplying examples, and this indeed has been done to death.[1] So let us try to get back to those elusive fundamentals.

This assumes that there *are* some fundamentals: some features of the human creature that predsipose it to "nationalistic" behavior. But this is dismissed by the "nationalism-is-modern" school, for whom the phenomenon starts not with Nature but with Herder (or a bit before in the precocious cases of England and France.) But let us observe that even the most diehard of the nationalism-is-modern school admit that "national sentiments" are very real. Thus Hobsbawm admits that "what is in doubt is not the strength of men's and women's longing for group identity of which nationality is one expression."[2] "What sceptics doubt," he continues, "is the alleged irresistibility of the desire to form homogeneous nation states..." Note the slippage here—from an admittedly "natural nationality" to a definitely resistable "nation state."

I doubt anyone would want to argue that we have inbuilt predispositions to form nation states. Natural selection would have to have been remarkably (and teleologically) prescient to have provided for that one—even for states! But nations (if not states) are formed out of *something*, and as Hobsbawm recognizes, "longing for group identity" is one thing (but not, as he supposes, the only one). Even more noticable is the slippage between the admitted "nationality" ("sense of group belonging") and *nationalism*—which can only be some kind of *doctrine* of nation-state primacy.[3] Truly the state can exist without the nation and the nation precede the state (or vice-versa), and some kind of *doctrine* to justify, glorify, and rationalize it all need only arise well after the historical fact

---

1. See the Summer 1993 issue of *Daedalus* for example. The article there by Tom Nairn "Internationalism and the Second Coming" (155–70) makes a good case for the durability of small nationalisms, but again does not get to fundamentals.
2. E. J. Hobsbawm, *Nations and Nationalism Since 1780.* (Cambridge: Cambridge University Press, 1990, p. 187.)
3. Isaiah Berlin in one of the most interesting, and hence most neglected, essays on nationalism, stresses the centrality of the doctrinal aspect, as well as the fact that no one predicted the durability of nationalism in the twentieth century: "Nationalism: Past Neglect and Present Power" in *Against the Current: Essays in the History of Ideas*, edited by Henry Hardy (New York: Viking, 1980). This version of his thoughts on nationalism in fact emerged as an address to a congress in Haifa in 1974, after a long conversation we had on the subject, which caused Berlin to ditch his prepared remarks and take up this issue instead.

(England) or alternatively precede and create it (Germany.) Commentators have made us familiar with, not to say sick of, all the permutations. But what the "nationalism-is-modern-not-natural" school are saying, slyly confounds these distinctions. Nationalism and the nation-state (and obviously the industrial nation-state so central to Gellner's theory[4]) are of course "modern." By the same token, appeals to human nature do not explain them. For Hobsbawm they are blatantly historical epiphenomena overdue for obsolescence. But as he too realizes, that naggingly persistent "national feeling" is somehow independent of all this historical jiggery pokery. (Isaiah Berlin also disclaims any attempt to explain the social psychology of nationalism. That remains for him a great mystery.)

Let us put it this way: Whatever the origins, historical, sociological, geographical, economic, military or whatever, of nationalism and the nation-state, the one uniformity is the relative ease with which "national" sentiments can be aroused and sustained in the populations of these "modern" entities. This gives the theorists of nationalistic "modernity" a deep sense of unease, since we are clearly dealing here with deeply atavistic sentiments and motivations. It is obviously disturbing to have to argue that some social phenomenon is "modern" and a "construct" but at the same time to have to admit that it derives its emotional energy from some unknown archaic dark corners of the human psyche.

This would only be strange, however, to a theory that insisted that sentiments and emotions themselves were solely the creations of historical conditions. Unfortunately this is the prevailing paradigm for the social and historical sciences. If, however, one accepts that man carries a baggage of evolutionary dispositions—mental as well as emotional[5]—then there is really no problem. The only problem is empirical: What social conditions "fit" these dispositions and what do not? I have spent a great deal of time complaining about the conditions that *fail* to satisfy these Palaeolithic motivations and mentations,[6] but it equally follows that, often serendipitously it is true, modern conditions will evoke and reinforce ancient (Palaeolithic) sentiments. Thus I have argued that bureaucracy will rarely ever work since the attributes it demands are so implacably anti-palaeolithic. Sociologists

4. E. A. Gellner, *Nations and Nationalism*, Oxford: Blackwell, 1983.
5. J. Barkow, L. Cosmides, and J. Tooby, *The Adapted Mind* New York: Oxford University Press, 1992.
6. R. Fox, *The Search for Society* (New Brunswick, NJ: Rutgers University Press 1989

too have noted the persistent failure of bureaucracy, but are frustrated in their explanations since they can only look for reasons within the historical conditions of bureaucracy itself.

Nationalism, at least in its form of real and obvious national sentiments, creates the same dilemmas. Here is something that taps and indeed thrives on atavistic motives and satisfactions—some benign, some generous, some horrible, that cannot be explained as creations of nationalism (and the nation-state) itself. The historical contingency school is left only with various forms of manipulative or conspiracy theories, by which the gullible masses are somehow brainwashed into various ecstatic states. Hobsbawm to his credit avoids this extreme nonsense, but equally he never comes to grips with the problem raised by his vision of a nonnationalist future: what will happen if you remove this source of human satisfaction?

There are three things you can do to the Palaeolithic hunter that we are. (Do I need to spell out again the argument that the tiny episode we call "history"—at best the few thousand years of the interglacial in which we live—has done nothing to change our basic psycho-physico-social nature that evolved over two and a half million years of the Palaeolithic?) The three things are: You can *deny* him his evolved needs either by simple deprivation or by imposing institutions that distort them; you can *satisfy* or tap those needs either directly or by modern institutions that utilize or at least do not frustrate them; you can figure out how to *fool* the evolved system so that we utilize atavistic motives to modern ends. (So far we only seem to have succeeded best in this third case with drugs, which fool the brain into thinking they are endogenous opiates. This fooling business is a dangerous road to travel.) The current task of history and the behavorial sciences should be to utilize the insights of evolutionary biology to help sort out where we are satisfying, where frustrating, and where fooling our Palaeolithic selves. Most contemporary savants are running in the opposite direction, and in circles to boot.

The evolutionary line leading to the powerful "sense of belonging" that the nationalism-is-modern school cannot deny but cannot accomodate is simple. In the nonhuman primates we find intense sociality within the troop, and equally intense xenophobia directed to outsiders.[7] In our clos-

---

7. Ralph L. Holloway, ed., *Primate Aggression, Territoriality and Xenophobia* (New York: Academic Press, 1974); Alexander H. Harcourt and Frans de Waal, eds., *Coalitions and Alliances in Humans and Other Animals* (Oxford, Oxford University Press, 1992)

est relatives, the chimpanzees, this goes beyond mere defense of range or territory to cooperative, predatory, cannibalistic, and ultimately geno- cidal attacks on other groups.[8] But above all there is the strong sociality and group identification. This is reflected in the earliest of hominid societies, the australopithecines, from at least three-and-a-half million years ago. Small groups wandered the east African savannahs, scaveng- ing and catching small game. As the scale of hunting increased with the advent of *Homo erectus*, the two-million year upsurge in brain size and social complexity took off on its upward trajectory. By the close of the Palaeolithic, larger bands making up "linguistic tribes" (up to five thou- sand individuals) with ceremonial cave centers emerged. Then came the Neolithic revolution, agriculture and herding, and the rest, literally, is history.

The sequence: primate troop → australopithecine horde → Palaeolithic band → linguistic tribe → tribal confederation → chieftainship → tribal state, and on up to city states, kingdoms, empires etc, is well enough known. What is not well understood is how each level draws on the lower levels. Thus the nationalism-is-modern school has a hard time dealing with the "tribal" elements of nations, and the political anthropologists often do not want to see the underpinnings of the human band or tribe as lying in the primate troop. But just as early human bands three million years ago drew on the socio-emotional strengths of their ancestral pri- mate heritage, so the tribe drew on the strengths of the band and ulti- mately the kingdom or state on the strengths of the tribe. At the heart of every nation then is tribal feeling writ large. And this is at once both the secret of the peculiar strength of national feeling and also its potential weakness. For when the nation is too large and too heterogeneous, as many modern nation-states and super-states become, then the bounds of Palaeolithic credibility become dangerously stretched, and we resort to the third alternative: fooling our Palaeolithic emotions. This, as we saw with the drug example, is a dangerous tack to take.

One thing that characterizes the basic hominid social unit is kinship. These are kin-related creatures. This draws on the primate roots where the same is true. The Palaeolithic linguistic tribe, while split into many bands or clans, preserved the idea that all those who spoke the same

---

8. Jane Goodall, *The Chimpanzees of Gombe* (Cambridge, MA: Harvard University Press 1986).

tongue were kin, usually by some legend of common descent. This was plausible, and explains what must often seem like a pathological devotion to language as a marker of social identity in modern nationalism (viz. the Serbian-Croatian example). But the linguistic tribe was probably never more than five thousand strong. When Aristotle set that limit to the number of citizens in an ideal city state, he knew whereof he spoke. Beyond that limit we must resort to *fictions* of kinship in order to tap (or fool) the emotions of group solidarity. Modern nationalists know this very well, and the linkage of language and "blood" (kinship) becomes an essential part of their rhetoric. Nations are big tribes. Thus rulers do indeed become "little fathers" of their people, and the nation itself a "mother-" or "father-land." When the "sibling-citizens" are clearly not of common descent, as in the U.S. or (former) USSR, then the focus has to be a sibling of a parent as in Uncle Sam or Uncle Joe. If we can all be children (or nephews) of the same ancestors ("We few, we happy few, we band of brothers") and speak the same tongue, then we can be fooled into thinking we are the same tribe: familiars—literally of the same family.

The fiction is very effective, and not only nations but religious orders and political and social movements freely use the rhetoric of kinship to arouse the same feelings of defensive solidarity. But by its very ambitions the modern industrial nation state (especially its superstate version) strains this fiction to its breaking point. Even so, "patriotic" appeals are never to self-interest but always to kin altruism ("Ask not what your country can do for you; ask what you can do for your country," etc.) But not only do very few people except a few cranks believe in the brotherhood of man, very few others believe that their co-citizens are really kinsfolk. If they did, they might behave better towards them. The fiction, in the end, ceases to be effective, especially if the pseudo-kinship has been forced on them. The "all those who speak the same language are kin" ruse fails miserably when one is *forced* to speak the language in question. The appeal to territory or a shared past—both elements of the troop-band-tribe scheme—is equally difficult to sustain as the territory gets too diverse and the past too diffuse or painful to be plausibly described as "shared."[9]

---

9. Other mechanisms for uniting large populations, like leader-worship and religion, often get inextricably blended with nationalism (or national feeling). But while they too have Paleolithic roots, we must here bracket them off and reserve them for later discussion.

We can draw on the primitive sense of kin-tribe solidarity just so far in supporting admittedly modern nationalism. The disaster comes when we try to force the fiction further than its bounds of plausibility. The palaeo-cynic in us rebels. The shotgun marriages of modern nationalism are suddenly on the rocks—maintained only by force, duplicity, and economic necessity.

One other way to maintain "national feeling" is the equally atavistic call to war. "Defense of the realm" or destruction of its enemies taps the deeply programmed "defend the clan" motivations. With nations, "the flag" replaces the clan totem, and "defending the colors" and "rallying round the flag" together with the appropiate songs, oaths, and almost religious devotion—witness the American horror at "desecration"—do an excellent fooling job on the Palaeolithic emotions. But this is difficult to sustain over long periods with any intensity, since "wars" were more in the nature of raids or brief skirmishes. It worked well enough with the incessant warring of small professional armies in the seventeenth and eighteenth centuries, but could only work in short bursts in the conditions of modern total war. The appeal works very effectively, but soon outstays its welcome.[10]

The moral of the tale told this way is very simple: The only nationalisms that will ultimately work will be *small* nationalisms in small national entities (states, tribes, or whatever). These can plausibly draw on the basic motivations to sustain themselves. If the larger nation-states and superstates are to maintain themselves through the "nationalistic" mode of social integration, then the paradox is that they must try to appeal to something other than raw national sentiment to achieve this. Rallying round white, European, English-speaking, Dixie-costumed, star-spangled Uncle Sam, will simply not do for the modern U.S. where at least a third of the nation cannot possibly feel kinship with him. As one of my Hispanic students put it almost vehemently, *"¡Uncle Sam no*

---

10. It was the formidable combination of Konrad Lorenz and Eric Erickson who taught us that the human mechanism of "dehumanizing" the enemy in effect rendered him a prey animal—a sub-human—and hence a "legitimate kill." Actually it works two ways: when we wish to despise and belittle the enemy we depict him as even less than prey—as vermin or worse; when we wish to arouse fear of the enemy we turn him into a superhuman—a monster, a "beast," a dangerous predator in effect. Churchill could deride Hitler as "Herr Schickelgruber" but he could also invoke the "Nazi Beast" or the "Nazi Menace" according to context.

es mi tio!" Some more subtle appeal, perhaps to enlightened self-interest ("you are better off here than in any nation on earth"), will have to re-place the raw national appeal, which cares nothing about having supe-rior economics but only about being superior people. This appeal to self-interest is what at the moment seems to be tenuously holding to-gether British and French Canada, and for that matter the English and Scots. The "national" sentiments here must work on a lower level, and as we have suggested, may give some aspirant but nonhomogeneous na-tions like Scotland their own troubles.

The Palaeolithic mentality and emotions cannot be indefinitely fooled, for they are what we are. We can, of course, destroy them with the likes of drugs, super nation-states and impersonal bureaucracies. But they will fight back and the fighting will get rough. Not only nationalism but a whole parade of so-called "modern social problems" from teen pregnancy epidemics and high divorce rates, to soccer hooliganism and religious fun-damentalism, may well prove to be, like "ethnic cleansing" examples not of system-driven pathologies at all, but of the Palaeolithic organism fight-ing for its survival, which is, after all, the most basic thing it knows to do.[11]

Appeals to rational self-interest are always at a disadvantage, for the interest may shift. The beauty of an appeal to "national sentiment" is precisely its nonrational and often irrational nature. It is an appeal often against self-interest and for self-sacrifice. Hobsbawm's skeptics may turn out to be wrong: There is an irresistable desire to form *something*, and even if it is not a nation-state, it is homogeneous. Perhaps we could call this irresistible desire "the perennial appeal of tribalism", and try to re-member that it allows for virtues that rational national bureaucracies no nothing of but which are very dear to our basic natures. Try heroism for starters. Hollywood and the sports world understands (and profits from) this very well, even if political scientists find no place for it in their dreams of the "rational actor" and other fantasies of academic life.

National states will continue insofar as they supply basic needs and are small and homogeneous enough to appeal to basic sentiments of be-

---

11. Soccer "hooligans" are egregiously, chauvinistically "nationalistic." Indeed they may just have discovered the elusive "moral equivalent of war" that William James saw was so necessary to "peace." I doubt this point will appeal to "Brus-sels" to whom the nationalistic soccer-patriots must appear as a recurrent night-mare of their worst frustrations.

longing. But let us never be complacent about super-national political entities when they come into competition with the perennial appeal of tribalism. A few hundred years is not even a blink of an eye in evolutionary time.

3

How Innovative Are We?

This was from another seminar organized by Alex Marshall, and the issue was military innovation, naturally. But as usual, the academics were simply asked to give their own thoughts on the general subject, not specific recommendations. With our typical arrogance, of course, we frequently overstepped the boundary and delivered up sage strategic opinions to our no doubt amused, but unfailingly polite, military counterparts.

Are we an innovative animal "by nature?" Aristotle thought we were a political animal "by nature." Others have thought we are an aggressive animal "by nature" or a conservative animal "by nature" or a religious animal "by nature." The list is long of proposed natural attributes. The problem has always been to know how to assess this. Mostly in the past, in history or theology or philosophy, or even psychology or anthropology, the "natural" has been whatever the analyst, for his own reasons, wanted to be there. This has varied from the "empty organism" (nothing is there) to genetic determinism (everything is there); from the "tabula rasa" (nothing is originally in the mind) to "innate ideas" (everything is originally in the mind); from "man is innately good" (Rousseau) to "man is born in sin" (the Church.) What we have today is not a simple formula to resolve this but rather a congeries of separate sets of evidence: from palaeontology, from neuroscience, from comparative ethology and particularly primatology, from sociobiology, from neonate studies, from evolutionary psychology, from psychobiology, from structural linguistics, comparative ethnography—and many other sources. By putting these together and bringing them to bear on particular problems, we can perhaps get closer to what we are "by nature." Thus to cast Aristotle's statement as a question: "Are we by nature animals that need to live in a *polis*?"—which is what he in fact said we are, we can answer: "No, we are by nature animals that need to live in small nomadic communities, but we can get by in a small, moderately socially differentiated *polis*, provided it is not run on slavery, does not fall prey to demagogues, and does not try to expand into a colonial empire." Athens, and Rome for that matter, if you remember, failed on all three counts.

Our question here is whether or not innovative behavior is "natural" to us, or whether it is something that must be artificially stimulated and supported to occur and be effective. Other social scientists who have studied innovation like Linton, Park, Barnett, etc., and more recently Clarke, Cancian, Layton, etc., have been concerned with the post-Neolithic period and with what, in the proverbial long-run, are relatively minor changes and inventions. They have usually been countering the notion of the stagnant or stabilized traditional society, and have been anxious to show that the old diffusionist theories ("savages don't invent, they import") were wrong and under what conditions "primitive" societies did innovate at whatever level. This is a worthy enterprise and a strong tradition in the social sciences and archaeology, closely tied to the study of social and cultural change. But our question is somewhat different. We are not so much concerned with the bits and pieces of change in traditional societies, which of course occurred (and continue to occur) and which can often be satisfactorily explained. We are concerned with the more fundamental question of how innovative an animal we are "by nature"—that is, is our bent more readily towards stability and long-term traditional societies? Or are we an animal driven to seek change and new horizons? It has been argued both ways, and different periods of history suggest different answers. And of course we do not have to suppose that either of these are universal personality traits. The need for new solutions may be normally distributed in any population with different circumstances favoring the adventurous over the cautious. But by the same token the distribution may be heavily skewed in one direction or another, giving our species as a whole a definite profile. If we want to find this "species profile" where should we look?

One place to start is our closest relatives, the primates. If they are innovative animals it would be odd if we were not. Do they innovate? The answer is yes, but infrequently. The best-known example of pure primate innovation is probably the potato washing of Japanese macaques. They were introduced to sweet potatoes, a new food, but these were covered with dirt. Some young monkeys took them to the water's edge and washed off the dirt before eating them. This was the only innovation of food habits ever noted in these animals. It spread quickly, and largely from mother to daughter. Sons picked up the habit but did not pass it on. Similarly, chimpanzees have learned to strip twigs and use the sticky stems to extract termites from mounds and eat them. This too seems to be passed on from mothers to children and then through the daughters. But primate innovation seems to be limitied to these two examples. Occassional accidental innovations occur, as when, at the Gombe Stream Reserve in Tanzania, a lowly male chimpanzee called Mike found that he could intimidate the other males by banging kerosene cans together and creating a noisy display. The innovation didn't last and the other males didn't imitate him. Other animals show similar capacities—like the birds that dropped pebbles into milk bottles to raise the level of the liquid, and beavers often show much original ingenuity in dealing with fairly complicated engineering problems in dam building. But again, these innovations are relatively minor compared to what appears to be a huge innate repertoire of these animals, on which they depend for their day to day existence.

Over the course of evolution we see hominids innovating at a cruelly slow pace. Hundreds of thousands, even millions of years pass from one innovation to another. Of course we can only largely infer such things as social innovations, but at least in the technological record we do not see rapid leaps forward. The Palaeolithic, the old stone age during which we were forged into the creatures we are, saw no change in stone-tool technology for at least two-and-a-half million years. [Since I wrote this, discoveries in Ethiopia show that stone tools were in existence for at least half-a-million years before that, so the period is three or more million years.] This puzzles commentators like John Wymer in *The Palaeolithic Age* (New York: St. Martin's Press, 1981), who find it difficult to "comprehend such slow development." But such an attitude assumes that innovation is in and of itself a good thing. We must come back to this issue, but in the meantime we must consider that innovation was not so much avoided in the Palaeolithic as that it was not necessary. If an animal is living at the top (or close to the top) of the food chain, and if life is satisfactory as it is, even if the animal has the capacity to innovate, why should it? This then is our question: are we "by nature" glacially (no pun intended) slow innovators, or are we just smart enough to know when we are ahead and to stay that way? The age of the discovery of fire-making is disputed, but even if we accept the sometimes-used 500,000 year estimate, it is obvious that what fire did was not so much push us forward as make the life we were living even more rewarding and so incline us to stick to it. Food could be cooked making tough parts usable, nights could be warmed making sleep easier, and predators and enemies intimidated. But this only encouraged us to make a better job of our nomadic hunting existence. We did not rush around forging metal or inventing steam power.

Even in the period we grace with the titles "history" or "civilization" our record is not much better given the opportunities. Compared with the Palaeolithic, this post-Neolithic period is almost an innovatory hothouse, but given our usual historic time scales, we still move at a leisurely pace. Thus from the invention of the sail, to the invention of steam-powered ships, we have a period of five thousand years. Ship design did not fundamentally change in this period. The innovation of the rudder improved steering and the platforms became larger and the sails taller. But nothing fundamental distinguishes the ships at Trafalgar from those at Actium. The major innovation from a military point of view was the mounting of cannon on ships, roughly in the 1490s. But this was not completed and perfected until 1650. In fact from the invention of the wheel and the sail until the advent of steam power in the nineteenth century there was no major change in methods of converting energy. And even here, consider that the original method of turning the wheels of steam locomotives was exactly the same when they went obsolete as when they were invented.

If we look at military "innovation" we get the same pattern. (And I draw these examples for John Keegan's wonderful *A History of Warfare* [New York: Random House, 1993].) We have already looked at sea warfare, but on land, for example, the basic principles of fortification did not change between the walls of Jericho and the nineteenth century—8,000 years. The composite bow—the brilliant weapon invented on the steppes of Asia which was the main weapon of the Mongol armies, stayed the same for 3,000 years. Cavalry tactics, since the invention of the stirrup (early 700s in Europe; 5th century B.C. in China) stayed fundamentally the same until World War II. According to Keegan, basic infantry tactics, especially deployment for speed of movement, were originated by the Assyrians in the 8th century B.C. and didn't change over the same period. Even after the invention of the cannon (by the French in 1490) and the musket, the pace of change was slow, with no new developments until the introduction of the bore in the 1850s. Even then military innovation lagged, and the musket continued to be the weapon of choice. Custer's Seventh Cavalry at the Little Big Horn were armed with single-shot rifles that jammed when they (rapidly) overheated. The Indians, who were armed with rifles as well as bows, spears, and hatchets, mostly had Winchester repeaters obtained from traders. Thus a modern army was not only outnumbered but actually outgunned by its "savage" opponents. In terms of tactics also, military innovation was abysmally slow. I recently watched the brilliant reenactment of Pickett's so-called charge at Gettysburg, for the film of that name. The tactic used—a slow march of long lines of men into the face of cannon and massed musketry had been obsolete at Waterloo, and had failed utterly at the Battle of New Orleans. Yet here, sixty years later, this ancient "line of battle" formation was still being used with carnage as the outcome. Lee (whose reputation as a great general continues to amaze me) did not even have the sense to have his men advance in columns, thus presenting a smaller target to the Union guns, only wheeling into lines at the last moment. But of course even more amazing is that in World War I the generals were still, in the face of machine guns this time, sending lines of men on frontal attacks. No doubt they were doing what they had been taught at the military academies, which makes one wonder what place these archaic institutions have in the world of modern warfare. Seeing how training proceeds at places like the Citadel one wonders (a) why on earth any intelligent woman would want to be there and (b) what possible role these institutions can have in training men for modern war. They would make excellent places to send incorrigible juvenile delinquents though.

The last 150 years have been a staggering exception to the evolutionary rule in almost every sense. An animal that is an almost painfully slow innovator has suddenly upped the pace almost frenetically. This has gone along with—although I am not confident to say has been caused by—an equally unprecedented and dramatic rise in population. But with both technology and innovation we must stop to ask what we are doing to an animal evolved to deal with small groups and innovative conservatism.

Let us return briefly to the primates. From these close relatives we inherited what ethologist Desmond Morris (in *The Naked Ape*) christened "neo-philia"—the love of the novel: a passionate curiosity and innovative capacity. Chimpanzees have it in abundance. Orangutans, given enough time, will learn to imitate the chipping of stone tools in order to open boxes of fruit. But with the primates, and so undoubtedly with our earliest, pre-tool-using hominid ancestors, this easily dissipates into fads, fashions, and idle curiosity. Cynics might argue *plus ça change*—and there is room for much discussion of our insatiable desire for the new for its own sake. "Fashion" is everything from clothes to ideas to gadgets. But while a lot of our neo-philiac activity is as dissipative as the chimp's, we are obviously also capable of something denied to other primates and, presumably, our early ancestors. We need the neo-philiac urge, yes, but we must add various other qualities, and these qualities must have evolved in that long drag of the Pleistocene—qualities like concentration, persistence, goal orientation, deferred gratification, inhibition and equilibration. I repeat, the rudiments are there in the great apes. But something quite significant had to emerge during the enlargement of the neo-cortex and the growth of cortical control that characterized our evolution in the tool-using period.

Let us take these qualities in order:

Concentration and persistence are there in the apes, but they had to be applied systematically and across a wide range of behaviors. The attention span, as we now like to call it, had to be lengthened and focused on something other than food and sex.

Goal orientation and deferred gratification are favorites of the psychologists, but in recognizing these they recognize something of great importance. It is not enough to be endlessly curious, we have to direct that curiosity/neo-philia to specific goals, and often long-term goals. And this in turn means that we have to be able to control our limbic urges and not seek immediate gratification of our needs and impulses but defer this urgent gratification—subordinate it to our long-term needs.

This could only be achieved with profound neural reorganization that allowed us to *inhibit* the immediate responses—emotive acting out—and to allow our neo-cortex to indulge in assessment of relatively long-term consequences of our actions in terms of equally (relatively) long-term goals. In fact the growing neo-cortex took on both roles: it acted as a center for such cognitive assessment and organization, at the same time as acting as an inhibitor of our limbic urges, including the neo-philiac ones.

Given these developments our neo-philia would not just dissipate or be concentrated in small areas, but could be directed to organized innovative activity over wide areas of behavior. The very slowness of innovation over this period is of course related to the slowness of the development of these mental capacities (although in evolutionary terms this was all quite swift—three times faster than the evolution of the leg of the horse for example.) Even when they are in place, as we have seen, we continue to be slow innovators and continue with the dissipative neo-philiac behavior of our primate heritage in large part. The flip side of this is that this "play" behavior (*Homo ludens*) is often a fertile ground for innovation in itself, as long as we know how to separate the possible cumulative and progressive (at least in a technological sense) elements from the purely playful. The Aztecs invented the wheel, but confined it to toys. The Chinese invented gunpowder, but used it only for fireworks. (This was either a good or a bad thing depending on one's view of "progress." I am just noting the tendency.)

Clearly here we are in the realm of evolutionary psychology, which has not had a lot to say about innovation per se. But some of its disputes on the origins and nature of human intelligence are relevant and revealing. Thus the sociobiological school, largely following my colleague Robert Trivers on the roles of deception and self-deception, has come to concentrate on what it calls "Machiavellian Intelligence" as the truly human intelligence. This means that as social interaction, during human evolution, becomes complex, so does cheating and deception, and there is therefore a strong selection pressure for methods to deal with this in manipulation, counter-manipulation, and cheater detection. Increased brain power is the consequence, and eventually even consciousness and self-consciousness can be seen as necessary outcomes of these pressures. Modern evolutionary psychologists, for example, put great emphasis on our skill, as evidenced in sophisticated experiments, on social contracts and the detection of cheating. We do significantly better on the same tests when posed in terms of cheater detection, for example, than when posed as straightforward logical problems.

There is no question that such Machiavellian skills have played their part in the evolution of intelligence. But criticism comes from those who see this as a one-sided emphasis which neglects what has been dubbed "Natural History Intelligence." Machiavellian Intelligence, they argue, is purely "inward turning" social intelligence—focused on the internal processes of the social group. In human evolution, they argue, selection would have been greater for intelligence that would deal with what Darwin called "the hostile forces of nature." There was a real world there outside the group (food, terrain, predators, prey, herd migrations, seasons, etc.) that had to be attended to even more sharply than in-group experiences, or the group would not have survived to have any experiences. Indeed, it has been argued, this "outer-directed" intelligence could cause a lessening of the intensely social pressures, which could easily get in the way of survival against hostile nature if they came to consume too much of the group's time and effort. Now what is interesting is that Cattarhine (old world) monkeys and apes, our nearest relatives, don't seem to show a very great natural history intelligence, while some eusocial New World monkeys (Callitrichids—marmosets and tamarins) who are much more distant relatives show a high degree of it. This would suggest that our earliest hominid ancestors did not have a particularly highly developed natural history intelligence. However, there is no question that we, *Homo sapiens* and our more immediate hominid ancestors, do have it. So what happened?

For years I have argued that while we are in many things, including Machiavellian intelligence, very like our closest relatives, we are very unlike in others (evidently including natural history intelligence). In fact it is the differences that are crucial, and we only study the likeness the better to understand the crucial differences. This relates to innovation as follows: "Innovative Intelligence" (and remember this was slow in developing) requires the above-mentioned components of neo-philia (curiosity) and manipulation, both compatible with Machiavellian intelligence, but also (a) careful and persistent attention to the natural world (i.e., natural history intelligence) and (b) inhibition and and equilibration to restrain demands for immediate gratification.

In my scenario for hominid evolution (as detailed, for example, in *The Red Lamp of Incest*), it would have been the changes in food acquisition (largely hunting) that brought about the attention to the natural world. Meanwhile, changes in the internal composition of the bands would have meant selection for greater inhibition and equilibration. It was the ethologist Michael Chance who first pointed out that the "attention structure" of old world primate bands was inimical to the development of natural history intelligence—but he rarely gets credited with this. So much attention was devoted to the dominant male(s) that there was very little time for anything else. He thought chimpanzees, with their more "hedonic" social system were less hampered in this direction, and indeed they do pay some attention to the environment as in "termiting" and the like. (And it is interesting to note in this regard that Lewis Feuer in his brilliant but also underappreciated work *The Scientific Intellectual*, argued, against the Weberians, that it was not the Protestant ascetics who founded and advanced modern science—whatever they might have done to foster modern capitalism—but rather almost exclusively men of a "hedonistic-libertarian" view of life.) But the change in our own ancestors to savannah living and a combination of hunting, gathering, and scavenging, would have forced an attention to the natural world that chimpanzees scarcely need in the forest. However, I went one step further and argued that systems of categorization developed in the internal (Machiavellian) struggle, with its growth of systematic kinship and alliance (essentially the invention of exogamy and marriage by exchange), could have then been used to classify and act upon the outside world (for example, classifying animals into different groups or "kinds" according to eatabilty or dangerousness, classifying fruits similarly, and so on. The origins of language may well lie in the need to maintain and communicate this classificatory system.) Thus the evolving hominids did something that no other primates ever had: they combined the two forms of intelligence to form a new kind of mental approach to the world. This is yet another example of the hominids not actually inventing something new, but taking two things that already existed in nature and forming them into a new, emergent, system with its own properties.

"Innovation" then requires the mature skills of both kinds of intelligence with the proviso that the exaggeration of one over the other is detrimental to sustained innovation. And note that the development of this intelligence was relatively slow, taking most of the Palaeolithic to develop, and only obviously coming to flower in the Upper Palaeolithic with a burst of creative activity within the last fifty thousand years. Even then, as noted, we have been slow to innovate until the runaway innovation of the last fifty years. But the need for the two kinds of intelligence to be in balance might lead to some fruitful thinking. For example, in bureaucracies is there an inverse relationship between internecine struggle and innovative effort? If most of the intelligent effort is absorbed in internal struggles—particularly status struggles, then there may be little left over for dealing with the outside world that the organization ostensibly exists to handle. Such redirection of "attention structure" will, as Chance showed, actually inhibit the intelligent manipulation of the real world outside the group. Joseph Needham in his monumental *Science and Civilization in China* suggested that the development of true science in China—as opposed to ingenious technology—was impeded because "Confucianism was so intensely concerned with human affairs that it ignored the world of non-human events." The quotation is from Feuer who adds the world-renouncing masochism of Eastern philosophy to the list of impediments. Innovations it seems are most likely to come from happy people who like the good things of this life and want to improve them!

Obviously there are other factors than these; for example, the lack of competition between bureaucrats would equally lead to stagnation in innovative effort. There is a balance and perhaps an ideal one, but we don't know what it is. We know what extremes to avoid, and that is surely something. In the chapter on bureaucracy we discussed factors that lead to dysfunction there, and most of the factors discussed would lead to the stifling of innovation in bureaucracies—which often seemed almost designed to inhibit innovation even when their ostensible purpose is to enourage it. I will mention here only the factor of the conflation of the bureaucrat's ego with the institutional form. We discussed this as regards cavalry, but today it may be just as potent in the clinging of various branches of the military to forms and means of combat that may be of dubious use in the future: tanks come to mind, as do supersonic fighter planes, and aircraft carriers. These latter had to win out painfully over the defunct battleship, but they too may have had their day. Built to deal with fast war planes, for example, they had to be rapidly converted to deal with massive helicopter lifts in the Haitian crisis. But one shudders to think of the difficulties in the way of rethinking their usefulness.

Variability is at the heart of selection. Without variability it has nothing to work on. This is why it is idiotic to expect evolution to produce uniform outcomes. Thus there will be variation among individuals in the qualities we have been discussing and it hence makes sense to ask if there is an "innovative personality" and particularly how this relates to its possible opposite the "bureaucratic personality." (The implication here is that a large part of these personality differences will be inherited. So be it. Numerous identical twin studies have by now shown quite precisely how heritable personality traits are.) We have already discussed the "inhuman" nature of bureaucracy as an institution. Does it follow that bureaucracies will attract people with low neo-philia and overdeveloped inhibitory systems? What we used to call the obsessive-compulsives— "anal-retentives" is a bit out of fashion now it seems. At the lower levels the answer must be often yes. The "Milgram type" is well enough known: obey all orders, go by the book, make no exceptions, and so on. Neo-philiac types work best outside the bureau (Darwin, Einstein, The Wright brothers, Edison with more than 1250 patents, etc.) But there is a catch. The innovative maverick in the modern world is relatively useless without a hiererchical, efficient organization to put his ideas into practice. If innovation is to "take" above the individual level it needs the bureau to institutionalize it. Thus we have another perhaps almost impossible balancing act to achieve here: we need to allow enough lack of bureaucratic regulation to allow innovative personalities to operate, and a flexible enough bureaucratic hierarchy to institutionalize it quickly. Perhaps the Manhattan Project worked in this way, but the two principles were constantly at war with each other, if the accounts are accurate. Many have pointed to the "Silicon Valley" model as the ideal, where the scientists are more or less left to their own devices, but where a very efficient industrial bureaucracy is in place to put innovative ideas into practice. Of course, these two personality types do not exhaust the inventory. There are plenty of noncompulsive types who are no more innovators than their bureaucratic bretheren. It may be true as Feuer argues (and I think he more than makes his case) that it is the hedonistic personalities who dominate innovation. But those who enjoy life too much can end up in a purely dissipative (if not dissipated) existence, where playfulness is high, but essentially imitative and not inventive. Look at the ski-slopes of the wealthy.

Someone is bound to ask about the "Japanese model" but that raises problems, since the Japanese, are seemingly not as hot on innovation as on imitation. (And we must remember that for centuries they, like the Chinese were mired in "Eastern masochism" and never developed an indigenous science.) However, their hierarchical bureaucratic industrial system does allow for the very swift implementation of imitated processes. It does seem that in our species profile the "imitators" will vastly outnumber the "innovators"—which is how it should be. It is the business of the imitators to take efficient advantage of the innovations. At the opposite end, for example, the British tolerance for eccenticity makes them high innovators—air defense, jet propulsion, cinematography etc.—but very poor at institutional, especially governmental, support, which means that many of their innovations end up being developed in other countries.

Within the United States military there seems to have been a conscious effort to move in the right direction with such things as LAMs

(Louisiana Maneuvers) and "Battle Labs" where "quick study and response" lead to changes while the battle is in process as it were, and thus
end the usual military problem of always fighting the last war. Perhaps
the "ideal" situation is where there is a maverick director of a powerful
and efficient—and autonomous—bureaucracy. Of course this is always
a gamble and can go horribly wrong. But innovation is always a gamble
anyway, and by definition we must take risks. This approach stresses the
importance of individuals and this is deliberate. It is wrong, but common, to assume that institutions and organizations innovate. This is the
fallacy of misplaced concreteness that unfortunately social scientists seem
to encourage. Only people innovate, only people institutionalize—insti-
tutionalization is a process requiring human action even if it is collective
action. "The Post Office" or "General Motors" or "Microsoft" never
invented anything.

We should stop here to note that we must not get carried away with the
idea that innovation is necessarily a good thing. The proposed "ideal
situation" is only ideal for getting innovations to "take"; it does not guarantee that they will be any good. There are plenty of examples of military
innovations that were disasters. Hannibal's elephants were certainly an
innovation as far as European warfare was concerned, but they bogged
down and died in the alpine snows. The elaborate heavy armour of medieval knights ended by making them unmaneuverable and vulnerable. The
creation of independent air forces led to fanatical attempts by the likes of
Arthur "Bomber" Harris and Herman Goering to prove that they could
win wars independently and so to the wastes and horrors of "saturation
bombing." One could go on, but the examples are all too familiar. There
are counter examples however that prove that when the ideal situation
exists the result is often spectacular. While we are knocking the air forces
let me mention Dowding and the RAF Fighter Command. Dowding had
two innovations to work with, radar and Spitfires. He realized the implications of this for effective air defense—if you knew exactly where the
enemy planes were you could get to them rapidly and hit them by surprise—and virtually created the efficient organization to link the two
that won the war in the air for Britain over the otherwise superior
Luftwaffe. The point is that innovations can go both ways, and in our
enthusiasm for promoting them, we should bear this in mind. Unfortunately the proof of this pudding is usually in the eating and there is perhaps nothing much we can do except point out the obvious.

"Thinking biologically" about innovations we can perhaps compare them to their natural counterparts, mutations. Mutations occur randomly—they are the "mavericks" if you like, and they are either:

- positively selected for (a few);
- negatively selected against (most);
- neutral—neither selected for nor against (large number).

So-called "non-Darwinian" evolution occurs with the accumulation of neutral mutations coalescing to make for a radical change in an organism. But ultimately selection will decide their fate. Are there social analogies to this? Some innovations will be taken up quickly, some dropped (like the vast majority of patents, for example), and some hang around in limbo for a while until their time is come. But perhaps indeed the rule is similar: nature is conservative with her forms. Only a few of the innovations, like the mutations, will take. After all, evolution is a record only of those that took; we have no idea how many were abandoned along the way, except that it was the overwhelming majority—99 percent of all species that ever existed are extinct. Modern theorists, like Boyd and Richerson, who liken cultural change to evolutionary change always seem to come up with this same conclusion: stability is the normal state. It has to be for cultural transmission to take place at all (as it has to be in the genotype for genetic transmission to occur.) Change—or innovation— will have to be the exception rather than the rule. And even then, many apparent innovations are in fact highly conservative in their outcome; that is, they may be radical changes—lung fish into amphibians, for example—but their effect is to render the organism more able to survive intact in changing circumstances (the legs of the lung fish enabled them to get *back into the receding water*). In biology this used to be known as Romer's rule, and perhaps it still is. Change is not sought for its own sake but will occur to help organisms maintain their integrity. The longer term result—land-dwelling, air-breathing animals—can of course involve quite staggering changes, but these are not what was initially sought.

What summation can we have regarding innovation and war? We face an uncertain future in which there is a strong possibility that "war" as we have known it is becoming increasingly irrelevant. There are two main possibilities: nuclear war and terrorist war. Neither is within the scope of war as we have known it. If the Gulf War "kicked the Vietnam syndrome" our problem in the future may well be to "kick the Gulf War Syndrome." Stealth bombers, microchips, and smart bombs and rockets, may all be useless against microbes in the water supply, or other terrorist tactics. In a way it is perhaps fortunate that the terrorists seem to prefer big bangs that get attention rather than microbial or viral warfare. The latter could be far more effective and deadly if the aim were really to inflict serious damage on large populations without much risk. And even here we may have to change our thinking. All the biological warfare experts I talk to seem to think that any such attack would be monolithic in its use of a large quantity of one deadly virus for example. But why should this be? There are literally thousands of viable microbial agents for use out there. Why not numerous attacks by many of these? This would have the advantage of not *looking* like a concerted terrorist activity (which of course for the moment they avoid since publicity is a major part of their aim). Indeed it might look like a plurality of "natural" outbreaks and occasion no alarm other than locally.

Consider over the last few years the growing spread of the HIV virus, the outbreaks of legionnaire's disease, the chronic and widespread growth of Lyme disease, the "Navaho" disease in the southwest, the food poisoning (*E. coli*) episodes in Oregon, the "reemergence" of tuberculosis, the freakish *Ebola* incident, the tampering with several across-the-counter medicines, cyclospora infections from coast to coast, the so-called Gulf War Syndrome, the rabies epidemic in the northeast, the "reappearance" of anthrax and smallpox, the numerous water pollution episodes (two-thirds of water supplies have been rated unsafe), and the outbreaks of often deadly "food poisoning" on several cruise ships. All of these have left death and sickness in their wake, and all are of course simply "natural" outbreaks. Of course. But if I were planning a biological attack on this country, and having seen, for example, the lengthy list of viruses the USSR was working on before the wall came tumbling down, I would be inclined to plan just such a slow draining of the population by multiple agents. My point is simply that this would be "war" but not a war that smart bombs and patriot missiles could touch. The armed forces of the future will also face many more "missions" of Somalian, Haitian, and Bosnian type (and if we are really serious about "human rights" and not just substituting moralism for a foreign policy, these could become the most urgent task facing the military), then perhaps a serious innovation would be to decrease the number of fast planes and cruisers, etc., and to increase the number and training of MPs, for antiterroist and "upholding democracy" tasks. These tasks are police, not army, jobs, and if the military has to do them, it should be to its police and even medical corps that the task should fall. All in all the military of the future will probably have to take on a much more protean style than the present outmoded division into "services" allows. My image is of a kind of Leggo system, in which specialized parts can be rapidly assembled and reassembled to meet rapidly changing needs without regard to their "service" identification. This would among other things make for a much easier integration of women into the military. But perhaps this goes beyond innovation into revolution, and hence beyond my brief. Still, military innovations in the past have often led to quite far-reaching changes in society at large, and the pressure of security can be as urgent as that of profits, and perhaps even a better model of what the society of tomorrow might be like.

Notes

The classic work on innovation is H. G. Barnett's *Innovation: The Basis of Cultural Change* (New York: McGraw Hill, 1953), where he stressed the role of marginality in cultural invention. The best of the more recent works is definitely *What's New? A Closer Look at the Process of Innovation*, edited by S. E. van der Leeuw and R. Torrence (London: Unwin Hyman, 1989). The best summary of the Machiavellian versus natural history intelligence debate is in Susan Cachel, "The Natural History Origin of Human Intelligence: A New Perspective on the Origin of Human Intelligence" in *Social Neuroscience Bulletin*, vol. 7, no. 1, pp. 25–30, 1994. Michael Chance's early work on "attention structure" appeared in "Attention Structure as the Basis of Primate Rank Orders," *MAN: The Journal of the Royal Anthropological Institute*, 2:4, 503–18, 1967. See also his "Social Cohesion and the Structure of Attention" in R. Fox, ed., *Biosocial Anthropology* (New York: Halsted Press; London: Malaby Press, 1975). Lewis S. Feuer's book—so underrated and so brilliant in its argument, is *The Scientific Intellectual: The Psychological and Sociological Origins of Modern Science* (New York: Basic Books, 1963; 2nd. Ed. New Brunswick, NJ: Transaction Publishers, 1992). The work of Joseph Needham referred to is his *Science and Civilization in China* (Cambridge: Cambridge University Press, 1956). The book on cultural transmission referred to is R. Boyd and P. J. Richardson, *Culture and the Evolutionary Process* (Chicago: Chicago University Press, 1985). On military innovation see Stephen Peter Rosen, *Winning the Next War: Innovation and the Modern Military* (Ithaca, NY: Cornell University Press, 1991). I am grateful to Dr. Joshua Lederberg of Rockefeller University (cited interestingly by Feuer as the only Jewish Nobel Prize winner in science to be of direct rabbinical descent) for an up-close view of Soviet (now Russian) resources for biological warfare. The idea that "social categories" may have been the source of "natural categories" is of course derived from E. Durkheim and M. Mauss, "De quelques formes primitives de classification," *Année Sociologique*, vol. VI (1903), but they did not put the idea into an evolutionary context. On the relation of military innovation to social innovation another neglected but original and interesting book is S. Andrejewski, *Military Organization and Society* (London: Routledge and Kegan Paul, 1954).

4

Sexual Conflict in Epic Narrative

This was a paper[1] first delivered at the meetings of the Evolution and Human Behavior Society at Ann Arbor in 1994. The session was organized by Joseph Carroll whose Evolution and Literary Theory *(University of Missouri Press, 1995) is a tour de force in the application of Darwinian ideas to literature. There is a growing movement of literary scholars, spurred on by the example of Frederick Turner, who are highly dissatisfied with the state of affairs in their discipline and want to utilize the insights of the evolutionary sciences. I had suggested in several places that the theme of sexual conflict—or at least a certain kind of sexual conflict—was central to epic literature, and that this told us a lot about what some of our atavistic obsessions really were. Here, then, Joe Carroll challenged me to spell this out.*

Can there be a sociobiology (using the word in its broadest sense) of literature? What would it look like? There is more than one answer of course, as there is more than one kind of sociobiology, and mine is a decidedly old fashioned model closer perhaps to the "ethology" of the Europeans. Here I suggest and illustrate one approach which is to take seriously the task of a sociobiological rewriting of Carl Jung on the "Archetypes of the Collective Unconscious." This is to go to the heart of the content of literature rather than to ask general questions about its function (which are no less legitimate) and to look at those enduring themes and characters that Jung and the folklorists have so diligently described and classified. It might also turn up some that, given the particular perspectives of sociobiology, Jung didn't see in the material of myth, folklore, literature, and alchemy. In the language of the now fashionable "evolutionary psychology" we could rewrite "archetypes" as something like "domain-specific information-processing myth-modules" developed in the "environment of evolutionary adaptation" (EEA). Clearly evolution demanded these archetypical myth-modules as an aid to survival and reproductive success, but to discuss this would take us into function rather than content, and having promised to deal with the latter, I shall go directly to it, and to the chosen topic of sexual conflict as it appears in the classical literary epics.

Let me summarize quickly what I take to be the situation of sexual conflict between the generations in the Palaeolithic (our effective EEA.) The hominids inherited the "primate baseline" of a tripartite division of the breeding group into (a) dominant males; (b) young females and those with dependent young; and (c) juvenile and peripheral males. The dominant male or males attempted to monopolize breeding during female estrus, with more or less success. The peripheral males were engaged in a constant struggle to gain dominance status and so enter the breeeding arena, and meanwhile to attempt surreptitious intercourse with the females. This baseline was gradually (but perhaps traumatically) changed by the evolving hominids into a system of kinship and alliances where the juvenile (or aspirant) males were constrained not so much by brute force as by rules and customs, and especially by lengthy procedures of initiation, made possible by the concomitant development of inhibitory processes in the evolving brain. The dominant older males continued in their attempt to monopolize fertile females (although no longer only during ovulation which ceased to have clear overt signals) by relatively permanent allocations as in "marriage" and systems of gerontocratic polygyny. The aspirant males continued to try to subvert the system to their advantage, by copulating with the younger females and eventually displacing the dominant males.

This transition, preserving the old drives and objects but reworking the system of allocation and control of females, continued to become more elaborate over two million years of relatively rapid brain growth. Leap-forward episodes were (a) the invention of weapons and fire and (b) the origins of language. The mechanics of the transition must have left a profound imprint on our evolved mental structures (or "domain specific algorithms" or whatever.) If we use the formula that I have frequently invoked (inspired by Freud) that "we constantly reproduce that which produced us," we should expect to find echoes of this significant species' *rite de passage* in our contemporary (i.e. within the historical period) mental products. Note this is saying more than just that we should find themes of sexual conflict per se, but themes of a specific kind of sexual conflict in which younger or subordinate males are often in deadly conflict with older or more powerful males for sexual access to fertile females. Even if the more dominant males are not going to mate with the females themselves, control of the fertility of these females is still important since it is through this control that they control the armed and dangerous younger males, aided by initiation, education, and warfare. The degree to which a society can cohere likely depends on their success—but that is to leap ahead.

Here I want to suggest that there are other places to look for evidence of the continuing power of this syndrome than in cross-cultural ethnography or current social surveys or experiments with college students, or all the other devices of the social sciences. These have their place, but they tend to concentrate on current behavior and attitudes which, as we shall see, are probably considerably distorted. If what we are interested in are the enduring mental patterns (the archetypes) we must look to a broader canvas. Here I would suggest that the resources of myth and literature are a rich mine of information for the enduring obsessions of the evolved hominid that we are. Jung has said as much, but without the insights of modern evolutionary biology. With these insights we can ask sharper and more focused questions about the "collective unconscious" starting with mental products that can be predicted from a knowledge of evolution rather than with our extensive but biased folk-categories.

I could start with oral mythology, and had intended to include a disquisition on the Trickster myth as a "module" dealing with the issue of deceit in social relations. But our brief is to deal with literature, so I will proceed to literary examples of the sexual conflict theme, noting that in the first instance many of these were transcriptions of oral mythology which may or may not have had a historical basis.

"My Lords, would you hear a high tale of love and death?" Thus begins what many commentators, like Denis de Rougement for example, consider the archetypical story of the "love triangle" we are exploring, *Tristan*. By the time of this "high" tale, in the twelfth-century medieval romances (of Beroul, Thomas, Eilhart, etc.) the genre had been much elaborated. But in the essense of its plot the tale was the same as its Celtic original where Diarmuid (under a *geas* or spell foreshadowing the "love potion") abducts Grainne from the older and more powerful Finn. The lovers flee through Ireland, where country people still point out the "table" dolmens as *leabaidh Dhiarmada agus Grainne*—"the beds of Dermot and Grainne (Grace)." Diarmuid finally dies, killed by a wild boar like Adonis (although ripped through the belly not the groin) and the doomed lovers are thwarted. (Tristan, like Odysseus, and the Fisher King, carried a scar on his thigh from a dangerous wound—perhaps a reference to some ritual of royal installation.) In the literary Tristan versions, where Isolde (Iseult) was stolen from the older King Mark, they are also thwarted and Tristan dies, with, in Wagner's operatic version, the exquisite *liebestod*—love-death song—sung over him by Isolde who herself dies of grief on his body. This theme of the doomed lovers who must die tragically because they have defied the "rightful" claims of the older generation, is to be repeated down the centuries, with Romeo and Juliet as its best known example.

Not all the conflicts have such gloriously unhappy outcomes. The Tristan version is often cited as the turning point where the ancient legend becomes "modern"—where it gives rise to the modern romantic-love complex. But mostly comentators have stressed the adulterous nature of the relationship and have seen the adultery as central. There could be no love within arranged marriages—particularly between young females and much older males—so "love" was born of adulterous attraction, always, however, fatal for the lovers. (And in most cases, interestingly, the woman takes the adulterous initiative, usually drastically severing a previously established male bond.) Surely the themes of adultery, cuckoldry, and female choice, are of great interest to the sociobiologist for obvious reasons to do with paternity certainty and parental investment, but I want to look at the "power triangle" aspects of the relationship because I think it enables us to take in some nonadulterous examples that are totally comparable but which we would otherwise miss.

Both Finn and King Mark are older royal personages who married younger brides, lost these to younger males, and started a tragic train of events. (Mark, being British, was unerringly decent about the whole thing; the Irish Finn was just plain vengeful, refusing to use his power of healing on the dying Diarmuid to the disgust of the other Fianna.) Now take something that looks similar in the greatest epic poem of them all, the *Iliad*. Menelaeus is the older kingly male whose young wife Helen is abducted by the golden youth Paris (willingly we suppose, but this isn't clear.) This abduction is the "cause" of the Trojan War in the story, but not the immediate cause of the events in the poem itself. These are, as every schoolboy knows, caused by the wrath of Achilles. And Achilles' wrath was caused by the High King Agammemnon's appropriation of Achilles' beautiful young captive Briseis. Achilles, in his fury, was about to draw his sword over this insult when Aphrodite seized him by his long golden hair and prevented the rash act. So he went to sulk in his tent, refused to fight the Trojans, and the rest is the *Iliad*.

Thus I think we can fairly claim that the greatest of the epics turns on the power struggle between dominant males and subordinates over the possession of fertile young females. (It is never actually stated that Achilles and Paris are indeed *younger* than Agammemnon and Menelaeus—it certainly feels that way; but they *are* subordinate.) The story cannot reach its resolution until *this* issue is resolved, and Achilles is brought back to the fight to be killed eventually, and ironically, by the arrow of Paris. Paris himself has to die and Helen be reclaimed, although not until the later *Odyssey*. But even in the successor story, although the main plot is to do with the wanderings of Odysseus, the "frame" for the plot is again a struggle between the young Telemachus—acting as surrogate for his absent father—and the older suitors, for Penelope. It is true here that Telemachus does not want Penelope for himself, which is why I cast him in the role of father surrogate, but it is interesting how often such switches are made in epic plots (see later comments on *El Cid*) to make them conform more to the basic pattern. If this interpretation is correct then, the adventures of Odysseus are in a sense a long subplot before we get to the final resolution of the sexual competition issue. (And it is of course possible to see the plot reversed in that Odysseus is the dominant male and the suitors, as subdominants, are struggling with him for Penelope. I think it is often the case that the basic pattern can thus be multivocally represented, adding to the richness of suggestion in the plot.)

If we look to the other great source of European epic—the Nordic— we find the theme repeated with incest thrown in. Actually the epics care little about incest since they concern divinities and royals who were allowed it anyway. The epic story of the Nordic gods and their human creations—the *Volsunga Saga*—was first recorded in the twelfth-century poetic (or Elder) *Eddas*, and movingly retold in prose by the thirteenth-century Icelandic author Snorri Sturluson. These and later versions were the inspiration for the best known synthesis, Wagner's *Götterdammerung*. I shall use his German version of the names since they are the most familiar. It starts with Siegmund stealing Sieglinde, his sister,

from her lawful husband Hunding, with the usual pursuit, battle, inter-
ference of the gods (Wotan for Siegmund, Fricka for Hunding), death of
Siegmund, and birth of the hero Siegfried. (Echoes here of a very old
theme as in Isis and Osiris verus Seth and the birth of Horus.) Siegfried
in turn pushes the story along in his struggle with Wotan over Brunnhilde,
ring of flame and all. It is of course the deceitful shape-changing Trickster Loki, with his slaying of Balder, who precipitates the actual
Götterdammerung—the destruction of the gods (*"Ragnarok"* in the original stories), so our two themes intertwine. But the basis of the conflict—
the sexual competition in its peculiarly hominid form—is there from the
beginning. (Brunnhilde is, I think technically, Siegfreid's aunt, so we
have whiff of incest here too. But then, as Anna Russell delightfully
reminds us, Siegfreid never met any woman who was not either his aunt
or his cousin. But we must remember that this this does indeed reflect
what was probably a Palaeolithic reality. The women a man met in his
lifetime would mostly have been, as W.S. Gilbert so prettily put it, "His
sisters and his cousins/ whom he reckoned up in dozens/ and his aunts.")

We started with the Celtic epics (taken down and elaborated by Christian monks from the tenth century on), and these eventually evolve into
the Arthurian legends. In the Welsh *Mabinogion* the triangle is again
represented in the conflict between Lleu and Goronwy Pevr over
Blodeuedd (the maiden created from flowers). In the Arthurian stories
we find the theme repeated in its elaborated medieval literary form in the
most famous of the adulterous versions: Lancelot versus Arthur for
Guinevere. This version took shape in the twelfth century in the works of
Robert de Boron and Geoffrey of Monmouth among others, and moved
on through Chrétien de Troyes reaching its culmination in Malory's *Morte
Darthur* printed by Caxton in 1485. Here there is unquestionably a contest between older royal male and younger subordinate male with a royal
female as the prize. And again it ends badly for all concerned. In most of
the epics it ends badly—usually for the youngsters, since these poems
and stories were obviously intended to bolster the official morality and
were made by older males for older males. The one exception is the *Odyssey* where Odysseus and Penelope settle down to achieve a happy old
age—we assume! Again in the Arthurian cycles it is the Trickster
Mordred—playing the Loki role—who with his deceit brings on the cli-
max and downfall of Camelot. Many of the subplot stories in the cycle
play with the sexual conflict theme also; for example, *Sir Gawain and
the Green Knight*.

Following the *Iliad* and the *Odyssey* is of course what is perhaps the first truly great "literary" epic, Virgil's *Aeneid*. In the first part—the Dido and Aeneas story—we have the premier "modern" love story with no trace of the ancient theme. It is a matter between the lovers: he has his noble task in the world (as the ghostly voice in Berlioz's great *Les Troyens* keeps reminding him—*"Italie! Italie!"*), and she has her great love to fulfill. She loses and kills herself; he goes on to found Rome and the Roman empire. A very modern story—no magic, no potions, just tragedy. But in the second half, once the hero is in Italy and seeking to create a kingdom and a royal lineage, the theme reasserts itself as Aeneas and Turnus battle with each other (Turnus standing in for the older male Latinus) for the right to the reproductive capacity of Lavinia and hence the founding of the Latin line that leads to Rome and history.

This had been an exclusively European survey so far, so lest we be accused of literary bias and a skewed sample, I will turn quickly to the great Semitic literary epics found in the Old Testament. The Old Testament is a hodge-podge of materials, but the actual story of the origin of the Israelites and their adventures before and after the Exodus has all the epic ingredients. Trickster for example is here again from the beginning as the serpent and crops up as Jonah and Samson or even Yahweh himself in many of his more whimsically amoral moods. Right up front we get the conflict of Jacob and Laban over Rachel (Genesis 29–31). Jacob does seven years' bride service for Rachel only to be palmed off with her older sister Leah and a weak excuse about the oldest having to marry first. He then does another seven years to get Rachel, and he and Laban continue to have a furious conflict until the covenant of Mizpah brings peace between them.

There is a long dry spell until 1 Samuel 25 when David begins his saga of wife-accumulation, and has his first run-in with Nabal the husband of Abigail. In 2 Samuel 11 David is fatefully smitten by Bathsheba the wife of Uriah the Hittite—one of his loyal soldiers. David contrives Uriah's death by a particularly nasty piece of deceit and gains Bathsheba. But the Lord kills their first born as a punishment. Relenting, the Lord allows a second son to live, and he is, of course, Solomon.

With David's descendants the incest theme reappears immediately afterwards in the lust of David's son Amnon for his half-sister Tamar. By trickery against David, Amnon rapes Tamar, and Absalom, Tamar's brother, biding his time, later has him killed. The subsequent tragedy of David and Absalom—the prototype of the all the later father-son tragic conflict themes—is well remembered; but that of Amnon and Tamar is often overlooked.

It is worth stressing that the perspective adopted here gives us a different view of the so-called "incest problem" which, at least in the way we pose it, is really part of our post-Victorian obsession with the nuclear family. Thus in the classic Theban cycle of Sophocles (to cite another of the great "epics") it was not the incestuous marriage of Oedipus that brought the curse on Thebes, it was the patricide: the killing of his father Laius. The incest was an unhappy consequence, not the cause of the problem. The plays can be seen to turn on the same triangular conflict— Oedipus versus Laius for Jocasta (and even later Haemon versus Creon for Antigone), with the brilliant twists that make this version of the story unique. In many of the stories, as we have seen, the woman in question is a relative, often close (the Palaeolithic reality again), but the real issue is the power struggle between the males and not either the much touted incest, or later, the adultery. And the struggle is not between equal males as we often loosely misread it, but between the contollers and the controlled, the elder and the younger, the uncles and the nephews, the kings and the subjects. Perhaps because we are further removed from the EEA than the writers of the epics and sagas, we tend to concentrate on what is important to our nuclear family-centered view of the world: the incest and adultery. We forget the actual or symbolic patricide, or at least the struggle with the father/king/uncle/god that the ancients found so riveting. This is a reason for starting with the sagas and epics, and we can of course go back in time to oral myth and forward to literature proper to find other examples.

One of the more obvious Western examples is the great Spanish national epic, *El Cid*. In the original *Poema [Cantar] del mio Cid* the conflict is between the Cid (Rodrigo Diaz), as the older male, and his sons-in-law who beat up his daughters and have to be punished. By the time Corneille tells the story in *Le Cid* (1637) it is between the Cid as the younger male and his father-in-law the (historically) fictional Count of Gormaz, whom he must kill in a duel to preserve family honor even at the cost of his wife's love. I used to think this was Corneille's own invention, but it seems he took it directly from popular Spanish ballads and plays (especially Guillen de Castro's *Las mocedades del Cid*) which make the switch by the sixteenth century. It is as though the popular imagination could not bear its romantic hero to be playing the heavy, and instead wanted him in the more Tristan or Lancelot-like role of younger male at odds with older, in a tragic triangle of good intentions gone sour and love put at risk.

I have deliberately stuck here with examples that will be familiar to my audience, but we could range farther to the Persian *Thousand and One Nights*), the Hindu *Rg Veda* (Shiva versus Daksha for Sati) and *Mahabharatha*, the Japanese *Tale of Genji*, the Georgian national epics, the Finnish *Kalevala* and so on for yet more in other literatures. One thing we shall find over time is a progressive decline of the influence of the "tragic triangle" theme, and its replacement by others. This probably reflects the waning influence of the older males on mate choice, and the growing independence of the young in this matter—although throughout the nineteenth century the younger lovers in *Madame Bovary* or *Anna Karenina* or *Wuthering Heights*, for example, continue to come to a bad end. (But note what relatively weak sorts of superordinate males Bovary, Karenin, and Edgar turn out to be.) This too however ceases to be true as the "happy ending" eventually substitutes for the "tragic triangle" when the pattern of the EEA gets more and more diluted and distorted in the twentieth century. Even in *Wuthering Heights*, despite what happens to the fated (and probably potentially incestuous) Heathcliff and Catherine—prototypes of the basic pattern, young Cathy and Hareton manage a neat happy ending in defiance of Heathcliff in his later incarnation as the dominant older male. Perhaps this is yet another of those "twists" we have previously noted that give unexpected depth to the plot, and often occur in narratives that reflect changing social and cultural circumstances: something that lines up *Wuthering Heights* unexpectedly, but not inappropriately, with the *Odyssey*. With the advent of contraception, democracy, universal suffrage, co-education, mobility and female employment in the workplace, and so on, the control of the older males (and females for that matter) over youthful sexuality has all but disappeared, and literature faithfully reflects this change. To spell this out with examples would of course be a whole other paper.

And I might add here that I do not wish in any way to suggest that the sexual competition theme has exclusive or even predominant significance within the whole structure of evolved human motivations and conflicts, or that it is always even the main theme of the narrative at issue. Thus, while the triangle obviously dominates *Tristan*, the story of the Cid, for example, is much more a hymn to feudal virtues than an epic of sexual conflict. And a complex epic like George Eliot's *Middlemarch*, while having the Ladislaw-Dorothea-Casaubon triangle certainly (and female choice dominant), is "about" the whole structure of its society. Even *Wuthering Heights* can be read, from one angle, as a plot about the skillful use of the law of entail as it existed before the 1834 Inheritance Acts (and, for that matter, the 1837 Wills Act), in Heathcliff's saga of vengeance. I only want to draw attention to the "sexual power triangle" as a pattern that does seem important by its sheer ubiquity, and one that very often provides the frame or motivation for plots that otherwise in their content wander very far afield indeed from the primordial patterns of the EEA.

You will have already probably observed that epic is close to tragedy in the strict dramatic sense—and that most epics (except perhaps the *Odyssey*) have a tragic ending. This opens up another line of enquiry into the very nature of the "tragic" itself, where the displacement and downfall of dominant males and the divided loyalties of females are certainly central. But the essense of the *agon* is usually different in tragedy, although no less related to our Palaeolithic heritage. I would venture that tragedy shows us the dangers of the tragic hero (Man) following some ideal or idea (good or bad) to its logical but terrible conclusion. This, combined with the "fall of the dominant male" theme, links us in fact to the brutal breakthrough into conciousness that langauge brought about but that failed to make us over into totally rational animals. We are less rational animals than rationalizing animals, wedded to ideas that are propelled by our palaeo-mammalian emotions. Tragic heroes and heroines rationalize their emotional dedications to wrong courses of action with a logic that has us weeping because it is at once so right and so inevitably appalling in its outcome. This is why Aristotle thought tragedy must be about "noble persons": the low born scarcely had the opportunity to get into such a fix. And indeed is it any less true today? When I ask students to name me a modern tragedy they inevitably say *Death of a Salesman* or *Of Mice and Men* or even *A Streetcar Named Desire*. But are these really tragedies or are they just rather depressing commentaries on dismal social circumstances? Are they tragic or are they merely pathetic? We shouldn't confound the two or we lose the possibility of that Aristotelian purgation of the emotions of terror and pity: the *katharsis* that marks out tragedy as its own. This raises of course the issue of whether we can even have such a thing as a modern tragedy. I won't argue this any further here, but it needs to be thought about. Tragedy then deserves it own evolutionary analysis.

So what of comedy? There is so much of it, and so many different genres, that sweeping generalizations are going to miss most of the subtleties. But does not sexual competition take place in comedies? Is it not even the heart of them as often as not? Agreed, but my impression from Aristophanes to Neil Simon is that the competition, while it can involve the "young male versus older males" theme, is of a subtly different kind than that in the epics. It is best summed up in the cliché formula "boy meets girl, boy loses girl, boy finds girl again." And the finding is consummated and a happy-ever-after ending is usually assumed. If all these ingredients produce an unexpected unhappy ending, then we have to resort to "tragi-comedy" to describe it. Who can decide whether most of Chekhov's plays are the one or the other? You might object that *Romeo and Juliet* fits this description perfectly and yet we assume it to be a tragedy. But is it? A good deal of it is comic, and while the young lovers are doubtlessly charming, their ending is sad rather than tragic. But I have already said it embodies some aspects of the "fatal love" theme that marks out the sexual conflict of the epics and this is true. The line is often hard to draw. Kill your young lovers off and you can soon turn the classical comic boy-girl romantic dilemma into something dismal. The essense of comedy is that it takes the conflict and turns it into a source of laughter. It is often a kind of parody (and often deliberately was) of the tragic love theme of the epics, except that in comedy we find the antics of the parties laughable rather than loaded with foreboding. The conflict in the comedy is usually either directly between the boy and the girl—some misunderstanding separates them, or between the boy and the girl's parents. He (sometimes she) is in some way "unsuitable"—usually of too low a social status. They require her to make a more suitable match, she balks, and let the comedy begin. It is rarely the case in comedy that the archetypical "epic" pattern emerges: older and more powerful male versus younger or subdominant, for the *possession* of the nubile girl. It is her disposition in marriage, that is, the alliance interests of the father, that are usually at issue. What the young lovers threaten to disrupt is the economic status quo of the older generation. Even when older males are involved in this version of the "love triangle" they are rarely dominant and powerful ones, but more likely ridiculous figures of fun, cuckolded, deceived, humiliated, and in the end, losers. (Of course, literature is not written to formulae, and part of its fun is in the changes it rings. Thus the Count in *The Marriage of Figaro* is bested by the women and underlings, but he is not a fool or a weakling. This is what makes for an interesting plot.) We have seen, however, that starting perhaps in the seventeenth, and throughout the nineteenth century, the older males tend to become weak, insipid, or ridiculous, which is why we have the problem with Ibsen. The men against whom his "tragic" heroines struggle so ardently are idiots. So, to overgeneralize riskily, and pleading time and length constraints, I can only say that while archaic sexual conflict motivations are definitely tapped in comedy, they are different from those in epic and most tragedy, and will require a different detailed analysis, particularly of their changes over time and the indications these give us of our continuing drift from the Palaeolithic pattern. The *sexual* conflict in the classic comedies is most often between equals (e.g., *The Rivals*) and is usually about the misadventures of courtship when it is not about the intruigues of cuckoldry (e.g., *The Country Wife*). We may even find that comedy, with its themes of inappropriate mate choice, cuckoldry, and deceit, is the older of the patterns; these themes go deep into the history of human behavioral evolution. Tragedy requires, ultimately, a conscious insight into the personal failure that has dragged everyone down. This does not to me have an archaic ring but is the stuff of a late-developing self-consciousness. "Pompous old fart gets cuckolded by young Don Juan who gets away with it" on the other hand, is perhaps the oldest joke of all.

I might suggest then as one general program for the "sociobiology of literature" that we first line up our expected archetypes—the mental content, particularly of social relations, that we would expect as a product of the EEA—and then see how it applies to the world's narrative literature, and how the themes change over time in reflecting changing circumstances. Ideally we would develop hypotheses that could be tested in cross-cultural studies of literature. In this way we could claim "comparative literature" back from the moribund state into which it has declined. Male bonding would be a perfect subject, for example, with a rich store of literary examples showing its stubborn persistence from Gilgamesh and Enkidu, and Achilles and Patroclus, through David and Jonathan, and Roland and Oliver, to Butch Cassidy and the Sundance Kid. The changes in the themes as recorded in literature may act as our best barometer of the distance we have travelled from the EEA mentality, and hence to the kind of problems we may be setting ourselves in the future.

Note

1. I would like to thank Fred Turner, Ashley Montagu, Robert Storey, Dudley Young, and especially Joe Carroll, for helpful comments and criticisms. To respond to them all would involve writing a whole book rather than a transcript of a twenty-minute paper, but the very number and quality of critical comments encourages me to think that at least I have hit on a worthwhile theme, even if I haven't covered all the angles in this short space. I have tried to do without references, but the rather cryptic summary of the "basic pattern" is fully spelled out in my *The Red Lamp of Incest* (New York: Dutton 1980; 2nd. ed. Notre Dame, IN: Notre Dame University Press 1983); and the obviously contentious point about the "secondary" nature of the incest theme, particularly in the Theban cycle of Sophocles, is dealt with at length in chapter 3 "The Virgin and the Godfather" of my *Reproduction and Succession* (New Brunswick, NJ: Transaction Publishers, 1993.) My own analysis of "The Fragmentation of Trickster" is in chapter 15 of *The Challenge of Anthropology* (Transaction Publishers, 1994.) Frederick Turner's work which was mentioned can be found in his *Natural Classicism* (New York: Paragon House, 1985) and *The Culture of Hope* (New York: Free Press, 1995.) Readers should also be on the lookout for Robert Storey's *Mimesis and the Human Animal* (Northwestern University Press, 1996.)

Interview

Political Correctness

with Richard Heffner

Richard Heffner's weekly interview program for public television, "The Open Mind," has always been a little island of intelligent discussion where public issues are quietly considered without regard to the demands of sponsors or even of audience ratings. (When I explained to one of my ever-skeptical daughters what I was going to do, she responded, "Ah yes: you're going to be on another of those programs that nobody watches.") In April 1991, Heffner had decided to ask the archpriest of postmodernism, Stanley Fish of Duke University, to give his views on the PC phenomenon, so he wanted to give the other side— whatever that was—equal time to make its case. He had just read my article on the Seville Declaration on Violence, in which I was violently critical of this kind of fashionable bullying, and since I was handy he asked me to pop into the Channel 11 studios in New York, where the program is taped, to do my part for the anti-PC crusade. While waiting to go on, I sat under large mural photos of scenes from "Star Trek: The Next Generation," one of that channel's great successes. I noted that the motto I was fondly familiar with and that was intoned at the start of all the old (which is to say the real) "Star Trek" programs: "To boldly go where no man has gone before," had been changed. It now read: "To boldly go where no one has gone before." The split infinitive, note, had been retained: grammatical correctness obviously being less important than the political variety.

HEFFNER: I'm Richard Heffner, your host on "The Open Mind."

And I want to focus today, as on several other programs, on the winds of change that have blown rather fiercely through even major American universities in recent years, and that cannot simply be dismissed as only "an academic matter" by those not immediately or intimately involved with the life of the campus. I refer, of course, to what's now called "politically correct" in the academy.

Indeed, *what* is deemed "politically correct" today—at Stanford or Michigan, or Duke, or Harvard, or wherever—may not make all that much difference to most thoughtful viewers right now. But *that* something, anything at all, *could* be labelled "PC" by today's university students, or faculty, or administrators, is what may come to haunt us all.

Back in 1948, when I first went to Rutgers University to teach American history and government, the very idea of being constrained academically by what was considered not "politically correct" in matters touching on race or gender or sexual identity, or just about anything else at all, would have seemed laughable. Less so now, however. No laughing matter as the academy seems—at least in some important places—to be driven today by notions of what *can* and what *cannot* be said or taught or perhaps even thought on campus and still be "PC"—politically correct.

So, today I want to discuss this tendency with the world-renowned anthropologist, Robin Fox, who there holds the distinguished designation of University Professor of Social Theory, and is my colleague at Rutgers.

Now, Professor Fox recently had the occassion to do battle within the academy with those who demonstrate a tendency to fanaticism…a passion, as he put it so generously, to lay blame upon and to punish those they find embracing ideas that are not, in *their* estimation, politically "correct." And what I would like to ask him first today is "what in the world is happening today to the life of the mind?"

Fox: That's the big question. What's happening, I think, is a narrowing down of the life of the mind, a diminishment. The broadness, the openess to inquiry, which is supposed to characterize the university, which is supposed to be what the university is *about*, is being whittled away by political pressures, by radical groups claiming "empowerment," by fashionable leftists, by feminists, by neo-Marxists. They go under numerous labels, but they are basically, I believe, the leftover characters from the Vietnam revolt who got tenured, stayed on in the universities, and now that they've no longer any real battle to fight have turned to using the university as a battle ground for their ideologies and for their political points of view. Their self-righteous moralizing is seductively attractive to the idealistic young, and they easily recruit followers.

HEFFNER: How can you explain the fact that while there seem not perhaps to be many enormous battles, this all seems to be making a very great impact upon the university?

FOX: Well, partly it's their own passion and devotion to what they're doing. People with a belief system and an agenda always have a tactical advantage. And partly it's the fact that most academics, like you and I, are sort of wishy-washy middle-of-the-road moderates: tolerant, decent fellows, who don't want to be thought ill of, and like to feel that they are up with the liberal tendencies of the times. We tend to be superindulgent of the lunatic fringes. So it's two things: one, they have the passion, the organization, the intensity to try and get their own way in these things, particularly in the humanities and social sciences. I don't think the music department's much affected by all this, any more than the natural sciences. So that's one thing. The other thing is the supineness of the tolerant majority in the university, which wants to be well thought of and which lets them get away with the nonsense.

HEFFNER: Would you have thought, thirty years ago when we first met, that you would characterize most of us as supine?

FOX: Yes. I did then. I think in those days I was a Young Turk, and I was trying to change my discipline for the better, as I saw it. Not, I think, politically motivated the way they are today, but intellectually motivated. And I was, I think, kind of depressed as many Young Turks are by the general willingness of the vast majority of academics to prefer the easy life to the intellectually hard and tough one. The attitude of most people then was, as it is now, "don't bother me, I've got these papers to publish, I want to get my next promotion, and I've got to put my kids through college, so don't push me too hard." Along with the fact that we all want to be thought "progressive." We none of us want to be thought of as whatever the current bad things are as conveyed by the fahionable boo-words of the time—sexist, racist, elitist; it used to be neo-fascist, militarist, and so on. The activists seize the high moral ground, and the rest go meekly along.

HEFFNER: What, then, is the downside? You don't want to be concerned about those who attack fascism and sexism and all the other "isms" that are out now, do you?

FOX: Well, what happens to people like myself, who would perhaps otherwise be inclined to shrug and ignore and get on with our lives, is that our toes get trodden on. We find our teaching interfered with, our freedom of enquiry endangered, our morality called into question, our freedom of speech censored, our students taught that right opinion is preferable to right argument. You might want to stay out of it and have the quiet life, but you can't. And there's another aspect of this which is that I think university administrations have changed. The faculty long ago lost control of the university. One of the big questions people usually ask is "why do the administrations allow them to get away with this?" Why do they allow, for example, the departments of English and history and political science and women's studies and sociology to be taken over by these people, by the politically correct, campus radical crowd? I think university administrations have changed considerably from being essentially people like ourselves who got sort of pushed into administration out of a sense of "noblesse oblige." We had to do our turn as dean or whatever, so we did it unwillingly but graciously. University presidents were expected to be emminent scholars. It's changed, and what we have now is a professional cadre of administrators who've given up on the scholarly life, whose business is administration, whose life is administration, and whose major concern is that they don't want trouble on their watch. No officer wants trouble on his watch. If an administrator has too much trouble, he's put down as a bad administrator, and therefore there's a tendency on the part of the administrators to do pretty much anything that will keep things quiet in the academy. And one of these things is to give in to the extremists—even to join them. You see, even if they *did* try to stand up to them, they'd really have no mobilized faculty support. The faculty who are mobilized are the radical faculty. I don't know if that answered your question...

HEFFNER: It does with a vengeance. The question now is...the point is that it answers it so well that I sit here wondering what then can be done? Where is that entry point into bringing about some change in what we're seeing?

FOX: Well, I think that those of my colleagues who have woken up to what's happening, and finally have decided that something has to be done, are divided on this. There are some real doomsayers who think Armageddon is around the corner for the universities. They think that, for example, in the private universities, once the parents and the boards of trustees and particularly the alumni figure out what's happening—at places like Duke in the English department, or Stanford generally—that once they realize there's going to be a terrible backlash against this and the villains will be rooted out. You might say, "how can this happen, all these people are tenured?" You know the expression "the tenured radicals" or the "Mercedes Marxists" as they're sometimes called...

HEFFNER: I like that expression!

FOX: Yes. Because they're all there on these handsome salaries, busily abusing the institutions that provide them. Anyway, one of the ideas is that there is going to be a backlash and even in the public universities the taxpayers are going to discover what is happening. They're going to discover that in sending their children to get an education in English language and literature they're getting an education in Marxism and deconstruction, relativism and nihilism, or the abuse of white males and the "canon" or victimology studies, or anything *but* English literature and language. And once the public realizes this they will rise up in their wrath. I'm skeptical, but there are precedents for the rapid decline of departments when they fall out of ideological favor. Modern language departments in the fifties and sixties were huge and powerful because they were compulsory subjects. Then suddenly it was decided they were not "relevant"—you remember "relevant"...yes, you remember "relevant."...

HEFFNER: I remember "relevant"!

FOX: Well, they were not relevant so they fell in numbers and importance. And the feeling is that this will happen to the politically correct subjects too: that there will be a backlash. I don't know about that. I really don't know how much the public and the alumni really care, or really understand what's happening on the campuses.

HEFFNER: You say "really care."...

FOX: Yes.

HEFFNER: You mean that?

FOX: I think they probably would care if they knew enough about it. But I think everyone is afraid of the spectre of McCarthyism; that is, of interfering with academic freedom and the like. And nobody, I think, wants to start up again the "Get the Reds out of Rutgers" sort of campaigns that idea-starved politicians used to run. So the answer to your question is that if there's going to be real reform it has to come from within the universities themselves and particularly from the silent majority of the faculty who don't in fact buy into the PC thing at all. But I don't see much sign of that happening, except for the formation of an interesting organization called the National Association of Scholars. I don't know if you know about that.

HEFFNER: Yes.

FOX: It now has branches on a whole lot of campuses. They publish a journal—*Academic Questions*—which published the article of mine from which you quoted, and which has of course been condemned by the American Association of University Professors, the Modern Language Association, and all the radical groups, as a right-wing, sexist, fascist rag...the usual litany.

HEFFNER: Okay. Let me ask you about that. How fair is it to say that the NAS has a political complexion of its own, that it is urging upon the universities the same course of action—"strike them down"—that the others you've described are doing, but that you are a reflection, or the NAS is a reflection, essentially of a conservative political attitude?

FOX: I think that, yes, there's something in that. If the PC pressure is coming from the organized left (broadly speaking), and the liberal middle is confused as usual, then opposition is most likely to come from the organized right. Certainly the people who join tend, I think, to be of a more conservative stance, but conservative with a small "c" as it were—not viciously right wing but more in the sense that they want to conserve what they see as being good about the academy and the academic life. And, at least this is the official line and the one I support, that what they're doing is what the AAUP should be doing but isn't, which is to defend academic freedom: freedom of speech and inquiry and freedom from the imposition of political ideologies.

HEFFNER: Haven't the universities always been in the business of imposing ideologies?

FOX: Yes. The radicals here have a good debating point. It's no good, they say, to long for a previous state in which there was a beautiful nonideological university. There were always ideologies. They have a good point because we are indeed colored by our times and our opinions and this will naturally influence what we teach and how we teach it. It isn't that long ago that "Christian Doctrine"—of the Dutch Reformed kind—was a compulsory subject for Rutgers students, along with compulsory chapel. And the feminists have a point in that most of the teaching was indeed done by the "phallocracy"—it was the white male view that was being preached largely to young white males. But I think the point is not that there were never ideologies in the university, but that the ideal of the university was that one should at least try to overcome bias. One should be at least a bit ashamed of it if it was too obvious. There was a notion that there were objective truths out there—that there was a real world out there that you had to measure your opinions against; that these opinions could be challenged; that they could be proved wrong! Now that's what's under attack. Among the radical deconstructionists, since everything is ideology, all that matters is picking your ideology and promoting it; not putting it up for test; not putting it up for grabs. I always tell students that the basic principle of learning in the university is that everything is up for grabs, except the principle that everything is up for grabs. That's what we want to see restored. At the moment, for example, feminist ideas are not up for grabs—except among feminists of course, where they squabble away like all good sectarians.

HEFFNER: Do you think that's possible? To restore rational debate?

FOX: I think it's possible if enough people wake up to what's happening, yes. But it's not possible as long as administrations and complacent or frightened or quiescent faculty go along with what's happening.

HEFFNER: You think the key is to be found in the administrations, I gather?

FOX: Well, I think they *could* do a lot.

HEFFNER: You don't expect them to?

FOX: Administrations are largely concerned with protecting their rears. But after all it was "administrations" that founded and built the universities in the first place, and they had some idea what went into them, and they made bold decisions and created departments and disciplines. I suppose it's not impossible to get an enlightened president who could forget about popularity and "management style" and who would say "I want a campus that's a real university campus, not something that's been politicized and intimidated and become a propaganda ground for radicals and feminists…"

HEFFNER: But when universities were founded there was indeed an idea of the university.

FOX: Yes, that's true. And that's slipping…it's slipping away. That's one of the things that alerted people to the crisis that is looming in the universities today. What's slipping is the idea of the university as a place for open, free discussion where theories can always be held up to the test of truth. Does it correspond with the facts? You have a whole army of people saying "there are no facts, there are only political positions…" We're in terrible danger I think. The whole point of having a university is being called into question. Universities are being turned into radical recruiting grounds and social reform operations.

HEFFNER: Well, you know, in your own essay that I briefly made reference to…when you're talking about this question of the human tendency towards violence or towards war, and you say, well, you don't necessarily know about that, but there seems to be "an innate tendency in the minds of men, a tendency more terrible than aggression, a tendency we are doomed to express and live by and that explains all this passion to lay blame and punish" and you point out that you were "impudent enough to suggest that *fanaticism* is just such a tendency." I really want to ask you, as an anthropologist, as a historian of man, do you feel that this involvement with fanaticisms of all kinds that I see about me is something that is a phenomenon, that is increasing, growing, in our times?

FOX: I think so. You see, when we had small cohesive societies everybody could be more or less fanatical about the same thing: their own totem, their own language, their own religion. And this was no bad thing; it probably served a useful function of social cohesion. They all shared these things and they didn't see any alternatives to them. Presented with different fanaticisms—from different tribes—they could reject and fight them. But when you become as big and diverse and complex as we are in modern nation states, there isn't a single fanaticism to share, and you get divided up into hundreds of different fanaticisms. But people adhere to them just as strongly. There is the same urge to belong to that tribe, to defend its totem to the death, to defend its gods against all comers. This is still very strong in us. So we attach ourselves to the little tribes we know: the feminist tribe (or one of them), or the Marxist tribe (or one of those), or the vegetarian tribe, or the gun tribe, or the pro-life tribe, or the lesbian tribe, or whatever. And we follow out the fanaticisms with regard to these rather restricted ideas.

HEFFNER: Is this your description of multiculturalism?

FOX: Well, it's what multiculturalism often boils down to…yes: the battle of one fanaticism against another.

HEFFNER: So that the larger a nation, the more disparate groups in it, the more fanatical will be the battling?

FOX: Yes. Particularly when people feel that they're fighting for their political and social and economic lives over these things. I think we always see that as a nation gets more diverse you get a greater diversity of fanaticisms also. The really interesting thing about the United States— the thing that drew so many of us to it who came from somewhere else— is its extraordinary ability to survive this kind of battering and still maintain a viable democratic political order. I think a lot of Americans take this for granted, but it is, in the history of the world, rather remarkable.

HEFFNER: But the battering is much more recent. I mean we used to absorb all this diversity.

FOX: Yes. Only one major civil war is still remarkable.

HEFFNER: In a program that Arthur Schlesinger and I did we talked about the Tower of Babel, and how that is much more important today than the unity of the nation.

FOX: We used to absorb the diversity because we had some firm idea of what was American, and what we could therefore require of people who wanted to join the club. It was a good club to be a member of and lots of people wanted to join. But there were certain ground rules, and you had to obey those rules, and there were certain forms and codes of behavior; there was a certain language that everybody spoke, and you had to know those things and abide by them if you were going to be an American. I think to some extent we've lost the sense of that. Take this whole move towards multiculturalism—another buzz-word that's moved in to replace real thinking. Every university president, if he wants to be accepted, has to declare himself a multiculturalist, and pooh-pooh the great books and Western civilization and the core curriculum and all those bad things in favor of multiculturalism. But what isn't understood it seems is that multiculturalism is fragmentation, and those fragments are going to tend to fly apart when infused with the energy of fanaticism, not come together. There's very little that holds together these disparate mini-cultures. You've got to have something. It almost doesn't matter what it is as long as you are confident about it and teach your young people confidently about it. The old Americanization programs where kids learned to brush their teeth and drink orange juice as they came in as immigrants, as well as saluting the flag, had something to be said for them. They produced people who had a rudimentary shared sense of what it was to be an American.

HEFFNER: I have to smile at that because you say "had something" to say for them, almost as if you and I still were back in those days, and we feel a bit embarrassed about those things.

FOX: We have to be apologetic now about saying that it's very good that people should be Americans, yes. We have to apologize because God knows we might expect them to speak English or do something terrible like that, which would immediately brand us a "elitists."

HEFFNER: Now, anthropologically...historically speaking, can you trace back many societies that lost that sense, that initial unity and, never regained it?

FOX: Oh, I think all those that fell apart. I mean they all got too big; they all got too diverse. Large empires—and America is a kind of empire—inevitably seem to collapse at some point. The center does not hold.

HEFFNER: They never regained their unity?

FOX: They never regained it. Rome went. There is no Rome! Yet to the old Romans their order seemed eternal.

HEFFNER: So if you are asked to be...to perform as a prophet?

FOX: As a prophet I would say that its extremely dangerous to push multiculturalism to the point where you don't have a central sense of belonging and sharing among all the people of a culture...yes. That's why sports are so important to us now. They are one of the few things we all share more or less incontrovertibly. So football especially has become a kind of great national secular religion, with "Superbowl Sunday" replacing Easter Sunday as the great ritual event of the year, along with the World Series and the NBA playoffs.

HEFFNER: You talk about sharing, but what do you do with the people whose participation in the sharing was so minimal? Historically it was so minimal. And you and I know that we can talk as white males about everyone sharing, but we know perfectly well that the sharing was largely left to us. Now what do we do about those people who were left out? How do we pull the teeth from their fanaticism today?

FOX: I really don't know that I have any very good prescriptions for how to do these things. I'm not a social engineer. I can see some of the ways you *don't* do them, and I see...

HEFFNER: The way they've been done?

FOX: The way they've been done. I mean...although, of course again you can't say this without getting all the bad labels, I think perhaps one of the worst things that was done was the affirmative action programs. These programs, it seems to me, have the opposite effect of what they're intended to have. A lot of the so-called "increases in racial tension" on campus, and racial incidents, are probably as much a product of affirmative action as a product of the nastiness or racism of white students. I don't see the white students as being as intolerant as they are painted. But I do see them as being under a lot of provocation. And I don't see black students benefitting particularly from the so-called affirmative action programs.

HEFFNER: You attribute this to some extent to affirmative action. To affirmative action, per se, or to affirmative action as poorly carried out?

FOX: As poorly carried out. As poorly conceived from the start. I mean the admission of large numbers of unqualified students to the university (and I've been there since this started) who then feel even more oppressed having got into a situation where they're expected to perform to standards they can't meet—more than 50 percent of them drop out. Or standards get lowered to meet them, as it were. So then they feel patronized because they're being put through a parallel system in Black Studies or whatever it is, that everyone knows is running at a lower standard than the rest of the university, so their degrees aren't taken seriously. I mean they're not being turned out as doctors, lawyers, engineers, and things like that, which the black community could use; they're being turned out with degrees in "oppression studies" as someone sarcastically called them.

HEFFNER: But that's our fault, isn't it?

FOX: Entirely our fault.

HEFFNER: Because we didn't put into this venture what universities might have put into the venture?

FOX: Exactly. We should have had a statewide coordinated effort to absorb these students gradually through the community college and state college system, giving them longer time to graduate and raising their standards by stages. Instead we panicked and threw them in the deep end without swimming lessons. What's happening here too is that a lot of resentment is coming from poor white students—if we can call them that. That is, students from white working-class backgrounds whose schools and neighbourhoods weren't in most cases much better than those of the black students. They see themselves being discriminated against, while blacks, Hispanics, and even someone with an American Indian grandmother are being favored even if less qualified. They don't think they had it so hot. They had to struggle; they had poor inner-city backgrounds as well. A lot of the resentment is coming from them, and that's where you'd expect it. The place to start with reform here is the community, the schools, and the homes and families. Until we sort that out there is no use the universities trying to pick it up at a later stage and somehow hope to reverse the damage done, without causing all these problems. Then, having caused the problems, turning round and pretending its an individual moral issue and saying the bad white racist students caused it and hustling them off to brainwashing sessions. And while I'm on with my catalogue of complaints...will you indulge me ?

HEFFNER: You'll have to be super quick!

FOX: Then let me just say that another idiotic outcome is the undignified corporate raiding that the rich universities are indulging in to buy up the very small pool of black (and other minority) faculty. This is not done for the benefit of the black community. It is sheer hypocricy. The administrations want to look good, so they want statistics of how many black faculty they've hired. But they're so few, and consequently even if you hire them they can get a better offer from a richer university. The logic of this is that they'll all end up at Harvard I suppose, which is fine for Harvard, but as I said, does nothing for the black community as a whole. We have to start at the bottom and change the whole system so that we produce and hold onto more qualified black undergraduates, and this is going to take time, money, and effort, and there is no quick fix.

HEFFNER: To get back to PC in general—and we have only a minute left—do you think that with resources, appropriate resources now, universities could do more...much more and perhaps turn the tide against the PC fanatics?

FOX: They could, but they'd have to rethink completely what they were doing, and they would have to give up all the shibboleths and holy cows that they've invented over the past twenty years and start, I think, from the drawing board—do it again from scratch.

HEFFNER: Anthropologically, once more. Are there examples in history of societies doing that...starting anew?

FOX: Picking themselves up and starting again after a self-inflicted disaster?

HEFFNER: Yes.

FOX: Certainly there are. We survived a civil war. The Europeans lost their empires but they still flouish in a more limited way. Russia is struggling through it at the moment, as is South Africa. Spain after the horrors of its civil war and dictatorship is a marvellous example of a society getting its act together again, thanks largely to a courageous and intelligent young monarch. And we're not speaking of a whole society or a mortal mistake are we? We're not asking to recreate the Roman empire, we're only asking for a few sensible adjustments in one institution within a society, namely the university.

HEFFNER: That's an optimistic and upbeat note to end on, it seems to me, when you talk about a *few* changes! Let's end it on that, and thank you very much for joining me today, Robin Fox.

Fox: My pleasure.
HEFFNER: Meanwhile, as an old friend used to say, "goodnight and good luck."

Afterword

Five years later, as I write, things are not much better, but I do think the greater public awareness I spoke of is beginning to assert itself, and there does seem to be a growing disillusionment with affirmative action, for example. California has plain abolished it, and action is pending in other states. Federal courts have thrown out a good many university "hate speech" codes and the like as being unconstitutional. The organized opposition within the academy continues through the National Association of Scholars, and many books have been written criticizing the PC phenemenon including its attacks on science. The New York Academy of Sciences recently had a two-day symposium devoted to attacking the attacks on science (see chapter 8 of this book). Several organizations have been formed and continue to grow, all opposing the fashionable trends. The National Alumni Forum headed by Lynne Cheyney is mobilizing that powerful lobby, and The Association of Literary Scholars and Critics is challenging the hegemony of the totally politicized and superpowerful Modern Language Association. In Canada, which has had its own disturbing history of the same nonsense, the Society for Academic Freedom and Scholarship has been founded to carry on the struggle there. But the nonsense goes on. My own university has recently notified the faculty to the effect that "sexual harassment" need not be either sexual or harassment, but can be the "creation of a hostile classroom environment." As my colleague Lionel Tiger was quick to point out, the most hostile classroom environments on campus were those of the feminist teachers with their diatribes against males, patriarchy, male science, and phallocracy. With whom do we file our grievances against this form of "sexual harassment" he asked? Needless to say, no one rushed to answer.

I was challenged on a couple of points, for example that over 50 percent of affirmative action students drop out. Actually the figure is probably higher. In 1992 (for which I happen to have the figures) Rutgers graduated 54 percent of the black members and 56 percent of the Latino members of the class (the white rate was 76 percent). But these rates include those blacks and Latinos who got in on merit and not by affirmative action. Of the latter, certainly more than 50 percent dropped out. And Rutgers ranked eighth among public universities in the nation in its minority graduation rate! These figures, in other words, are among the very best. I was also challenged about the "two track" system, without which these figures would be infinitely worse. I can only point to thirty years of experience with the system which, at Livingston College in the late 1960s, I was instrumental in helping to start up—although I had grave doubts at the time about the wisdom of what we doing in "nontraditional recruiting" and the like; but these were dizzily idealistic times, and I was tentative foreigner. Of course, the deliberate lowering of standards for minority students will be denied by the administrations and the black studies departments and the like. But I have been through the system and seen how it works and I know what happens. I speak from direct personal experience here. And I hope my point is not lost: I consider this a disservice to, and a sell-out of, these students, who do not need this kind of patronization that is designed largely for administrative cosmetic purposes, but a total system that will make sure they receive *from the start* an education that will enable them to compete equally with their white peers in college. Pretty much everything else is a band-aid on this social wound—it benefits a few minority students and faculty but does not solve the basic problem. It is merely a salve for the ever-agonizing liberal conscience.

It is tempting to say, regarding the PC question in general, that we have never lived through sillier times in the academy. But these strange institutions have been swept by all kinds of fads and fashions. Academicians live in a hothouse of ideas, and since ideas have so little restraint from the real world, they can easily, like the tail of the peacock, run dazzlingly wild. And academicians have so little real power that they can easily become intoxicated by the illusion of it. The universities are full of people filled with self-righteous anger about perceived social injustice, with no-one to vent it on except students and colleagues. Fortunately, they do little harm to the world at large (except to the language), and we should be grateful for this small mercy and meanwhile bear the cross with patience. It will pass.

5

Moral Sense and Utopian Sensibility

This chapter began life as a contribution to a symposium of the American Political Science Association on James Q. Wilson's book The Moral Sense *(1993). It was later published in a symposium in* Criminal Justice Ethics *(1994), with a reply by Professor Wilson. The first part of the chapter is the original contribution, to which I have appended Professor Wilson's comments, and my response to them. This book, by the "other" Wilson, is a momentous contribution, and one that I see as being in direct line of intellectual descent from* The Imperial Animal, *like, for example, Melvin Konner's* The Tangled Wing *(1982), another milestone in biosocial thinking. This is not at all a review of the book—it has been massively reviewed elsewhere—but rather a commentary on the issues it raises; issues that are fundamental to any claim on our part to have any relevance to morality, and hence policy.*

One of the oddest things about cultural relativism is its almost perverse obsession with the specific content of moral systems as opposed to their general form. The anthropologists I talk to who have done fieldwork in exotic societies and are committed social relativists or social constructionists will never tire of pointing out to me how the content of moral rules is quite different in "their" society from "ours" and how this proves the essential soundness of their relativistic premises. I then ask them if they know of any society that does not have moral rules, and an elaborate moral discourse surrounding them. They do not. I ask them if "their" society has rules about, for example, the fair distribution of resources. It does. They are different from our rules, but it has them. I ask if it has rules about the legitimate use of violence. It does. Again they are different from our rules, but it has them. I ask if it has a theory of blame—of the attribution of responsiblity for breaking the rules. It does. Different again, but it has it. I ask if it has a system of rewards for keeping the rules and punishments for breaking them. It does. I ask if it has standards for assessing personal worth, and a system of moral discourse for evaluating it. Well, yes it does. There are good people and bad people and ways of distinguishing them—but of course the standards are not ours. Of course not. I ask if children, at different stages of their lives, show a different understanding of the nature of the rules. Well, yes they do. I ask if this is taken into consideration by the adults in assigning responsibility to children. Well, yes it is—but not in the same way as we do it. No, certainly not.

I then ask them why they think people might be so stupid as to apply completely nonapplicable moral rules to themselves? Surely they will only apply relevant ones? Rules against embezzlement are useless in a society without money, but rules against the unfair use of property there will surely be and sure enough there are. And does this not depend on some notion of "fairness" that is independent of the actual content of the rules? Similarly does not the praise-blame system depend on some notion of responsibility independent of what is actually praised or blamed? And if there is some concept of treachery (and there always is) then does this not depend on some notion of loyalty regardless of the boundaries of the unit (i.e., those to whom treachery is a crime)? I could add to the list of queries but you have the idea by now and can add to it yourselves.

I usually succeed in driving my colleague away rather than driving my point home. There is a profoundly curious reluctance to conduct the debate at this level. The anthropologist wants to keep it at the level of specific rules to illustrate the vast differences between moral systems: I want to move quickly to general features of moral systems to illustrate how they are all fundamentally about the same things, even if the casuistry differentiates them. But my colleague suspects that I am going to spring a trap about universals, and then grab him with some nonsense about innate moral propensities or the like, and either backs off, accusing my "universal framework of moral discourse" argument of vagueness or something such, or, if he has done Philosophy 101 at some point in his career, will trump my ace with accusations of the Naturalistic Fallacy. I don't let him get away with that one since I did Philosophy 201, and rapidly point out that I am not saying anything about prescriptions following logically from descriptions at all. I am simply saying that we know of no societies where there is not a recognizable *framework of moral discourse*, and that the contents of this discourse are pretty much the same everywhere, even if the actual prescriptions differ a lot—which one would expect, since people are not totally out to lunch and so will usually make their specific rules relative to their actual situations.

Now the point I am making, and have been making for more than thirty years, is not peculiar to me nor did it originate with me (I learned it from Morris Ginsberg in the early 1950s), and students of that odd branch of Western thought we call Ethics, will recognize the issues well enough. But I fear that they too are trapped in their assumptions, and as we have seen, provide ammunition (if blank) for the relativists in their resistance to the idea of universal standards of moral discourse (note I don't say universal standards of morality; I agree there aren't any.) This is because, ever since the Greeks, we have been hung up in Ethics with the notion of The Good. This is after all what Ethics is supposed to be about. And two and a half millenia later we still can't agree on it, which should tell us something. One thing it might tell us is that this pursuit of The Good is not a very promising route to follow. I agree heartily with Mae West that goodness has nothing to do with it. It is the obsession with goodness that gets us into tangles about the Naturalistic Fallacy and the like, and to "disproofs" of evolutionary ethics and so on (the good cannot be equated with the more evolved etc, etc.) It also leads to incredible philosophical silliness as in the case of G. E. Moore's unbelievably influential "disproof" of the Naturalistic Fallacy and insistence that "good" was a "non-natural object" and so on.

That this should all have stemmed from Hume's innocent observation about how people, in the process of moral discourse, often jumped from statements of "is" to statements of "ought" without any justification, is significant. People do do this all the time; Hume was a good anthropologist to pick up on it (even from the literature alone, although I'm sure it was obvious to his acute personal observation of honest gentlemen and modest women.) And indeed when it came to framing a moral theory of his own, Hume (following mostly his Scottish moral-sense colleague Hutcheson) did the same thing. He only complained that people did it "without justification"—he was willing to supply justifications for his own conclusions at length.

What Hume had observed then was what I have chosen to call a feature of the *universal system of moral discourse*: that people do not usually just arbitrarily announce moral judgments out of the blue; they associate them with statements of fact and assume that the judgments and the facts are related. Often indeed they do not fill in the "justification" since it appears obvious to them that, for example, torture causes pain and pain is undesirable so one ought not to do it; it is not a good thing. It takes the philosopher to create a system of meta-discourse in which this becomes a "problem" because of the "good" business. But, one is forced to ask, before the advent of cultural relativists and antinaturalistic philosophers, how in God's name did we ever manage to run our families, raise our children, and preserve civil order? The answer is that we did what the overwhelming majority of people still do: we ignored these issues and got on with our moral lives. We stated our facts and made our judgments; we assigned praise and blame and argued over the standards; we assumed that people were (with exceptions) responsible for their actions; we rewarded and punished our children to make them, we hoped, into the kind of adults we wanted. Our lives were, and are, dense with morality, as all good novelists know and make the basis of their art.

But while evaluative words are indeed an essential part of the universal moral discourse, they are a practical not a theoretical part. People do not argue about the meaning of "good" in the normal conduct of affairs, although they may argue a lot about what is or is not good. And at the level of content, of course, the relativists are trivially right: notions of the good and the good life differ, often sharply. We, in the Western rationalist tradition, have been so overwhelmingly concerned to establish just what this could "mean" that we have lost sight of the fact that people operate perfectly well in their often well-ordered social worlds without any such definitional problems. They know what is good and what is bad. They will argue the casuistry of these things, and even change their notions over time quite radically. But they are not arguing about the meaning, only the application. And they will argue within the limits of the universal framework I hinted at at the beginning and that James Q. Wilson in *The Moral Sense* explores in such admirable detail. But we shall return to that.

If goodness—or at least the definitional problem of goodness—has very little to do with morality, what does? We find this hard to swallow precisely because of our confusion of "moral" with "good." Let me put it graphically: to say that we live moral lives has nothing to do with saying that we live good lives. Many Nazis lived very moral lives. Headhunters and cannibals live very moral lives. Inner-city gang members live very moral lives. Maximum security prisoners live complicated moral lives. Colombian drug lords live very moral lives. Most terrorists live supermoral lives. You are shocked because you assume that this must mean that they lead "good" lives according to your notions of the good. But whether or not these are bad people, and some assuredly are, they still live according to rules and standards of morality framed in the universal discourse. Drug lords will argue fiercely about the fairness of the division of spoils according to effort versus the division according to investment. Gang members will reward the loyal and punish the treacherous and assume that those so acting are responsible for their acts. Nazis would insist on strong family values, sound racial hygiene, and devotion to the fatherland. Headhunters will despise a man who cheats in his method of taking a head. Terrorists will give up their own lives in the name of a higher value, and argue that in their struggle there are no innocent victims since all are in part to blame for injustice even through passive acquiescence. (They have problems with children, although I have heard elaborate justifications here too.) In fact only a relatively few psychopaths and sociopaths and total sadists (i.e., people who are consitutionally incapable of developing a social conscience) can be said to live outside the iron necessity of operating within the universal framework of moral discourse.

Thus groups of people doing what seem to us very bad things still do them in very moral way. And this is my point: since they are organized groups of human beings trying to live highly social human lives—whatever their aims and objects—they have no choice but to live according to a moral order. This is what human groups and societies are; this is the only way they can operate. Do a simple thought experiment: try to design a society or organized group that operates according to "pure reason" taking everything on its merits without preconceptions, making no prescriptions on the basis of descriptions, assigning no responsibilities, and so on. It is inconceivable of course. It would not be a human society. Nor would a society operating on the "greatest happiness principle" or the "categorical imperative" or the "original position" or any other of the fantasy states of the philosophers. Even the designers of utopias have to accept the framework of the universal moral discourse; they simply alter the content to suit their own prejudices about the good life. The more they depart from this, the more lunatic their creations appear. The only real alternative to the moralizing, moralistic, and morally obsessed human society is ultimately the genetically engineered caste system of Huxley's brave new world, or Hellstrom's hive. The totally rational and nonjudgmental society of Spock's Vulcan might exist, but as all "Star Trek" fans recognize it is not a human society, and Spock is only made plausible by being half human himself.

In other words, *moral* should not be equated with *good* but with *human*. To be human is to be moral, that is, to act within a definite framework of specific judgmental concerns in interacting with other humans. Another way of putting this, which some Western philosophers to their credit, even before Darwin, recognized, is to say that we have, as humans a "moral sense"—indeed Darwin counted himself as one of their number. I agree that we have a moral sense for the same reasons Darwin gave. Natural selection would have favored the development of what we call morality in any organisms that developed the levels of intelligence, consciousness, foresight, and sociality that humans did. Those individuals that acted towards others in a "moral" way would be more likely to survive and have offspring and so on, until genes favorable to this moral behavior came to dominate their amoral alternatives (which did not necessarily disappear however).

A major component of this morality is what I have stressed as "inhibition" or "equilibration" (after Michael Chance), and which Wilson deals with under "self control." It is the psychologists' "deferred gratification" and without it living according to rules (morality) is impossible. Other major components are sympathy, without which group living would be impossible, a sense of fairness or "justice" without which the settlement of inevitable disputes and the control of cheating would be impossible, and the attribution of responsibility without which praise and blame, the system of rewards and punishments, and the raising of children would be impossible, and again, the sense of duty or group loyalty without which (along with sympathy) true altruism would be impossible. In the parlance of modern evolutionary psychology, these would be "domain specific algorithms" (or modules) showing a high degree of design adaptedness— perhaps we should always talk of "moral senses" in the plural.

Wilson has caught them all (except perhaps the attribution of responsibility) and done a fine service in showing the psychological underpinnings that make them work. I am only concerned that he too is perhaps still stuck with assuming that they should produce a "good" result. I agree with him that most of the time they do, in the sense that people do get on with their lives, morals and all, with a minimum of harm to other people, despite the temptations and distractions towards selfishness and greed that are all pervasive. But I find no built-in guarantees. As he sees, the "moral sense" in this sense, is fragile. It is easily overwhelmed. It has a narrow range of application. Universal moral standards are not part of the universal moral discourse—only the meta-discourse of the philosophers. We may all operate in all our societies around a fixed set of moral senses, and this will give a remarkable "sameness" to human moral systems despite their surface differences of rules and standards. (Much as there is a sameness to all human languages in the jobs they do despite often staggering differences in surface grammar; the same with kinship systems.) But it does not mean that there is a universal basis for "goodness"—only for morality.

The moral senses are basically, as Darwin pointed out, the social senses: they are the equipment we need to lead a human social existence. If perhaps we substituted "social sense" for "moral sense" it might make the point—as indeed various prescient philosophers other than the Moral Sense school have done; people as various as Royce, Bradley, Bergson, and Thomas Jefferson (although the latter was much influenced by the Moral Sense philosophers.) The social senses will not guarantee utopian or good outcomes because they were not evolved to do this. They could not anticipate these latter-day demands of civilized society. They evolved, like the rest of our domain specific modules, to cope with survival in the (often loosely defined) Pleistocene, and specifically in the Palaeolithic period of the last two million years when our brains underwent a tripling in size and developed the complexity of function that now charaterizes them. And the evolutionary process was not concerned with producing some type of ethically ideal "good" person, but with a person who could survive. You are constructed to survive in a world without philosophers, popes, or policemen, but with an often hostile environment, including groups like yours but hostile to it, and your own kin as your only resource.

The moral/social senses that evolved to cope with this would be particularistic, nepotistic, and xenophobic. Altruism would not extend automatically beyond the "familiar"—literally "of the family"—in these circumstances, and sympathy would be hard to extend to the stranger. Thus dealings with strangers would be heavily hedged about with rules and rituals to contain the potential hostility. I have been watching the excellent PBS Civil War series recently, and one of the striking things about this remarkable conflict is how the officers of each side conducted themselves with great "fairness" to those on the other, and usually scrupulously observed the rules of war. But these "enemy" officers were mostly fellow West Pointers and saw themselves, in what may now appear a perverse sense, as members of the "same" group. But this didn't stop the Confederate troops under (the non-West Point) Forrest from conducting a brutal massacre of surrendering black troops and "Tennessee Yankees" at Fort Donelson. These unfortunates were outside the group, or traitors to it, and the rules no longer applied. This result, as well as the many examples of gallant actions towards the enemy, is a direct product of the Palaeolithic moral sense.

We have to face the fact that the products of the moral sense are not always pretty. The sense did not, as we have seen, evolve in a nice democratic bourgeois liberal world, and a good deal of it is inimical to that world, as any gang member or terrorist will tell you in some detail. That is why rationalistic exercises like those of the ethical philosophers—attempts to find universal standards as in Kant or Rawls—are largely beside the point and only interesting as prescriptive exercises. They are not descriptively or theoretically adequate when it comes to explaining moral behavior. Thus while the moral sense may inspire sympathy, self-control, and fairness, these are all directed to fellows, to the familiar. That same moral sense—as duty or loyalty—can tell us to kill the dangerous unfamiliar, or better still torture the traitor, without sympathy or compassion. And this is just as moral. And it worked very well in the small societies of our "environment of evolutionary adaptation"—to use the jargon to describe the world we evolved to cope with. It did not produce moral utopias, but it did produce viable societies which rapidly rose to the top of the food chain, and that was what was at issue.

Unfortunately, the system can break down and even backfire in the large, impersonal bureaucratic, peasant and industrial societies of human history. We simply cannot fool the Palaeolithic senses into believing that the rest of the society is indeed a kind of kin group, despite the ingenuity expended in this direction by prelates and politicians. As William James saw so clearly, perhaps only with war can we manage it, and this is our greatest moral and social parodox to date. The pleas to social morality we receive are essentialy versions of "try to behave as if you lived in a small community consisting largely of your kin and close friends." But we don't, and we know we don't, and enough of us just don't care. The lure of even a little money and petty power is enough to overwhelm the fragile moral sense of being part of the social organism. So we fall back on the gang. Within the gang there can be loyalty and altruism and sympathy; there is indeed honor among thieves. But the society at large is hard to see as anything but a feeding ground of prey animals. And the gang can be a corporation, a social movement, a government department, a branch of the military, an ethnic enclave, a profession, a university, a religious sect, or a Mafia "family." We are used to the vocabulary of "special interest" politics, but we don't see this as evolutionary business as usual, as indeed we fail to see most of our so-called social pathologies from teenage pregnancy epidemics to high divorce rates.

Thus, in conclusion, I am obviously with Wilson and against the relativists when it comes to the existence of innate moral senses. Absolutely. But I am perhaps not as sanguine as he when it comes to pinning much hope for a good society on the innate moral senses given the alarming shift in circumstances in which they are now required to operate. If we can't persuade the few Serbs and Croats—who speak exactly the same language—that they are at least a pseudo-kin group, what are we going to do with nearly ten billion people in the year 2000? I'm still waiting for the utopian solution to this one.

* * *

In his reply Professor Wilson commented on my comments as follows:

But if by these means I have narrowed whatever difference may exist between Professor Gauss and myself, I may have widened that between Robin Fox and myself. I would very much regret that, since I regard Professor Fox as one of the most sensible anthropological students of morality I have encountered and one whose own writings have done much good in exposing the mindless cultural relativism of some of his colleagues. But perhaps because he has been engaged for so long in a war to reclaim the soul of academic anthropology, he may, in desperation, have yielded too much of the high ground in his effort to avoid losing the war. In his essay, he recounts his attempts to get relativists to admit that morality is a universal feature of human societies. His strategy is to get them to acknowledge that there is no society, however exotic its specific moral rules, that is without a moral code or that fails to engage in moral discourse about the justification for that code. By conceding to his opponents the absense of any universal moral rules, he concedes, I think, a bit too much. Just how much is suggested by his striking, and I think unwarranted, statement that "to say we live moral lives has nothing to do with saying we live good lives." Or in another place: "*moral* should not be equated with *good* but with *human*." If "moral" and "good" are entirely different concepts, then I confess that I no longer know the meaning of either. It is no answer to say that this radical distinction is proved by the fact that Nazis, cannibals, criminals and terrorists "live very moral lives." It is certainly true that many Nazis were good fathers, many cannibals respectful of private property, some criminals fair in the distribution of their booty, and many terrorists capable of self-sacrifice. It is more correct to say that in *some aspects* of their lives, these people behaved morally, but that in other aspects they were utterly immoral, by which I mean bad. That they followed moral rules with respect to some matters shows, as Professor Fox has argued, that human society is impossible without such rules, but it does not show that these people can be regarded as moral. I agree that there are few universal moral rules, though I think there are some: the rule against incest, for example, or that against unjustified homicide. But I do think that there are universal moral sentiments, and I think Professor Fox agrees with me, for he provides a list of such sentiments that is quite similar to my own: self-control, sympathy, fairness, duty, and the attribution of responsibility. Moreover, we agree that lives led more or less in accordance with these sentiments tend to produce a good result, though he is at pains to put inverted commas around "good" so as to suggest its problematic status. And finally we agree that these moral sentiments are fragile and easily overwhelmed. Where we apparently disagree is whether these universal sentiments imply some universal judgment about what is good (and good without inverted commas)—that is, about how people ought to live and about what actions ought to be condemned. My view is that these sentiments, taken together, imply a respect for innocent human life. Our sympathy is most easily engaged by the sight of a suffering baby; infancy necessarily implies innocence, and all but the psychopath feel, or can easily imagine, grief at the suffering of their own infants. Fairness, (or more broadly, justice) implies a standard for judging who is innocent and who not. Self-control implies a recognition of our impulsive and self-regarding nature, and thus the desirability of holding our impulses in check, so that harm to the innocent will be avoided. We have many duties, but our highest is to those most dependent on us and least able to fend for themselves. The central problem for moral reasoning is to determine the range of people and circumstances over which these sentiments ought to rule: whose life is innocent and in what does respect consist? Moral reasoning is not, as Professor Fox suggests, "beside the point," but it is, as he says, usually quite parochial. The tragic and gruesome events in Bosnia and Rwanda remind us of that. How, then, ought we to draw the circle within which our moral sentiments are governing? I know of only one way to answer that question, and that is to be, or become, disinterested spectators of the way the circle is drawn and the behavior that occurs within its circumference. Nazis, cannibals, criminals, drug lords, and terrorists are self-interested judges of their behavior, just as we middle-class American professors are self-interested judges of our own behavior. But for both groups it is possible to imagine a disinterested spectator—not only possible but essential, for without a belief in the possibility of disinterested judgment there is no possibility for any moral standards to exist at all. We remind ourselves of that every time we criticize a player for cheating at a game in which we are an observer but not a participant. It is an empricial question, susceptible to an answer: how will disinterested people, given all of the facts, judge genocide, infanticide, cannibalism, terrorism, and criminality? I think both Professor Fox and I know the answer to that question: such acts will be condemned absent extraordinary justifying circumstances.... If disinterested people do not condemn the unwarranted sacrifice of innocent human life, then, indeed, goodness is a chimera, and morality rests merely on a prudential calculation about how best to get along in a given social situation.

* * *

Here, then, are some counter comments:

I certainly did not intend to give up any high ground to moral relativists! I don't think I even gave up any low ground. I said what I have always said: that at a descriptive level there exist considerable differences in moral judgments between societies both in space and time. This is unanswerably the case and those of us who seek to combat relativism waste our time in denying it. What is at issue is what we can or cannot infer from this moral variability. The "weak" relativist would infer that moral judgments are infinitely variable and we have no easy way to reach any universal moral judgments. The "strong" relativist would insist that we cannot in principle reach any universal moral judgments; that we are hopelessly trapped in our local versions and that they are, in the end, incompatible. Professor Wilson and I both disagree with the relativists. But where we seem to differ is in the way we wish to frame the disagreement. And as is the way with these things we have to recognize an initial quibble. I think it is possible to make up a list of moral prescriptions based on my idea of "humanness" that we should all follow. I make no bones about this: I am interested in moral prescriptions; I want to rewrite the ten commandments with Darwinian hindsight. And in doing so I would hew very closely to what Professor Wilson describes as the basic moral principles. Indeed my list is, as he says, quite similar to his own because it *is* his own, with only my addition of the attribution of moral responsibility. But we must separate this prophetic function of making moral prescriptions from the business of analyzing what actually goes on in the world. And here I think perhaps we do a little bit part company. He thinks that people develop quite specific notions of the "good" which are essentially universal. I think their notions of the good are widely diverse, but that *something* is universal, and that this is something on which we can build. The something that is universal is what I have chosen to call the *universal moral discourse*. I tried to show that however much they may differ in their specific moral rules, people universally agree that there should *be* moral rules and what is more that these moral rules should concern some pretty specific things: the things in fact that Professor Wilson and I agree on as the basic principles of morality. I argue, much as Darwin did, that intelligent social animals gifted with foresight and hence the ability to forsee the consequences of their actions could act in no other way. They would have to be, in this sense, "moral" animals; that is, they would have to conduct their lives according to some rules of morality. Now I think we can pretty well predict what those rules of morality would be about, but I do not think we can ever predict quite what the rules themselves would be, for again pretty obvious reasons to do with human adaptability to varying circumstances.

The "universals" in my scheme then would be "rules of discourse" without which society would be impossible. Let me try to elaborate this point with some other examples to make clear what I mean. Universal discourses exist not just in the area of morality but in all areas important to our social lives. They consist of an often hierarchical but certainly "chunked" set of ideas or topics that serve as information storage and gathering devices, that in turn enable the dialogue to proceed. I repeat: at the local level there will be great divergencies between the extremes that are inherently possible in the terms of the dialogues, but the terms themselves will be universal. The hierarchy we can view in the familiar way as sets and subsets. Thus "my father" is a subset of "kin term for males" itself a subset of "kin terms" itself a subset of "status terms" and so on. (And it is interesting to see what is universal about such a term. If we define it as "male married to my mother" for example, or even "male parent" this is not universal since many males not married to my mother and who are not parents are, in various kinship systems, called "father." But if we define it as a term that includes in its definition "man married to my mother" and "male parent"—a term that is distributed according to a limited set of rules among males, then this is universal. No kinship system lacks such a term.) To take some examples of areas and terms we can look at the commonly accepted ethnographic categories as first approximations: Kinship (descent rule, group membership rules, degrees of relationship...); Kinship terms (address vs. reference, reciprocals, sex linkage...); Religion (sacredness, worship, rituals...); Etiquette (propriety, salutations, deference...); Economics (goods and services, rules of exchange, value...); Law (legal persons, rights and duties, torts and crimes...); Marriage (exogamy, preferences and prescriptions, rights of parties...); Taboos (persons, objects, food, names, topics...)—and so on. These traditional categories are certainly ethnocentric in their vocabulary, and they are not discrete, nor are they meant to be. But they are useful first approximations rooted in intense cross-cultural observation, and can be refined and made more abstract as one proceeds. We can add Wilson's category of Morality (fairness, duty, obligation, self-control, sympathy) and my addition of attribution of responsibility. This category in turn pervades all the others. As I said, they are not discrete but rather constitute "chunked" areas of concentration within the overall category of "Social Dialogue"—areas which distinguish themselves by their very universality: we know of no societies that do not conduct dialogues on these topics and order their lives according to them, even though they may come to radically different conclusions.

Again then I stress that this is where the universality lies, not at the level of specific content. The analogy I have always used is the Chomskian one of language where the universal grammar is one thing, but the actual spoken languages are wildly different and mutually unintelligible. At the level of speciic content one gets the obvious wide divergences that so entrance the relativist, but which to the universalist must be simply local instatiations of the universal discourse. Societies will in fact be distributed in interesting ways along the continua that we may extract once we have found the extreme polarities of the various terms. Take "murder" or "unlawful killing" for example. Theoretically societies can differ from the extreme of "no killings unlawful" to "all killing unlawful" as on the axis described below:

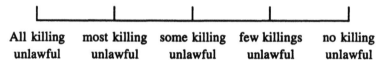

All killing unlawful	most killing unlawful	some killing unlawful	few killings unlawful	no killing unlawful

One would suspect here that the distribution of societies would follow a more-or-less normal curve, the majority being bunched up towards the center (if only because most societies do not regard the killing of enemies as unlawful for example.) On the other hand, take the curve of "exogamy"—the rule of marriage outside the group of near kin, however defined. This can range from "comprehensive exogamy"—all relatives (e.g., all the descendants of all sixteen great-grandparents) banned in marriage, to "total endogamy"—no relatives banned in marriage. The latter is indeed a purely theoretical category since no known instances are known. The first category occurs but is not common (Southeastern Bantu; Medieval Christian Europe). Again we can arrange the possibilities on a continuum:

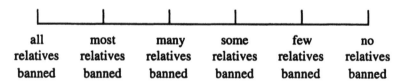

all relatives banned	most relatives banned	many relatives banned	some relatives banned	few relatives banned	no relatives banned

This curve would, I suspect, be skewed somewhat to the left, unlike the murder curve: most societies ban quite a few relatives as marriage partners. It is possible to have more precise and technical definitions. I am simply trying to illustrate here in a rough-and-ready way with everyday vocabulary.

To return to Wilson. We would find a similar distribution for the subcategories of "Morality." There would not be universal agreement; there does not have to be to posit the existence of universals. This is, and always has been, my point. Universals do not exist at this substantial level, and evolutionary theory would not propose that they do for a species that was expanding into wildly different ecological niches very rapidly (in evolutionary terms) and depending very heavily on cultural adaptation to survive. It would be decidedly maladaptive to have some kind of fixed rules encoded in the genome, rules that would simply be inappropriate in many of the local circumstances. On the other hand it would be equally maladaptive to have no inbuilt constraints, since the organism would be in a state of informational confusion most of the time. The answer is to have, not inbuilt rules of conduct, but inbuilt rules of discourse, in my usage, or inbuilt "information processing modules" in the words of the evolutionary psychologists.

These would provide a framework for categorizing and assessing information, and subsequently setting up rules for acting on it. As I keep insisting, the local rules would differ; they would have to; this is the object of the exercise. But the categories and rules of the dialogues that establish them would be universal. Societies do not always do the same things, but they talk about the same things and in the same formats. I have had totally intelligible moral discussions with people as diverse as Pueblo Indians, Irish Republicans, middle-class American Wasps, Hassidic Jews, Mafia bosses, Lebanese Christians, Colombian Indians, born-again Louisiana fundamentalists, Chinese intellectuals, Kenyan tribesmen, Mormon Elders, Franciscan monks, Hindu priests, Marxist Bulgarians, Jordanian Muslims, New England Unitarians, Australian Aborigines, and even Frenchmen. We often could not differ more radically on specifics, but we were able to differ intelligibly and recognize exactly what the issues were and the rules of discourse surrounding them. We agreed perfectly on the grammar, but not on what to say. In the old language of the ethologists, the grammar is species-specific. The problem with the ethologists was that they, and the social scientists who latched on to them, thought only in terms of "behavior." (We were the "behavioral sciences.") Now we know that it is more fruitful to think in terms of cognition—of innate information processing modules, or algorithms, or discourses. I like "discourses" since it not only steals one of the relativists' favorite terms and restores it to the universalist environment where it belongs, but because it stresses the social nature of these innate predispositions to *talk about* and *discuss* the world in certain a priori ways, and then to act upon the results of these discussions. It thus does not deny that social institutions are "culturally constructed" but it does insist that these constructions rest on a foundation of categories of universal discourse. As such, then, cultural constructions, deriving as they do from the evolved brain and its subfunction of language, are derivative of human evolutionary biology. It could, if you think about it seriously, be no other way. But I must resist the temptation to preach to my anthropological colleagues here and return to the issues raised by Professor Wilson's comments.

Let us try again with the "good versus moral versus human" issue which seems to cause confusion where I meant to introduce clarity. I will try to use a philosophical type argument to make the point, although this is dangerous because I am a bit rusty at it, but here goes. Every closed moral system has its own definitions of "the good." If our criterion of choice between such systems depends solely on our pronouncing some good and some bad, then we cannot escape the relativist trap for we can always be accused of simply using the definition appropriate to our own closed moral system, and by definition this only has the same status as any of the others. We are also open to the Logical Positivist objection that all we are doing is expressing approval or disapproval of the systems on which we pronounce. Yet we obviously wish to choose between the systems, for some do indeed revolt us however good they may seem to their participants. Now Wilson's answer is that of the "disinterested observer" and this is the same trap that John Stuart Mill fell into when he painted himself into a Utilitarian corner with "the greatest happiness of the greatest number" as the criterion of goodness. Since this led to obviously vulgar preferences triumphing (a fact cheerfully accepted by Jeremy Bentham—pushpin *was* better than poetry) Mill had to insist that the voters must be "those best qualified to judge." Which is to say, of course, him and his philosophical radical friends. Similarly, Wilson and his educated, sensitive, democratic friends would constitute the "disinterested observers" who would pronounce on the goodness and badness of moral systems. A communist dictator or priest of the Inquisition need not apply, clearly. But this raises the same problem: who is to judge the "disinterestedness" of the fabled observers? We are left with no ground on which to stand unless we invoke superior moral intuition or such, and here we are back on Mill's shaky ground again.

No. If we are to try to decide between competing moral claims—competing claims to goodness—then we must have *a criterion independent of goodness* to make the decision. I have always argued that "human-ness" is such a criterion since, unlike goodness, it can be stated objec-tively and does not need specially disinterested observers to utilize it. The factors that make up the moral sense for Wilson indeed make up "humanness" for me; as I have said we are in complete agreement here. But I am trying not to get caught in the relativist trap (far from conced-ing anything to the relativists) when I want to say: "Yes, the Nazis led moral lives insofar as they operated according to the universal rules of moral discourse, and they were consistent in their application of their own definitions of the good within their closed system; but their system was not a human one, and therefore should not be preferred to systems that are more human." Now note here that I am not claiming that the Nazi system should be condemned for being "immoral" or "bad" or any-thing such. It probably should, but I am arguing that this gets us into relativistic difficulties and hands the high ground back to them indeed, leaving us with only our disapproval and no objective standard of refer-ence. I am assuming here, of course, that the standard of "human" is objective and does not need privileged observers any more than a stan-dard of, say, "freezing" does. And I think that this in fact is the argument that Wilson himself has made. I just feel that if he could overcome his cultural prejudices that insist that we must use "moral" and "good" as synonyms, and that we must reserve the right to define them for our-selves as morally superior people, then he could escape the logical bind into which such a position is bound to drive him.

Let us take his insistence that the innate moral sense will drive us all to conclude that there should be a "respect for innocent human life." It does, of course, no such thing. Even a superficial knowledge of the world's history, or a look at current events, shows that "innocent human life" is an almost meaningless term in the face of universal child-killing atroci-ties. And I doubt if a truly "disinterested" observer would be as quick to condemn as an interested one: in the sense of someone who is both com-passionate and angry. I remember as a young man unskilled in the ways of the world, wanting to throw up on January 14th 1956 when the Cyp-riot terrorist organization EOKA announced that for every Greek child killed by the British forces they would retaliate by killing a British child. It was the stupidity on one side and the cold bloodedness on the other that appalled. But I was far from disinterested. Of course compassionate people will condemn such things, but equally passionate people will perpetuate them and justify them. The old have always been willing to sacrifice the young in their own interests. Respect for innocent human life has in fact been low on the agenda of almost every society known to history.

What does happen is that the universal moral discourse forces us to engage in a dialogue about what constitutes the terms "life" and "innocent" and "human" and to reach some conclusions about their referents. Take a brief look at the current abortion debate to see both the intensity of the dialogue and the near impossibility of getting agreement on the terms. In my argument both sides are acting "morally" and in terms of what they conceive of as "good." In fact some of those most guilty of offenses against innocent human life are the ones who argue with most conviction that they are "morally correct" and that what they do is "good." I can see us getting nowhere if we stay, as Ethics has since the Greeks invented the word, within these terms of reference. Let us grant that all these disputants in all cultures will indulge in moral argument and definition and come up with different and contradictory answers. Then let us simply sidestep the arguments and say: this does not matter; it is indeed beside the point; the point is whether the resulting system of rules and action falls within "human" limits or not. If it does, unfortunately, it will not necessarily be a nice, liberal, pacifist, tolerant, democratic polity. But it will be a society that, for example, respects all the parameters of moral discourse and does not disallow any one of them. It will be a society that meets the full range of human needs, and does not arbitrarily squash any of them. It would not be Nazi Germany, and it would not be the contemporary USA, but neither would it be the Congo pygmies. In fact, my suspicion is that it would probably be a Palaeolithic tribe or small Neolithic village, and that everything subsequent would fall short. What we would be left with would be a kind of scale on which some societies scored better than others. And the list might be upsetting to our notions of the good life. It certainly would be dismal news for pacifists.

But I use these examples to drive home my point that we are not here concerned with the "good" and its numerous local definitions. We are concerned, if you like, with societies that "work." I don't think societies governed by religious fundamentalists will fail to "work" because they are immoral or bad—they are in fact highly moral and definitely good according their own definition—but because they are inhuman: because they lack enough dimensions of humanity to be able to sustain themselves; although as I again have often pointed out, even societies lacking important human parameters can rumble along for a long time, because, paradoxically, the ability to be duped by systems of belief is an essential part of being human. So "work" here has always to be in quotes, and qualified by "in the long run" with the proviso that it can be a very long run indeed (Pharoanic Egypt for example, or caste in India.) Of course, to decide on the degree of humanity, while one does not have to be disinterested—one can be passionately on the side of humanity for example—one does have to be *informed*. One has to know what kind of animal we are and what kind of society we evolved for. It isn't hard to guess who the bench of magistrates should be here, and, how strange that like Mill I should conclude it would be "me and those who are informed as well as I am." But again I insist: we would not, like Mill's or Wilson's judges, be deciding what was good or better or immoral or anything of the kind; we would be deciding the functional equivalent of "what freezes." We would not need moral judgments, innate or otherwise, just the equivalent of a thermometer. Those whose temperatures we are taking would be the ones who, being human and having no option, would be moralizing and do-gooding themselves into a frenzy.

I cannot resist one last point to my philosophical argument. Something that has bothered me ever since as an undergraduate I was introduced to ethical argument has been this thorny problem of the definition of "good." The problem is that to define something you have say it is something else. Yet if we say that good is something other than good, like "the more evolved" or "the greatest happiness of the greatest number" or "the product of moral intuition" or "that which advances the cause of the proletariat" or whatever, then we leave ourselves in a definitional pickle, for we leave ourselves unable to say "the more evolved is good" without ending in a tautology that "the more evolved is the more evolved"—or whichever example you take.

Students of Ethics are well aware of the huge literature that surrounds this problem and of the various nonsolutions that have at one time or another held sway. One popular one was that words like good and bad are not really definitional words at all but are the equivalent of saying "hurrah" and "boo." This emotive theory would have such words be merely expressions of approval and disapproval. Now this gets us out of the definitional difficulty but it leaves us with another: it makes perfect sense to say "I think that is good but I do not approve of it." And perhaps more obviously "I think that is bad but I approve of it." In other words, "ordinary language"—the language in this case of the universal moral discourse—allows a distinction between approval and goodness. This would seem to shoot down the "hurrah-boo" theory, except that common sense suggests that there is a connection between approval-disapproval and good-bad; but what is it? When I say "I think that is good..." even if I am going to follow with "...but I disapprove of it" then I am implying that *someone* would approve of it, or perhaps that it is worthy of approval by someone, if not me. It may even only be worthy of approval by a hypothetical person, never having been put to the test, but this approval is implied. It is also assumed that the person approving would have some reason for the approval, which might very well be that it was "more evolved" or something such. If then we write the formula for "good" as something like *"worthy of approval by...because..."* then we escape the trap and make, I think, good common sense of the word. Of course, a lot of the time, we will indeed be using it in an emotive hurrah-boo fashion, but we need to take care of the awkward fact that we can say of a piece of modern art, "I'm sure its good, but I hate the bloody thing." Try it. In any such case you may substitute my formula and it makes perfect sense. In fact it makes such perfect sense that someone is bound to have thought of this already. Then why haven't I heard of it?

Well, philosphizin' is definitely fun. But I hope that in the argument preceeding the above I have managed to clarify where Wilson and I truly agree in substance about the moral sense, but disagree about how to frame the argument concerning its reality and ubiquity. In shifting the burden from goodness to humanity, and in making "moral" a neutral not an evaluative category, I hope to have left the relativists with no ground— high, low, or middle—to do anything but gesticulate from, without having to invoke the disinterested observer or any other of the *dei ex machinis* that have plagued this argument since Plato's philosopher kings. It only remains now for us to get on with the business of defining what it is to be "human," for how can we achieve it if we don't know what it is in the first place?

6

Left Ideology and Right Archaeology

Jonathan Benthall, the editor of Anthropology Today, *had the idea of doing a series on "large scale" publishing ventures in anthropology. To start this off he asked me to do an appraisal of the* One World Archaeology *series—all twenty-two volumes. The publishers had to send them by air from the U.K., and the first shipment was almost totally destroyed when its packaging burst and it got thrown about the baggage compartment or wherever they keep the air mail parcels. A second shipment arrived in slightly better condition and I spent most of a summer vacation reading through it. Why undertake such an overwhelming task? Well, I am interested in where archaeology fits into the scheme of things in the social sciences, and I am even a dabbler in a marginal sort of way (see chapter 11 of* The Challenge of Anthropology). *So I learned a lot. And perhaps this little "review essay" will explain why I even find a ray of hope here for the future of our currently fragmented endeavors.*

The changing patterns of publishing in academic life should be of interest to more than just intellectual historians. How our material and ideas get circulated and to whom should be something not just taken for granted within the profession. It helps to define what we are as a profession: how we see ourselves as an academic enterprise. If there has been any general move, it has been away from the strictly professional arena of publication to the growing flirtation with "trade" style. The trade style was always there with regard to *books*, since academic presses were few, and anthropologists could count on a curious lay audience for books about strange customs in distant lands. Deliberate attempts were indeed made to appeal to this audience ("The Sexual Life of Savages") and Raymond Firth recollected to me how he was prevailed upon to change a somewhat stuffy chapter title on initiation to "Firing the Ovens of Youth" for popular consumption. But the majority of publishing, before World War II and for a while after, was done in museum series and special series of governments and learned societies or particular universities. My own first publication was in the London School of Economics Monographs on Social Anthropology series, and my ambition was to have work appear as a Memoir of the American Anthropological Association, or a Bulletin of the Bureau of American Ethnology, just as my Africanist friends looked to the Rhodes-Livingstone Institute, or others to the Polynesian Society, and so on. It is hard to find anyone now who cares to use these outlets. The growth of trade presses with anthropological "lists" and the even more phenomenal growth of university presses, the larger of which (Oxford, Cambridge, Harvard, Chicago) behave essentially like trade presses, has taken over the intellectual publishing world. The reasons for this lie, as does so much else in contemporary life, with the baby boom and the subsequent explosive growth of academic jobs and markets. In the U.S. at least "one book" came to be regarded as a minimal qualification for promotion and tenure in the arts and social sciences, and the ever increasing number of faculty and students in the sixties, seventies, and eighties, fueled both the supply and the demand.

Archaeology was perhaps more consistently conservative in this respect than its sister (sub)disciplines. Although there was always a general audience for pop archaeology (and no shortage of pop archaeologists to meet it) most of the source material came out in what was charmingly known as the "grey literature": museum, governmental and contract agency reports, and series. This continues and often makes bibliographic research a nightmare. Also, in both archaeology and anthropology generally there were the periodic "Proceedings" produced by the large international societies, which were simply the bound papers presented at the huge international meetings. These were usually the most pointless and certainly the most boring of all the "professional" publishing enterprises. The papers were usually skimpy affairs written to ensure the presenter a travel allowance. Rarely did anything new or unknown get presented. The conferences themselves were largely extravagant social events and were simply not taken seriously as marketplaces of ideas. Most of these tomes went straight onto the library shelves and stayed there gathering dust. I remember taking down a twenty-year-old one from the shelves of the Peabody Museum in Cambridge, Massachusetts, to find the pages still uncut!

But the combination of growing markets and trade interest might have changed all that—or at least given the opportunity for change. Certainly the *One World Archaeology* series, being as it is the "proceedings" of the World Archaeological Congress held at Southampton (UK) in 1986, could have been yet another of these monuments to boredom like so many of its predecessors. But the conference itself was born of a far from boring controversy, and the initiatives that gave birth to it have in turn taken advantage of those publishing and marketing opportunities to produce something unique. In a sense, it is a record of the proceedings, but a record organized to make a point and attractively produced in hardbound, self-contained volumes, each of which has a subpoint to make. That a commercial publisher (first Unwin-Hyman, now Routledge) would take on a twenty-two-volume series of this kind is a sign of the times: the market must be presumed to be there.

The controversy of which the series was born is not something I want to dwell on, even though it is not irrelevant by any means to the interesting outcome. The World Archaeological Congress as it is now known, was created after a break with the old IUPPS (International Union of Pre- and Proto-Historic Sciences) over the issue of the inclusion of South African and Namibian scholars, in those heady days when it was assumed that such grand gestures actually had effects in the real world. Academics often get these fits of wanting to feel useful and relevant; something to do with their guilt over their privileged positions, probably. (Those who want an account of the shenanigans leading up to the fateful break should read prime-mover P.J. Ucko's [1987] obviously self-serving but lively, amusing, and even quite moving memoir.) I have little sympathy with this moralistic maneuvering, and would not have supported the breakaway group even if I had been invited (they knew better than to ask.) But this at least puts me in the position of a skeptical observer of the outcome: I cannot be accused of partiality towards this series, quite the opposite.

So my question is: regardless of its avowedly left-wing radical origins, what can we say about the result? First: this is absolutely not just another bound set of conference papers. The volumes are of course largely composed of such papers (except for those commissioned later), and some do not rise much above mere accumulation. But the best of them constitute lively debates on the topics they cover. Part of this stems from their having been organized into conference topics that were intitially "problem oriented" rather than just "sub-discipline oriented" in the old style. Perhaps we should begin with a survey of the volumes to give the reader an overview of the whole enterprise. I have divided them into six rough categories according to my own reading of their cross-referencing. These are not hard-and-fast and there is much overlap. For the details of how they emerged from the conference consult Ucko's excellent introductions to each volume. In the hardback edition all are published by Unwin-Hyman except for the two by Routledge so indicated.

1. Animals and Art: *Animals into Art*, 1989, ed. H. Morphy. *Signifying Animals*, 1989, ed. R. G. Willis. *What is an Animal?*, 1988, ed. T. Ingold. *The Walking Larder*, 1990, ed. J. Clutton-Brock.

2. Politics in the Past: *State and Society*, 1988, eds. J. Gledhill, B. Bender, M. T Larsen. *Center and Periphery*, 1988, ed. T. C. Champion. *Domination and Resistance*, 1989, eds. D. Miller, M. Rowlands, C. Tilley.

3. Politics of the Past: *The Politics of the Past*, 1989, eds. P. Gathercole, D. Lowenthal. *Archaeological Approaches to Cultural Identity*, 1989, ed. S. J. Shennan. *Who Needs the Past?*, 1988, ed. R. Layton. *Conflicts in the Archaeology of Living Traditions*, 1988, ed. R. Layton. *The Excluded Past*, 1989, eds. P. Stone, R. MacKenzie. *Archaeological Heritage Management in the Modern World*, 1990, ed. H. F. Cleere.

4. Ecology: *Foraging and Farming*, 1989, eds. D. R. Harris, G. C. Hillman. *Hunters of the Recent Past*, 1989, eds. L. B. Davis, B. O. K. Reeves.

5. Theory: *The Meanings of Things*, 1991, ed. I. Hodder. *The Origins of Human Behavior*, 1990, ed. R. A. Foley. *What's New? A Closer Look at the Process of Innovation*, 1989, eds. S. E. Van der Leeuw, R. Torrence. *Archaeology and the Information Age*, 1992, (Routledege), eds. Paul Reilley, Sebastian Rahtz.

6. Descriptive Archaeology: *The Archaeology of Africa*, 1993, (Routledge), eds. Thurston Shaw, Paul Sinclair, Bassey Andah, Alex Okpoko. *From the Baltic to the Black Sea*, 1990, ed. D. Austin, L. Alcock.

Two volumes, which I have not read, on the world in 18,000 B.P., will appear in the paperback series to be published entirely by Routledge.

Now what follows is not going to be a twenty-two-volume book review. Each of these volumes has been individually (and usually quite favorably) reviewed already. My brief, as one interested in the current identity crisis in the anthropological "sciences" is to read them (and I have read them all quite conscientiously, although I admit skipping through some of the more turgidly descriptive chapters) and to offer an overview or assessment of the total effort. One thing is certain right away: anyone reading through this series is going to get quite an education. Perhaps few people will read it straight through, but as one who has I have come out the other end dizzy with information and ideas, and a curious kind of optimism, which I will explain later.

But there was an intial disappointment. The controversy that spawned the conference also ensured that it would be deficient in a major area. The African palaeontologists were simply absent; some because they were from South Africa, and the rest in obvious sympathy with their excluded colleagues. Nothing can make up for this loss. The rather lighweight *Origins of Human Behavior* does nothing in this direction, and the *Archaeology of Africa* while a magnificent volume in its own right, deals only with the more recent archaeology, not the four (or five) million years of hominid history that are missing. Ucko descibes how they tried to put together such volumes but gave up in despair for lack of material (introduction to *The Origins of Human Behavior*, p. x). The two on 18,000 B.P. are again welcome, but not a substitute. Now that the brouhaha is over and the South Africans are in again, the organizers might think of making amends by commissioning volumes to fill this gap.

This is spilt milk over which we waste time crying. The obvious imbalance however is made more noticable by the group of books that make up the biggest category, what I have called (after one of the volumes) *The Politics of the Past*. This involves a lot of archaeological navel gazing on the theme of who wants/needs/controls/interprets the past. Here also we get the majority of the third world input on the indigenous response to the past and to the archaeological treatment of it (sacred sites, bones of ancestors etc.—*Archaeology of Living Traditions*). I was prepared to be impatient with all this agonizing, but it actually turned out to be quite interesting and to raise some important problems. I couldn't get too worked up over passionately different schemes about where to put the rest rooms at Stonehenge (*Archaeological Heritage Management*), but the issue of "objectivity" in the interpretation of the past is a real one and one of the livelier debates in the series. And it obviously overlaps with the currently fashionable debates in anthropology (and the social sciences generally) where an aggressive relativism is reasserting itself.

For the archaeologists the issue is one of whether their traditional approach to the past—let us call it the Rational Objective Scientific (ROS) approach, is really not just a culturally relative subjective viewpoint and therefore of no more validity than indigenous versions. Interestingly, the weight of argument in these volumes urges a modest and modified objectivism (see especially Wylie in *Archaeological Approaches to Cultural Identity.*) The proponents of the extreme subjectivist/relativist approach (in archaeology best exemplified by Shanks and Tilley, 1987), by raising the indigenous peoples' concepts of the past to the level of those of the scientific occident, often seem to forget that the "archaeology" they wish to share on equal terms with the rest of the world is itself a peculiar product of the whole process of scientific rationality that characterized the West and nowhere else. (China had technological ingenuity—not the same thing.) This is Gellner's (1989) "miracle": the exclusive cultural innovation that formed the basis of inquiry for Weber's sociology, and of which social science is itself a product. Certainly, as Layton and his contributors emphasize in *Who Needs the Past?*, we can see that all peoples have some interest in the past of some kind. But the issue here is not simply an interest in the past, but the *kind* of interest: the archaeological interest is a rational objective scientific interest (ROS), which prescientific indigeneous peoples do *not* have. This to not say that our "rational" approach to the past is untainted by ideology, chauvinism, greed, power, and all the other ills that rationality is prey to. But it is to say that if archaeology is to be made a common property of the whole world, then this is an offering comparable to experimental science or actuarial statistics, with all the implications thereof.

Indigenous cultures take an interest in the past, but it is not an ROS interest—an interest in the past *for its own sake*; for the sake of pure knowledge; for the sake of adding to our ROS knowledge of the past. Their interest (like that of nonarchaeological Westerners) is for mythical or dynastic or power purposes. Old-fashioned as it may seem, archaeology is really interested in the *truth* about the past, however elusive this may be. To cite at length pre-scientific notions about past divisions of time (as in the Rg Veda for example) does not equate such efforts with those of (even attempted) scientific objectivity.

We cannot have it both ways. If we do the relativistic and postmodern thing and equate the two views, then we cannot ask "them" to pursue an end that is not indigenously theirs, and only becomes so insofar as "they" assimilate to "us" and our otherwise incomprehensible goal of ROS knowledge of the past. And I stress it as a goal rather than a fully realized achievement. The important thing is that it is the goal that has driven our scientific endeavors, and we seem in danger of losing our way in a sudden fit of guilt and disillusion. We are in danger of falling over backwards in our respect for indigenous traditions and interests. Intrepretation may be "subjective" but, even subjective interpretation, by ROS rules, is open to scrutiny and disproof. Archaeological propositions are so open (as are, I suppose, oral histories, in principle). But myths and legends are not, nor do they wish to be. Few indigenous peoples would thank outsiders for putting myths and legends—or oral histories for that matter—to objective test; they are indeed automatically protected from such scrutiny by their metaphysical status. This is the difference, surely: however contaminated by bias ROS propositions are (and we get an earful of just how contaminated in these volumes) they are in principle open to scrutiny and potential disproof. If they are not we have a right to dismiss them as metaphysics. To elevate native myths to the same level is to say that *their* bias is OK, but *ours* is not! Peculiar.

It does not help to argue, as Layton does, that they may serve useful functions in context. Thus Ptolemaic theories of the universe or Linnean theories of fixed species may be wrong, he says, but reliable star maps can be constructed from the former and useful classifications from the latter. This may be so, and by extension, one supposes, theories that people emerged from the ground in situ can serve useful functions in context too. But that does not make them right. To use a graphic example (suggested to me by McCann's chapter in *The Politics of the Past*) the Nazi theory that Jews were a subrace descended from dwarfs while the Aryans were their superiors descended from Atlanteans certainly had its uses for the Nazis. It was "subjectively correct" for them "in context." So do we we allow it to be equally valid to ROS theories of evolution and racial origins? Of course, you will rush to say NO. But at the same time, you of the relative-truth persuasion will insist that a theory that a tribe came up through the ground via a reed and that they are the first people in the world and have always been there, is to be treated seriously as an alternative subjective theory to the "Bering Strait Theory"! The latter—for all its possible cultural contaminations, is, by ROS rules, open to correction and disproof. It has to display its evidence for public scrutiny and accept principles of refutation. Religious myths do not have to do this and indeed would resist it. Yet we are in danger of allowing to indigenous "theories"—in principle as unprovable and as racist as the Nazi theory—a priviliged position that we refuse to allow to ROS theories. We are in a kind of twilight zone of good intentions gone crazy. By all means let us give their own past back to indigenous peoples so that they can be as ethnocentric about it as Western societies are. But let us not confuse this with giving them access to ROS archaeology. The best of them in these various volumes seem to know the difference better than their Western mentors, and they get on with science. Indeed, the archaeologists generally are better at getting on with science than with agonizing over the theory of it; something we shall come back to.

But let me change tack and ask another general question that arises persistently from almost all the volumes of this series except the most methodological (*Archaeology in the Information Age*) or the most descriptive (*From the Baltic to the Black Sea.*) The question is this: *What were all those social anthropologists doing there?* Let's do a few quick counts from the volumes in category 1. In *Animals into Art*—one of the particularly impressive volumes and a very beautiful one too—I count (roughly) ten archaeologists, ten social anthropologists, and two historians. In *Signifying Animals*, a volume subtitled *Human Meaning in the Animal World*, only one contributor out of nineteen is an archaeologist! Similarly in *What is an Animal?* Tim Ingold has assembled ten assorted philosphers, biologists, etc., and only one archaeologist. Even in *The Walking Larder* (which could equally well have gone under the "ecology" heading), I count ten out of twenty-seven as social anthropologists. Overall rough total for these volumes: twenty-seven archaeologists, *forty-three* social/cultural anthropologists, and eight "others" (including historians, philosophers, biologists, zoologists, etc.) Indeed, an observer wandering into Ingold's or Willis's sessions might have been forgiven for asssuming he was at an international cultural anthropology conference.

This is perhaps going to upset some purist archaeologists. It might have been a serendipitous outcome of the political stuff (if we can't get the "reactionary" archaeologists, let's invite the "liberal" anthropologists— well known for their ingenuous dedication to any and all radical causes), but I don't think so. I think there is a serious hidden agenda to all this. It is never stated as such, for example by Ucko in his careful and interesting introductions to each volume, but it is there by implication. Let us call it: "The Revival of the Comparative Method." This much derided tool of social evolutionary anthropology was based in fact on a perfectly sound premise: that contemporary social structures provide clues to past structures at the same level of techno-economic development. Thus the excitement over Australian Aborigines, continued in this series, who were taken as "living examples" of the Palaeolithic. And in some sense they surely are (as the Marxists who pop up here and there are forced, by their theory, to recognize also.) The mistake of the evolutionists lay not in the general premise, but in the fatal assumption that "Palaeolithic society" could be read off in some one-to-one fashion from modern Aborigines; for example, that palaeolithic society must have been based on matrilineal totem clans or patrilineal exogamous marriage classes, or whatever.

We have of course no guarantee of this, we now realize, and palaeo-society would probably have been as diverse in this respect as modern "Palaeolithic people" are. But the problem with the comparative method was only in its spurious degree of specificity, not its basic premise. There is no reason why, at some very general level (and in the case of art even some very specific level) we should not assume that modern palaeo-tribes are not substantially like true palaeo-society. The likeness may not lie in matrilineal totem-clans, but it certainly would involve a "totem-like" relationship with the animal world, and an almost certain linkage of this symbolically with the human reproductive world; that is, with kinship and marriage. It is fascinating to see then, fairly extended discussions of the whole man-animal "totemic" relationship here, as in *What is an Animal* and *Signifying Animals*, and Layton in *The Meanings of Things*. Once we divorce "totems" from their specific relationship with descent groups, as Goldenweiser and Lévi-Strauss have done for us, then the way is open, and is here taken, to a discussion of the symbolic use of animals in human representations, with the present giving us valuable information about the past.

Because the *specific* sociological connections could not be made, social anthropology and archaeology drifted apart, thinking they had nothing to offer each other. This was an almost fatal mistake for the Science of Man; another nail in the coffin of a holistic discipline. In one broad and generous sweep, the One World Archaeology series has restored the dialogue. And the interest is that the move came from archaeology, not from anthropology. The anthropologists feel they can do without the archaeologists, but obviously not vice-versa (except for some lunatic fringe elements not, thank God, represented here).

My examples were from the Palaeolithic, but the Neolithic example is even stronger. Many of the "primitive" cultures that anthropologists traditionally study fall into the "living Neolithic" category. And this is particularly strong where there is continuity between the past and the present as in, for example, the incredibly old (9,000 years) agricultural traditions of New Guinea, and their modern descendants (see the excellent discussions in *Foraging and Farming*.) I would put in my two bits for the Americas too where the continuities between the "dead" civilizations and the living descendants are alive with clues to past practices and a better understanding even of the present. (Fox 1994, chap. 11) Layton, whose work with aboriginal painting (see *The Meanings of Things*) exemplifies the best of this tradition, puts it the most strongly when he asserts that in many cases, "Access to meaning may only be gained through ethnography" (*Who Needs the Past?*). Before we get too excited on this score, let me say that not much dialogue about all this took place at the conference. The social anthropologists did their little numbers and the archaeologists theirs without much reference to each other. But the stuff is now on record, the issue is live, and a real dialogue can be opened on the basis of what we have before us here. How to use the present to interpret the past is a very live issue. How to use evolutionary theory to link both is something it seems neither side is quite ready for yet (but see Rindos in *Foraging and Farming*.) I've ridden that hobby horse enough, and for those who have ears to hear, let them hear.

I have said that the archaeologists are at their best not when arguing about what they ought to do but when actually getting on with it. *Foraging and Farming* is a good example. Here again, Part II has seven chapters concerned with contemporary ethnographic analogues/homologues of past practices, and Harris (the editor) has a sensible model of gradual domestication that includes, at each stage of "increasing input of human energy per unit acre of exploited land" an ethnographic counterpart from "burning vegetation" up to "propagation of phenotypic variants" (e.g., maize). This volume shows how, with a minimum of conceptual difficulty (despite the sniping in the opening theoretical chapters) archaeologists, geneticists, chemists, biologists, ethnographers, agronomists, etc. can put their heads and data together to provide an increasingly sophisticated picture of this absolutely crucial aspect of human social evolution. Add *Hunters of the Recent Past* for a complete picture, and the whole (perhaps misnamed) "agricultural revolution" or "Palaeolithic-Neolithic transition" gets a fresh and exciting look. Of course archaeologists are going to worry constantly about "interpretation" but perhaps they should worry less. Social anthropologists worry just as much and their subjects are alive! At least archaeological data stays still, as it were. One of the great strengths of the subject in an age that is drifting away from science and objectivity in an alarming fashion, lies in what it sees as its limitation: it must always come back to face the brute facts of physical remains, its subject matter. This is a strength, not a weakness. By being forced to deal with recalcitrant real objects and the constant reality of change through time, it has something to offer the timid sciences of "function" and "equilibrium" and yea, even "interpretation" where human scientists have to face human subjects in a series of mutual protean shifts.

Enough preaching. In dealing with such a huge series one is forced to leave something out, and indeed I have said least about some of the issues and volumes that actually interested me the most, such as those of category 2—*Politics in the Past*: the section on literacy in *State and Society* for example. Also, some volumes are simply encyclopedic and fulfill a need independent of the series: *The Archaeology of Africa* is simply a majestic book; the subtitle, *Food, Metals and Towns* puts the necessary stress on agricultural Africa, for, as we have seen, Palaeolithic Africa is sadly missing. But this should not detract from the value of this remarkable compendium. *What's New?* proved to be a surprisingly lively and attention grabbing volume on innovation. One could teach a great course out of it—something equallly true of most of the volumes. *Archaeology in the Information Age* is going to keep the computer buffs happy, and is visually a beautifully produced volume. Some are truly for the specialist. You have to love the subject to get through *From the Baltic to the Black Sea*, yet I found myself drawn with fascination to the details. How can you resist "Merovingian Skull Deformations in the Southwest of France"? And a nice discussion evolves on archaeology and history; another hardy perennial. If I have to pick a favorite it must be *Animals into Art*, but as an act of necessary self-denial I will not go into details as to why. Of all the hard pieces of physical evidence left behind, pictures and sculptures are the most endearing always. And, as this volume shows, not by any means as enigmatic as they have been painted.

The issue will always be "what were they doing?" or even "what did they think they were doing?" And the utilitarians will battle with the symbolists, and the processualists with the cognitivists, and so it will go. The fact remains, "they" were humans like ourselves at the core, and in some metatheoretical way we "know" what they were doing; it is only the cultural details that are elusive, and some of these always will be. But this splendid series, with its cunning and timely hidden agenda, makes a great gesture in the direction of drawing the squabbling (or even indifferent) sciences of mankind back together into at least a conversation, a powwow, an intellectual jamboree. The cheeky perpetrators may have done more than just reshape the agenda of archaeology, and I for one look forward to a time when the wretched disciplinary distinctions will have ceased to matter and when we *all* gather for a "human sciences" conference as lively and productive as this one, but even more comprehensive and inclusive. The "Science of Mankind" (and the Enlightenment project of its Universal History) may perhaps be reborn from the boldness of a few archaeologists and anthropologists in Britain in the 1980s. Why not?

References

Ucko, P. J. 1987. *Academic Freedom and Apartheid: The Story of the World Archaeological Congress*. London: Duckworth.

Shanks, M., and Tilley, C., 1987. *Re-constructing Archaeology*. Cambridge: Cambridge University Press.

Gellner, E., 1989. *Plough, Sword and Book*. Chicago: University of Chicago Press.

Fox, R. 1994. *The Challenge of Anthropology: Old Encounters and New Excursions*. New Brunswick, NJ: Transaction Publishers.

7

Self-Interest and Social Concern

This is from one of series of seminars bringing together academics, businessmen, and even some denizens of the Beltway (the director of the Congressional Budget Office, for example) to discuss the relevance or otherwise of theoretical academic thinking to the real world of business, financial, and governmental decision making. They were organized by the late Albert Sommit for The Conference Board, an organization of far-ranging interests but which is perhaps best known for its index of leading economic indicators that can have immediate impact on the markets. It addresses the topic of "self-interest" and this brings it into the debate concerning "individual selection" versus "group selection" on the theoretical side, and "free market" versus "communalism" on the social front.

If economics is the science of self-interest, then so is evolutionary biology (and hence anthropology.) Organisms strive to reproduce themselves, or their relatives; that is, those who have genes in common by descent ("inclusive fitness"). They may, under conditions dubbed "reciprocal altruism" also aid the productive and reproductive efforts of genetic strangers if there is a payoff for their own relatives. "Altruism" in this scheme of things might seem a misnomer since organisms in being altruistic (giving up their own reproductive fitness to benefit the reproductive fitnesss of others) are simply being selfish in that they are protecting replicas of their own genes. But this is not a new paradox. Long before we knew about genes, even after we knew about natural selection, we struggled with the problem of the relationship between the apparent selfishness at the base of human action and the equally apparent facility we had to lead, at least to some degree, unselfish social lives in ordered societies.

But the picture painted by modern evolutionary biology, is both compatible with the assumptions of the "gloomy science" itself, and gloomily "Darwinian" in its own right. Since Mandeville in the early eighteenth century (*The Fable of the Bees*) set the tone of the debate, economic and social theory have struggled with the problem of the "harmonization" of self-interest and social-interest. On the one hand the Hobbesians argued that only a strong central power could impose such harmony, while the followers of Shaftesbury have argued for the "natural" harmonization of the two: private vice becomes public virtue in Mandeville's own words. Adam Smith's "hidden hand" and David Hume's "conventions" were two of the Scottish Enlightenment's contributions to the harmonization debate. All the "harmonizers" wanted to show that the pursuit of self-interest would naturally result in public good either by the establishment of conventions or by the play of market forces or because "reason" would reveal the necessity. Alexander Pope became the poet laureate of the movement, and in his *Essay on Man* (1733) hammered away at the moral in his impeccable heroic couplets:

> That reason, passion, answer one great aim;
> That true self-love and social are the same;

> Self-love forsook the path it first pursu'd
> And found the private in the public good.

> The same self-love, in all, becomes the cause
> Of what restrains him, government and laws.

Darwin, while proclaiming himself a true member of the "moral sense" school in ethics, nevertheless seemed to enter the fray on the side of "self-love" in proposing that individual selection was the basis of evolution. Individual organisms pursued their own reproductive ends in competition with each other and with the "hostile forces of nature." Those that could adapt survived; the rest fell by the wayside. When it came to self-conscious Man, Darwin insisted that such an animal would indeed develop a "social conscience" but this was not out of some kind of moral superiority but because it was in his interest to do so. The "moral" individuals would stand a better chance of success in the reproductive struggle than the others. It was a constant problem for the self-love or self-interest theorists then to figure out how social cohesion and moral and political cohesion could "naturally" arise without introducing divine intervention or political despotism. The vitalists like Bergson or Teilhard de Chardin or George Bernard Shaw had no trouble with this since they could introduce a "life force" or some *telos* or cosmic goal ("noosphere") towards which the universe was evolving and which would impose its own teleological cohesion.

But for true Darwinians as well as their brothers-in-arms in economics, self-interest must rule and such order as we achieve cannot be at its expense, but must be its (often paradoxical) product. Indeed, various critics have insisted that Darwinism is simply the imposition of classical market economics onto the natural world, and Darwin did acknowledge his debt to Malthus, who can legitimately be claimed as ancestral to both lines of thought (with Alfred Marshall standing for economics where Darwin stands for biology). The most modern version of "ultra-Darwinism" takes this all a stage further down the biological scale: inclusive fitness and reciprocal altruism work at the level of the gene itself. Organisms are, in Dawkins' striking phrase, simply "gene machines"—clumsy vehicles that serve the purposes of the blind replicators that have no other "purpose" than their own replication. It is ultimately then the gene itself that is "selfish"—concerned only to produce more replicas of itself, and this in turn produces organisms that carry out the genetic mandate.

We would be correct to ask whether or not the conditions created by modern *Homo sapiens* do not mitigate this picture of a war of all against all; but before we get to that let us note the constraints built into the raw evolutionary picture itself. The war for a start is not of all against all but of some against others, and the some and the others are groups of kin—at the kin-selection ("inclusive fitness") level, or groups of cooperating but familiar non-kin at the level of reciprocal altruism.

Thus while "ultimately" (tricky word!) the genes may be "selfish"—interested only in their own replication, their organism hosts are bound, if the theory is correct, to cooperate and even sacrifice to preserve the selfish interests of the genes they host.

This is not such a bad initial outcome after all. Both kin and non-kin will end up acting "altruistically" to each other whatever the sinister purposes of the genes. Indeed, these selfish purposes cannot be achieved without such cooperation and even sacrifice by *groups* of gene-host organisms.

The situation in modern *Homo sapiens* may be homologous with this—another argument—but even if it is not, then the raw evolutionary conditions are not a bad analogy for our present condition. Thus even if we are the self-interested rational calculators of economic theory, this will not prevent us from acting altruistically, *as long as there is a payoff*. The "cultural" payoff is not as easily defined as the genetic payoff. If we continue the analogy we should behave altruistically if there is a *productive* payoff, as opposed to, or as well as, a reproductive payoff. Actually what we do is to *increase* our production and decrease our consumption. This is most conspicuous with children where we increase our productivity but radically decrease our consumption to their advantage. Here of course there is an almost complete overlap with the raw genetic situation, since children are our measure of genetic fitness. All such "economic" activity is then equally "reproductive" activity: investment in the next generation of our own genes.

But equally, particularly in times of war and privation, we increase our productivity and decrease our consumption for the "general good"—that is, for non-kin (although we may need the stimulus of kinship language to motivate us—"brothers in arms" "defend the fatherland" "Uncle Sam needs you," etc.) Following the analogy we can be said to do this insofar as we gain from everyone else's doing it; hence the righteous anger against and punishment for traitors, cheats, free riders, deserters, draft dodgers, and black marketeers, who threaten the balance.

Even working from the raw situation something else of importance follows: In any social animal, genetic self-interest often works best in a collective social situation. Thus once sociality has evolved, only the most social organisms will be likely to prosper genetically. There will, if you like, be selection for sociality. Darwin recognized this quite clearly. We do not have to depart from the model of genetic self-interest here, but we must see that it is in the interest of the organisms to behave socially, for example, cooperatively. One does not have to be an advocate of group selection (i.e., maintain that traits evolve for the good of the group) to see that the properties of some social systems (e.g., defense against predators) increase the reproductive efficiency of their members. Such systems will win out over "individualistic" alternatives in the evolutionary struggle. This is the differential selection of groups rather than group selection, and offers a profound check on individualistic behavior from the start. Individual sacrifice on behalf of the group makes sense, because the group is an efficient protector of one's kin-related genes (even if it is not entirely composed of them; see the case of Horatius and his brave companions).

As Darwin saw so clearly, in any animal with highly developed sociality of this kind, where consciousness and language evolve, so too will a

Horatius the Maximizer
A Sociobiological Lay of Ancient Rome

Horatius calculates his immediate reproductive success and the degree
of his parental investment,

then contemplates his obligations under reciprocal altruism.

He then calculates the degree
of his inclusive fitness,

and only then goes forth to perform the ultimate altruistic act.

"morality" develop to reinforce and extend such behavior. Again, looked at "selfishly" it will pay us to support and indulge in "moral" behavior because such behavior will be protective of our own and related genes. The "categorical imperative" is therefore the primitive response to the group "ought"—a position wholly compatible with Durkheim's, by the way, even though arrived at by a different route. The specific content of the "ought" will of course differ from group to group (from clan vengeance to universal brotherhood), but the power of the moral imperative is constant. Systems of praise and blame and responsibilty, and of reward and punishment, will in turn follow. And indeed no human group has ever been discovered that lacks these—although only some few highly literate ones make a problem out of it (called "moral philosophy" or "ethics").

Thus group norms and sanctions, in this view, are simply a conscious creature's reinforcements and articulations of evolved group sociality. In the short run they may appear to run counter to "self-interest" narrowly defined, but in the notorious "long run" they are in fact (unless they become totalitarian and repressive of self-interest) protective of genetic self-interest—even to the point of protecting the self-interested organism against its own worst excesses which might damage its reproductive interests. (Drug rehabilitation, laws against suicide, abortion, etc.)

Since it has profound implications for how we view self-interested behavior, let us ask "what is the self-interested organism interested in?" The standard reply of current orthodox evolutionary biology tends to be "maximization of its own reproductive success." But the question is whether this really describes the proximate motivations of the organism or some long-run teleological goal. If the latter, it cannot represent a proximate motivation since the organism is not aware of long-run teleological goals. It will be, as Keynes so shrewdly observed, dead long before they are realized. Even genes only "seek" to replicate *themselves*—not make as many copies as possible, and certainly not to make as many copies of copies of copies as possible.

Observation of most K-selected (high parental investment) animals, including humans, shows them in fact obeying a variety of proximate motivations which, if successfully accomplished, result in reproductive success. But except in a few cases, maximum reproductive success is rarely pursued as an end in itself. (Although *optimal* success can plausibly be regarded as a proximate motive: not "I'll have as many kids as I can" but "I'll have as many kids as I can afford to rear properly.") The proximate motivations followed are many and various but can be generalized as: acquisition of resources and status; sexual intercourse; security from enemies; pleasure in companionship and children, and so on. Obviously the details of these will differ widely according to species, but if they are successful, reproductive success as such will usually follow. Even where reproductive success is consciously repudiated or physically impossible, these proximate motivations continue to operate: among homosexuals, eunuchs, and castrati for example, and even supposedly celibate clergy.

This point is important since it helps us to understand the "raw material" of the self-interested actor that we are searching for. Thus, in the pursuit of status and resources, for example, males must engage in a great deal of intricate social behavior, and in the competition for mates females must do likewise. There must therefore have been selection for males who gain satisfaction from such intensely social behavior, and against those who do not—hermits, rapists, outlaws, and misanthropes of various stripes. Men will therefore pursue sociality *as an end in itself*. And we should not get confused here with terms of disapprobation like "antisocial." Youth gangs for example are anything but antisocial; they are imbued with a powerful primitive social attraction in a way that school simply is not. Given their miserably poor employment chances even if they attend school, inner-city youths in choosing gangs over education are making a sensible choice. And it does nothing to harm their reproductive success as inner-city birth rates testify. In the vast majority of cases this pursuit of sociality by men as an end will indeed pay off genetically in the form of offspring, themselves protected by the social system these fathers have fostered. The same, with somewhat different strategies, goes for females, and often even more so. (Welfare mothers are almost totally dependent on the "non-kin" universe of their society for support.)

But this paints a very different picture from the simpleminded, fitness-maximizing selfish gene-machine of crude sociobiology. This creature is no more "real" than the rational self-interested actor calculating marginal probabilities and maximizing marginal returns of classical laissez-faire economic theory, or the even more ghastly dehumanized actor of the rational social contract in Rawls's theory of justice. In both reproductive and productive activity then, actors are, to coin a phrase, seeking to *maximize sociality*. To this end they will buy dear and sell cheap, exchange economically useless items with expensive and even dangerous ceremony, and even destroy their accumulated wealth in ostentatious public displays. In the end they will sacrifice themselves and their own interests, and even their families and kin for the "common good." None of this would be intelligible on the basis of "fitness maximization" or the rational calculation of marginal returns. But it is this "nonrational" behavior that we depend on to have societies at all, and the paradox (if it is a paradox) is that it is all in fact derivable from the needs of the selfish gene to replicate with maximum efficiency.

The implication of all this for the questions raised by the issue of "selfishness" in both biology and economics should be obvious. I propose three pertinent conclusions:

1. The major proximate motivation of self-interested social animals is the maximization of sociality.

2. The self-interest of organisms (genetic, economic, or both) is constrained by sociality not only from without but from within the proximate motives of the organisms themselves.

3. The optimal social organization then would be one that recognized self-interest (reproductive or productive) as a primary driving force in individual motivation, but that also reinforced the sociality-maximizing motives of individuals such that they produce positive benefits for the individual and the society which is both his product and his producer.

The last is of course the pious wish of good philosophers everywhere. But the difference is that they mostly come at this solution from purely "rational" arguments while we are looking at it as a totally natural phenomenon produced by evolution. It need not have been so. In "solitary" species it is not so. The range of possible "good" societies from this point of view is very large and varied; but this view is antirelativist in that it does provide a standard by which to judge the relative success of the various experiments in sociality that human history and ethnography present. At the extremes, totalitarianism and anarchy both fail. It is the finer gradations that cause the problems that we endlessly discuss.

Translating this into more familiar historical or sociological terms for our own social system, we must ask how to reconcile the ideology of contractual individualism that inspires both economic entrepreneurship and runaway litigation, with a necessary revival of civic virtue in a society where cynicism about politics and office holding is at an all-time high, and where untrammeled egoism and greed are even touted as virtues. We must ask how, even if rampant self-interest indeed is the fuel of an expanding economy, whether we can afford such an economy if the price is a decline in national civility to the point of near anarchy in the cities and total disillusion with the system in the suburbs. Somehow, while tapping the motive of self-interest we are failing on the reciprocal altruism front. Reproductive rates in the middle classes are at an all-time low and divorce rates at an all-time high. Women are abandoning their children to strangers in the pursuit of economic gain and "self-fulfill-ment." Men default (up to 80 percent) on child support payments. And still the economy does not prosper consistently. We have a long way to go to get forward to the past.

Notes

1. Since some people have missed the irony intended in my little cartoon on Horatius, here are the relevant verses to jog the memory.

From: Lord Macaulay, "Horatius: A Lay Made About the Year of the City CCCLX" in *Lays of Ancient Rome*, (London: Longmans, 1874)

> But the Consul's brow was sad,
>   And the Consul's speech was low,
> And darkly looked he at the wall,
>   And darkly at the foe.
> "Their van will be upon us
>   Before the bridge goes down;
> And if they once may win the bridge,
>   What hope to save the Town?"
>
> Then out spake brave Horatius
>   The Captain of the Gate:
> "To every man upon this earth
>   Death cometh soon or late.
> And how can man die better
>   Than facing fearful odds,
> For the ashes of his fathers
>   And the temples of his Gods,
>
> "And for the tender mother
>   Who dandled him to rest,
> And for the wife who nurses
>   His baby at her breast,
> And for the holy maidens

Who feed the eternal flame,
To save them from false Sextus
That wrought the deed of shame?

(Herminius and Spurius Lartius volunteer to help defend the bridge)

"Horatius" quoth the Consul,
"As thou sayest let it be."
And straight against that great array
Forth went the dauntless Three.
For Romans in Rome's quarrel
Spared neither land nor gold,
Nor son nor wife, nor limb nor life
In the brave days of old.

Then none was for a party;
Then all were for the state;
Then the great man helped the poor,
And the poor man loved the great;
Then lands were fairly portioned;
Then spoils were fairly sold:
The Romans were like brothers
In the brave days of old.

Any modern textbook on economics will deal with "economic motivations" and the "rational consumer," etc. Readers might want also to note the "rational actor" theory in modern political science. For a critique of this kind of economic reasoning see: Robert Frank, *Passions Within Reason* (New York: Norton, 1988). The basic concepts of sociobiology can of course be found in Wilson's great book of the same name, *Sociobiology: The New Synthesis* (Cambridge, MA: Harvard University Press, 1975), while the selfish gene is again dealt with in the book of that name by Richard Dawkins, *The Selfish Gene* (Oxford: Oxford University Press, 1976). For reciprocal altruism and parental investment see Robert Trivers, *Social Evolution* (Menlo Park, CA: Benjamin/Cummings, 1985). For the relationship of such thinking to morality and the social order see Richard Alexander, *Darwinism and Human Affairs* (Seattle: University of Washington Press, 1979). For Darwin's place in this line of thinking see Robin Fox, *The Search For Society* (New Brunswick, NJ: Rutgers University Press, 1989). For the ongoing debate on the role of group selection versus individual selection in evolution see, David Sloan Wilson and Elliott Sober "Reintroducing Group Selection to the Human Behavioral Sciences" in *Behavioral and Brain Sciences*, 17:4, pp. 585–654, 1994.

8

Scientific Humanism and Humanistic Science

This started life as an article that Edie Turner, as editor of Anthropology and Humanism Quarterly, *asked me to write as a contribution to a "state of the art" issue. For space reasons the version that appeared was much cut down, so when Norman Leavitt and Paul Gross were organizing a symposium for The New York Academy of Sciences on "The Attack on Science and Reason" I took the opportunity to restore the missing stuff and add some further comment. I ended the actual talk with a homily on "why now?" which explored the possibility that there was a cyclical fin de siècle phenomenon of which "postmodernism" was just the late twentieth-century version. But since that angle has not yet been fully worked out, I left it out here. It is, however, something to ponder. The nihilistic, anarchic, relativist, neo-Idealist, eclectic, subjectivist whirl seems to come around at the end of centuries both confident about progress and yet shattered by fresh evidence of our inability to use the fruits of progress wisely. As the Chinese curse has it: "May you live in interesting times."*

I have been challenged to explain an apparent inconsistency in various published pronouncements on the issue of humanism and science. On the one hand I appear as a champion of science and the scientific method in the ever-more acrimonious debate on the status of anthropology as a "science." (Fox 1993, 1994) On the proverbial other hand, I appear as a gloomy critic of the "academic/scientific enterprise" in its entirety. Now I could just claim with Emerson (no, not Winston Churchill, although he loved to use the phrase) that a foolish consistency is the hobgoblin of little minds, and slither past this one. But the great Ralph Waldo did say a *foolish* consistency, and no one wants to admit to that who claims either scholarly or scientific status, much less both.

No, I'm afraid I must protest my innocence here and hence claim not to have been inconsistent at all. I would not bother, except that I think perhaps there is a little lesson to be learned in understanding why, a lesson very relevant to the current debate. So let us back up a little and take an autobiographical peep into the Golden Age of Anthropology. I admit I came in on the tail end of the shining epoch—the boring fifties. But I was just in time to be socialized into the notion that there was no other game in town but science if one wanted academic and epistemological respectability. People called their books *The Science of Culture* (White) or *The Natural Science of Society* (Radcliffe-Brown), or even *A Scientific Theory of Culture* (Malinowski); anthropology was still unashamedly "The Science of Man." They might have quarreled about whether the subject matter of the science was indeed culture or society, or custom or behavior, (was that ever settled?), but they did not quarrel about the science bit.

The symbolism of their quest for scientific status was marked: the archetypical image was not clad in academic robes but in a white lab coat, preferably with a slide rule (remember the slide rule?) sticking out of the pocket. Everyone wanted "laboratory" status. I worked at Harvard in both the Laboratory of Social Relations and the Laboratory of Human Development, and even in France the burgeoning structuralists at the Collège de France instituted the Laboratoire de l'anthropologie sociale— still there and still flourishing under the same title. Both Britain and the U.S. then had a Social Science Research Council, and would have settled for nothing less. The vindictive Tory government in the U.K. has recently stripped the Science from its research council title—surely to revenge themselves on the pesky Fabians from the LSE. Signs of the times, indeed. We anthropologists understand these symbolic gestures, no? But back then it was science or bust. The terror of being excluded from scientific grace was palpable. The last thing a PhD candidate wanted to hear was that he was being "unscientific." Words of doom.

Just what constituted being scientific was in turn much debated. At Harvard it raged between the statistical crowd—analysis of variance qualified you for scientific heaven—and the Freudians. But even many of the latter who were in turn anthropologists tried manfully (as we used to say) to "operationalize" psychoanalysis and so wring science out of it. This meant mostly that "Freudian hypotheses" were "tested" by statistical methods—Yale to the rescue waving the HRAF files and flurry of T tests and Chi squares and assorted other measures of association. Triumphantly, ancestral claims to legitimacy were established through a once-forgotten article by Sir E. B. Tylor, and everyone breathed a collective sigh of scientific relief. The strict ethnographers, not having hypotheses to test and anything to predict, strove to claim at least the status of the "observational sciences." They were more like natural history or astronomy than physics, but they were sciences nonetheless. As Popper taught us—and taught me personally at the LSE—it was method not subject matter that distinguished science, and insofar as we were dealing with "public" data, objectively gathered and both confirmable and refutable, then we were doing science at however humble a level.

Again, simply doing science—while the only road to truth (what else was there, theology, metaphysics?)—did not mean that one was automatically right. It is true that in the first flush of Popperian enthusiasm this seemed to get forgotten. We were all so concerned with the *status* of simply doing science that whether what we were doing was worth the effort was a question rarely raised. Thus there could be both wrong science and trivial science, but this mattered less than being science. After all, it was part of the price one paid for being on the track of truth. It meant however that a great deal of pseudoscience got through unnoticed except by a few curmudgeonly critics like Pitirim Sorokin. We tended to forgive anything so long as it was, at the very least, conducted in the scientific spirit.

Now this might seem cynical but it isn't meant to be. I am wholly in favor of proceeding in the scientific spirit at however low a level, rather than abandoning the effort simply because a lot of it is trivial. Let that be clear. On one shoulder sits the spirit of Popper demanding science in the form of falsifiable hypotheses, and on the other sits the ghost of Dean Swift parodying the crazy scientists of the Royal Society trying to extract light from cucumbers. I love Swift's humor, but I defer to Popper's judgment: at the very least we should try to emulate the virtues of science. If we do not then we are either merely expressing opinions—however erudite and insightful—or worse, doing metaphysics. Metaphysical statements let us remember, can be *verified* but not falsified—this was the basis of the Popperian criticism of Logical Positivism. Thus "all events are ideas in the mind of God" could be verified by producing God and showing the correlation between events and his ideas. But in the absense of God and his ideas, or in the presense of alternative hypotheses ("all events are the products of previous events") the metaphysician can still hold fast to his belief in his mind-of-God hypothesis, and he can't be proved wrong.

He can't be proved right either; that was Popper's clincher. To be truly scientific the hypothesis had to be vulnerable to disproof, otherwise, as David Hume said, commit it to the flames. If there was a lot of trivial science then there was even more trivial metaphysics and worthless opinion. The only other game in town in those days that commanded a lot of attention was Existentialism. (Actually I found they had barely heard of it at Harvard.) And some of us remember A. J. Ayer's perfunctory dismissal of it as "a simpleminded misuse of the verb to be," or, even better, that "nothing is not the name of something." (I believe it was also Sir Alfred who said "existence is not a predicate.") As for the ancestors of Existentialism: Heidegger, Husserl, and Kierkegaard, they represented the worst excesses of continental idealist metaphysics and, according to Ayer and the others of his persuasion, were talking literal nonsense. It is amusing to me therefore to find almost forty years later that I am expected to come to terms with these monsters and be held accountable to their excesses of unreason.

No thank you. Even trivial science had the virtue of vulnerability, and since there were a great many aspirant scientists and not many good ideas, triviality was the price we had to pay for the few gems that made it into the permanent record. It used to be an old joke that the strictures of the NSF made it impossible to get a grant for anything that had not already been done anyway. Rats were run silly in an attempt to achieve "replicability." At the same time, any daring new idea was almost bound to be turned down since it was novel and hence its "replicability" was in question.

But here we must draw a very necessary distinction between the ideals of science and the way science is conducted. And an even more necessary distinction between the results of science and the uses to which they are put. And a yet more necessary distinction between those same scientific ideals and the failure of many scientists to live up to them.

The conduct of science can lead to boring triviality. Even great results can be used to evil ends. Scientists, being children of Adam, can be fools and charlatans or even just blind and biased. Indeed, my own despair at the "academic/scientific enterprise" which raised the initial question is a despair over the inevitability of human frailty, not over the ideals of scientific discovery. Since science has no value agenda of its own it is always subject to hijacking by fanaticism and idealism. Thus, when I am told that some particular theory—Mendelian genetics for example—has been used to bad ends by eugenicists, racists, sexists, and fascists, I am depressed but not surprised. It is part of the basic "design failure" of human nature that leads to the intial despair (see the essay of that title in *The Violent Imagination*). But this does nothing to shake my faith in the truth of Mendelian genetics. This will be established by the testing of Mendelian hypotheses, and if these are falsified, fine; we are still doing science and the result will be—as it was after Morgan and de Vries discovered mutations—a better genetics. And again, and perhaps most important of all, one should not confuse the valid results of science with the *provenance* of those results.

I seem to hear repeatedly today that science is somehow disreputable because it is the province of European white bourgeois males (or something such). (I was once accused in print of being a "bourgeois establishment scientist." I immediately rushed off a copy to my mother so she would have had printed proof that I had made it.) Mendel was such, he was even an Augustinian monk, but he got it right about the wrinkled peas; and it wouldn't have mattered if he'd been a black handicapped Spanish-speaking lesbian atheist. These incidental facts about *scientists* tell us a lot about the history and sociology of science. They are indeed, and always have been, the province of the sociology of knowledge. Many critics of science today in anthropology speak as though they have just discovered the idea that knowledge is relative to class, race, sex, religion and so on. This idea was in fact at the basis of modern sociology with Weber's question about the role of religion in the development of occidental rationality (and, for that matter, Marx and Engels on the nature of "superstructure.") But the next erroneous step was one that Weber never took: to say that the *truth* of propositions so generated was relative in the same way as the generation of them. (Marx and Engels unfortunately did take that step, and announced that revolutionary proletarian truth was the only truth. But it is worth noting that they never doubted that the issue was truth or that their truth was "scientific"—indeed they made much of this distinction in their pursuit of "scientific socialism.") Truth is independent of the source. Bias and prejudice and the like there will always be, there *has to be* in order for ideas to be generated at all. We do not think in a rational vacuum. As David Hume again said, "Reason is, and ought to be, the slave of the passions."

My despair sprang from a belief that human beings can never use their reason for disinterested ends. I still believe this. The sociology of knowledge, the very mechanisms of the brain, and all the complaints, for example, of the feminists and deconstructionists, confirm this belief for me. But at the same time I do not accept that bias in the generation or use of science affects the status of scientific propositions themselves. There is, in other words, no such thing as "feminist science" any more than there is "Aryan science" or "Jewish science." When feminists claim that there is "Eurocentric white male science" what they are talking about is bias in the choice of subjects or the conduct of experiments or observations, or even more in the use of metaphors to popularize science. All this may well be true. But here is the nub: *the very ideals of science itself are the only real antidote to its misuse*. To insist on putting "feminist science" in place of "male chauvinist science" makes no more sense than putting "Aryan science" in place of "Jewish science," if what we are interested in is the truth of the scientific propositions themselves. Here the only solution is to put "good science" in place of "bad science." That is, science conducted according to objective, rational, empirical procedures aimed at eliminating observer bias as much as possible.

Even so, scientific hypotheses have to come from somewhere. In this sense there always has to be "bias." The metaphor of "bias" derives from the fact that according to quirks of its construction, a freely rolling ball may tend to run in one direction rather than another. But if it were not for such biases we would never take a direction. Let me return to the issue of wrong (and/or trivial) science in order to cull an example. In the era I was describing, the dominant paradigm (as we have come to call it post-Kuhn) of behavioral science was Behaviorism (disregarding for the moment the Marxists and "scientific" socialism.) Nothing escaped its influence from philosophy to linguistics to anthropology—and even communist doctrine via Pavlov and Lysenko was happily Behavioristic (indeed Pavlov was one of its founding fathers). Even if its influence was indirect, as in a lot of anthropology, it nevertheless helped to reinforce and underline the prevailing environmentalism of the subject, and its metaphors were all-enveloping.

Cultural determinism was in fact a form of Behaviorism in which a blank-slate organism, the "culture carrier," was molded through "enculturation" (read "conditioning") without any regard to what happened in the "black box" of the organism's brain and consciousness. In many culture-and-personality versions the Behaviorism was quite overt and its language and theories used to "explain" cultural traits and behavior.

Now there was no question that Behaviorism was "scientific." It passed all the tests. It sought disconfirmation of hypotheses. It worked on the logico-inductive method. It was objective and its results replicable. It had only one slight fault: as a total theory of human behavior and culture it was wrong. It explained some things about human behavior, but when it tried to push into other areas, chiefly for example in language, it simply failed to account for phenomena that it claimed to explain—language learning by children for example. Alternative theories became available, for example those of the ethologists, which could account for animal behavior where Behaviorism failed. Experimenters began to produce falsification of the theory of "reinforcement schedules" by showing how animals resorted to "instinctive" behavior patterns under repeated trials. So great was the Behaviorist bias that these initial results were simply not believed. One editor of a leading psychology journal, confronted with the findings of John Garcia and his colleagues, announced that he would believe the results when they found bird shit in cuckoo clocks. Well, the bird shit cometh, and indeed hiteth the fan. Chomsky demonstrated how children could not possibly learn language by conditioning. And so it went. The paradigm of Behaviorism had pushed too far and had run up against phenomena it could not explain. Its hypotheses were disconfirmed. Back to the drawing board.

The Behaviorists went kicking and screaming. Scientists are human. They put vast investments of time, money, prestige and ego into their work and they don't like to see it faulted. What is more they had a three-hundred-year tradition of tabula rasa philosophy and psychology behind them to give strength to their prejudices. But the opposition equally had its biases. Chomsky derived his from Cartesian linguistics, Garcia from the natural behavior of animals, the ethologists from Darwinian evolution, and the social science fellow travellers initially from the ethologists but ultimately from a plain dislike of the Behaviorist/Environmentalist paradigm as evidenced in, for example, the shocking case of the scientific tyranny of Lysenko and Stalin among other things.

In other words, a whole mixture of information and "bias" went into the questioning of the Behaviorist wisdom, and hence the search for information and the design of experiments to disconfirm the Behaviorist hypotheses. In the process, other biases than those motivating the Behaviorists (both capitalist and communist versions) became enshrined in the new natural sciences of behavior. These in turn will undoubtedly be challenged and if they push too far, disconfirmed, by people with other biases. The robust findings of Behaviorism and Ethology will be retained, but science will push in new directions where they could never go. Indeed, many would claim that it was the very failure of Ethology to explain its own firm observations on the basis of "group selection" theory, that led to the development of the alternative of "sociobiology" based on individual selection. The debate still rages, as it should, but it is a debate that rages within the confines of a basic set of assumptions about how such issues should be settled in science. It is, in other words, a truly scientific debate, not an ideological or metaphysical one.

The point then that science can be "wrong" is beside the point. It is the business of science to be wrong. That is one way we know it is science.

The point that science can be "biased" is equally beside the point. We have to have biases to motivate us to look beyond established paradigms.

The point that science can be "trivial" is beside the point. We have to have a lot of trivial science to keep scientists employed, for out of the trivia some pure gold will emerge, often serendipitously, and since we do not know in advance where or how it will emerge we have to put up with the trivia in the meantime.

The point that science can be used for evil purposes is beside the point. Art and music can be used for evil purposes, but no one proposes abandoning either. Anything can be used for evil purposes. I am not going to stop listening to Wagner just because Hitler liked him.

All these objections are beside the point if the point is the *truth* of science. The truth of scientific propositions is independent of these objections, including my own despair at our human ability to use science wisely.

It was my own "bias" against the "inhumanity" of Behaviorism as exemplified in the Skinner box and *Walden II*—my own deep-rooted organicist Burkean conservatism if you like—that led me to search for other and more plausibly "human" theories of human behavior, and has taken me from Ethology through the evolution of behavior to neurosociology, cognitive science, and the developing breakthrough in the philosophy of mind and human consciousness. My "bias" was against socialist totalitarianism (just like Orwell's—although he thought it was socialism gone wrong, whereas I thought socialism was wrong to start with.) I freely admit to the bias. I am proud of the bias. I am glad to have lived to see the day when I can turn round to lifelong critics on the political and the scientific front and say: "I told you so." But the scientific truth of the theories I was driven to explore as alternatives to the totalitarian ideology of Behaviorism will have to stand on its own regardless of my bias, even if intellectual historians might find the connection interesting.

To return to the original issue then, of whether or not I was inconsistent, the answer should be clear: I was talking not of the truths of science, but of the uses of science when I despaired of science. I was, in short, taking a "humanistic" position with regard to science and aligning myself with H. G. Wells at the end of his days, with George Sorel, with Albert Camus, with George Orwell or William Golding or D. H. Lawrence or T. S. Eliot or a host of humanists who have deplored the uses of science in the twentieth century in particular (although the seeds of this attitude were firmly planted by Ruskin and Carlyle, Dostoevsky and Mary Shelley, and others in the nineteenth as well.)

There has been a chorus of dismay about the consequences of scientific hubris. But what I want to argue here, and what the build-up has meant to establish, is that this humanistic despair is misplaced if it is directed to science itself as opposed to the uses, or the biases in the generation of, science and technology. Indeed it is the marriage of the former to the latter, when technology turns sour, that really frightens the humanists. What frightens them is not Einstein's discovery of the relation of energy to mass and the speed of light squared, but the translation of this into atomic weapons. It is not electronics and wave theory, but the use of this to produce television and mechanical control of thought. It is not Mendelian ratios as such, but their use to prove that some races are inferior, and not natural selection as such but its use in arguments for exterminating less-fit races.

It is true that the humanists do not always make this distinction. They do indeed blame science as such for the mess. But these are usually the religious humanists for whom science challenges the truth-claims of religion, and so is to blame for separating us from God. Few current anthropological humanists I think fall into that category. Yet they too seem to be making the same mistake. They blame the gardener because the tree has poisonous fruits. Again they are often confusing science and technology, which is not altogether their fault since we all tend to equate them. But there was technology long before there was science. Science is a way of knowing: an epistemological system. It has in fact nothing to do directly with technology which can flourish without it, as it did in China. Edison was not really a scientist in the strict sense. He was a technological *bricoleur* who operated by trial and error and hunch and know-how and cumulative successes. But science and advanced technology are inextricably linked in fact if not in theory, since advanced technology is dependent on the findings of science.

But a disillusionment with the fruits of technological advance (weapons of mass destruction, worldwide pollution, thought control and totalitarianism, consumer materialism, etc.) really has nothing to do with the question of whether or not anthropology should or should not be a science. This question, which I answer in the affirmative, has to do with the claims of anthropology to be able to answer real questions about the real world: to establish scientific truths. It has nothing to do with how such truths might be misused, or the provenance of their discovery.

In theory. In practice, if I am consistent, I will have to say that of course they will be misused. This is part of my "humanistic" complaint: that we are fated to misuse knowledge by the very nature of our devotion to ideas (see again "Design Failure" in *The Violent Imagination*). This hypothesis, I must admit, verges on the metaphysical. It could only be falsified by oberving an indefinitely long period of human progress free from the misuse of science and the fanatical devotion to ideas. No one lives long enough to test such hypotheses. So far, human history roundly confirms it, but I cannot speak for the future. I would dearly like to think I am wrong—at least I would know I am doing science and the spirit of Popper would be appeased. But this is why I insist that this is a humanistic observation, an opinion, a judgment call, not a scientific hypothesis. Because it seems to me we have no real alternative. Unless we are to abandon the search for "truth"—which is evidence about the real world established by the testing of falsifiable hypotheses within the framework of a revisable theory connecting them—then we are stuck with "science" and we have to go with it whatever our nervousness about its possible misuse. We have to use our humanistic imaginations to try to second guess the misuse and so avoid it as much as possible. This does not amount to controlling or censoring science as such, but to constructing the possible scenarios for its abuse and seeking to avoid these.

This is what the humanist-scientist Michael Crichton did in his brilliant morality tale *Jurassic Park*, and what indeed the best of many of the science fiction writers do, which is why they turn out to be better social scientists than we are much of the time—I cite Frank Herbert's wonderful *Dune* series and the collected works of Asimov, Heinlein, Brin, and Bradbury. This area has been too little explored by "humanistic" anthropology—let us call it "the anthropology of the future"—and this is a pity since it is a perfect area where humanistic imagination and sensitivity and scientific knowledge (and technology) best come together. The possibilities of scientific hubris are here accepted, but so is science as a way of knowing. The ideal—often unstated but always there—is the melding of humanistic and scientific ideals in the service of mankind, not their bitter opposition. In this, science fiction at its best transcends the gloomy pessimism of the Sorelian antiscience tradition, while keeping a level head about the possibilities of a scientific utopia. My point is that it recognizes the distinction I am urging between the the truths of science and the biases and uses of science, and searches for humanistic ends without ditching the search for scientific truth.

But, some of you have been itching to interrupt, hasn't the whole issue of "objective scientific truth" been called into question? Isn't this the point of the "humanistic" objection after all? What is the point in trying to seek a rapprochement if there is no scientific "truth" and all truths are relative? Are we not then only left with the humanistic modes of interpretation as practiced in the humanities proper? For this type of objection (having its roots of course in "deconstruction" and neo-idealist philosophy) it is not the fruits of science (although these may have been the source of this particular "bias") that are at issue, but the status of scientific truth itself.

But the arguments get all muddled up. Thus, the argument goes, there are no absolute truths since all knowledge is relative to the social condition of the knower: the Marxist and sociology of knowledge position. In the latter-day version this social condition has been expanded from social class to ethnicity, race, religion, class widely defined as position in the social dominance system, historical period, ideological position (which should be a product but has become a producer), generation, "gender" (an egregious solecism meaning, in essense, sex[1]) and Lord knows what else.

---

1. "gender, n., is a grammatical term only. To talk of *persons* or *creatures of the masculine or feminine gender*, meaning *of the male or female sex*, is either a jocularity [permissible or not according to context] or a blunder." H. W. Fowler, *A Dictionary of Modern English Usage*, Oxford: Clarendon Press, 1926, p. 211

Thus we can get such monsters as "Eurocentric white male heterosexual bourgeois Protestant science."[2] This "science" has no claim to universal absolute truth, the position holds, *because* of this provenance. It is only "true" in this "context" just as, for example, in the Middle Ages, the pre-Copernican theory of the universe was "true" in the context of a society governed by Catholic theology. But there is no universal truth of science outside these relative truths of particular sciences. There is much invoking of Einstein on relativity and quantum physics and the Heisenberg principle—often in startling ignorance of the the real principles involved in each—and of course Derrida, Foucault, Feyerabend, and sometimes Dilthey (by the better educated.) The hapless Tom Kuhn (who is horrified by this particular mangling of his theory of paradigms) and Richard Rorty, are invoked like gods to justify an ultimately totally relativistic epistemology, as is Quine despite his being an uncompromising materialist.[3]

These arguments have been so well ventilated now, and by people better able to deal with them than I, that I am not here going to fight the battle all over again.[4] Obviously I do not agree with the relativist position. While accepting the connection between social position in all the above senses and the generation and use of scientific ideas, I clearly do not accept that this relativity affects the truth value of scientific propositions per se. A proposition, so long as it is in the form of a falsifiable

---

2. I was on a student committee, in 1957, for the relocation of Hungarian refugee students after the uprising. It goes without saying that we were very unpopular with the student Left. We interviewed a candidate who told us he had been studying at a Marxist-Leninist institute. His subject was "proletarian philosophy." He told us he wanted to continue his studies at Oxford. What did he want to study there, we asked. Without hesitation he replied, "bourgeois philosophy." We figured he would survive just fine.

3. I remember almost thirty years ago being one of the few people in Princeton willing to talk at length with Dick Rorty about his enthusiasm for Idealist philosophy, which no one else seemed to share. He put me on to reading Royce, and I fired him up over Bradley. I might add that I was not too enthusiastic about their theories of reality, but I was interested in their social theories. Tom Kuhn and I, also in Princeton, discussed, while feeding his pet monkeys, the "paradigm shifts" in behavioral science I have described above. Thus do the wheels of history turn in strange and crooked ways.

4. See Gross and Leavitt, 1994 for the best summary, but also the interesting critiques of the "Dallas School" of humanists who do not accept the mainstream anti-science position of their colleagues, as in Turner 1995, and Argyros 1991. A massive tour-de-force on these same lines is Carroll 1995.

hypothesis, is not "invalidated" by being placed in a different social "context." This is where the Heisenberg principle is so often and so strangely misunderstood and misused by such critics. The proposition in question might never have arisen in another context, or might have arisen in a very different form, and this is in itself an interesting question for the sociology of knowledge to pursue. Indeed it was the starting point for Weber's brilliant, and soundly scientific, comparative sociology of knowledge based on the principle of concomitant variation first propounded by John Stuart Mill. Strange how Weber is so often cited then by the relativists as though he were a founding father of their movement! This is based on a misunderstanding of his principle of *Verstehen*, loosely translated as "understanding " and which is certainly concerned with the subjective states of the actors. (Basically Weber was asking "what did they believe they were doing?") But he never thought this removed analysis from the burden of objectivity and proof.

At the risk of being boring I repeat: the truth value of a proposition, even a proposition about subjectivity, is not affected by context. This is the whole point of science; the whole point of the revolution in thinking that Weber set out to analyze under the heading of "rationality." And he saw it applying across the board—to music, mathematics, business, theology, law and religion, as well as science. (How many "humanistic" anthropologists so free with Weber's name read him on the rational evolution of music in the West? Not many to my knowledge.) And it happened once in history in one particular place, but, and here is the revolutionary thing: unlike every previous system of thinking its truths were potentially universal in their application to reality. Unlike religious or magical beliefs its truths were totally independent of social and cultural context. We will get nowhere trying to control the world with the principles of sympathetic magic as practiced by a Siberian shaman, and indeed they will only be intelligible in their cultural context; but the same shaman will do very well with the observation of Boyle's law, or by following genetic principles in his breeding of reindeer—and so would his Zulu counterpart.

It was because of this principle that Weber was able to conduct his "scientific" investigation of comparative civilizations and ideological systems. If Weber were the relativist he is made out to be he would have had to dismiss his own lifework as inherently false. Weber would have seen quite clearly the impossibility of the relativists' position: if it were true, then it must be false. They are caught like the Cretan liar (who said that all Cretans were liars): if all truths are indeed epistemologically relative and have no universal application, then the proposition that all truths are epistemologically relative is itself relative and has no universal application and we have no reason to accept it. It is the product of its own context, biases, social conditions, and so on.

Indeed, it is. This brings us back to the question we started with about anthropology and the quest for scientific status in the heyday of the scientific paradigm. At this point most anthropologists would have been what it is fashionable to call "value relativists." This was an often incoherent position but at its most general it said that "we" could not judge other societies on a scale with ourselves at the top. All societies were ethically equal in this view. The great sin was "ethnocentrism." This position itself is not logically sound, but leave that for a moment. It was essentially a humanitarian attempt to oppose the view of the "natives" as "savages" and to plead for a deeper understanding of customs that appeared at first, to the "ethnocentric" observer, as cruel or disgusting. But I know of no anthropologists who extended this to epistemological relativism—to the view discussed in the previous paragraph. There was no way they could do this and maintain a "scientific" status. Paradoxically, it was argued that value relativism was more "scientific" than "absolutism" or other nonrelativistic positions in ethics, and the Logical Positivists (and their linguistic philosophy successors) were often invoked as philosophical backup for this view: ethical statements were "emotive" not "descriptive" hence there could be no absolute ethical standards, and so on. The world of anthropology was thus kept safe for science. The "Natural Science of Society" for Radcliffe-Brown was essentially what we now know as "structural-functionalism" and he (mistakenly) thought that this meant it should look for "general laws" of social functions on the model of "general laws" of physics. None were ever found, nor should they have been, since science does not proceed by looking for general laws, which are, in any case, always provisional hypotheses in real science as opposed to pseudoscience (for example, the "evolutionism" of Herbert Spencer—the "development hypothesis" as he misleadingly called it.)

Scientific "truth" is indeed not fixed and absolute "out there" in the world waiting to be discovered, but is *a special kind of relationship between the knower and the known*. The nature of this relationship, however, as we have seen, is unique and confers a unique status on the propositions (hypotheses) that result. The Functionalists did not understand this. Radcliffe-Brown himself declared that he was an evolutionist of the school of Spencer and his "science" was a nineteenth-century mechanistic version that never caught up even with Popper (and despite my loyalty to my old teacher I have to admit that we have progressed in the philosophy of science since!) (See Schilpp 1974.)

Thus, in Britain and France, a reaction set in against the scientism of Functionalism. In those early days it was seen essentially as a shift initiated by Evans-Pritchard and Lévi-Strauss from explanation to interpretation, from cause to meaning, from science to symbolism, from social structure to mental structure. It saw itself as reviving the historical division between the natural and cultural sciences (after Dilthey, after Kant) and coming down in favor of *Kulturwissenschaft*. It therefore saw itself as moving away from "science" as such since "science" was associated with the discredited Functionalism. For the French, the paradigm of linguistics (de Saussure, Jakobson) was first invoked as an alternative; later hermeneutics and rhetoric got their turn, and the rest is history. In the U.S. Clifford Geertz (who also ended up down the road from me in Princeton) led a group of young resistance fighters against Functionalism in its Culturalist versions and in particular in its evolutionary or ecological materialist varieties, and "symbolic anthropology" here too lined up against "science" and with the new European symbolical and structuralist movements.

In its origins, this move from "function to meaning," from science to humanism, was anything but radical. On the contrary, some of its manifestations were positively reactionary, or at least seemed so to the scientific rationalists of the time. In the U.K., at Oxford, it was an affair conducted largely by Roman Catholic (some converts) anthropologists (Evans-Pritchard, the Lienhardt brothers, Turner, Douglas, etc.) who were in a frank reaction against the positivist-rationalist tradition of Sir James Frazer and his admirer, Malinowski at the LSE.[5] (For the record, I too was reared in that tradition, and in some sense still consider myself a Malinowskian social anthropologist.) I remember the suspicion that this

---

5. Malinowski's admiration for Frazer actually seems to stem from his permanent residence in England and applies to his writings in English. I gather his early writings in Polish are quite critical of Frazer. But it was the *Golden Bough* that drew him into anthropology.

latter-day "Oxford Movement" engendered. Sir Raymond Firth, Malinowski's successor, groaned deeply, and shook his head sadly, when Turner decided to call various stages of Ndembu rituals "stations." And the superpositivist Max Gluckman of the rigidly empiricist Manchester school (which he created of course), referred to the whole movement as "The Oratory." Edmund Leach at Cambridge responded with a series of "structuralist" deconstructions of the Old Testament—just to keep them on the defensive. Cambridge as a whole was still in good rationalist hands with Fortes, Goody, and Leach, who, like most of their generation (including Evans-Pritchard) hailed from the LSE graduate program. (During World War II the LSE was evacuated to Cambridge, so a natural affinity existed: if anything Cambridge was more left-wing than the LSE, despite the latter's reputation.) The Cantabrigian counter-movement was to come from young and as yet unknown sociologists who reacted equally against the Fabian empiricism of the still-dominant LSE, and who were eventually to kick off the "cultural studies" movement, aligning themselves with Paris and Frankfurt.

In the U.S., we largely associate this trend with Geertz and Schneider, and perhaps with Bellah in sociology—all, like myself, products of the Harvard Social Relations Department, and all reacting against it. Again, they were seen at the time as more reactionary than radical, especially by the Left and very especially by the Marxists. When I was there in the late fifties, there were always one or two people around busily quoting Suzanne Langer, or Kenneth Burke, or Alfred Schutz, but no one took them seriously. We were wrestling with Parsons's grand synthesis, and this was the point of departure, pro or con. Actually Geertz seemed to start in the direction of trying to build a "general theory of social action" to use the jargon of the time, but then backed off into "thick description" and "interpretation" and the like and away from grand Parsonsian generalizations. He never seems to have given a coherent reason for this switch; it seems more a matter of taste than anything else.

But my point is that none of these initial movements were "radical" either intellectually or politically. They were even just the opposite. They predated the "spirit of '68" and the philosophical revolutions in continental Europe. And, despite the currently fashionable conspiracy theories of knowledge, I am inclined to see them as genuine, perhaps even predictable reactions to the overlong dominance of Behaviorism and Functionalism, positivism and empiricism. They were in this sense genuine intellectual movements. They were also genuine movements in the direction of a "humanistic" as opposed to a "positivistic" view of the role of the social "sciences." But at least initially they did not attack or denigrate science as such. They simply quietly differentiated themselves and what they did from it. The Oxford Catholics, for example, saw no future in attempts to "explain" religion according to reductionist psychological schemes such as those of culture-and-personality anthropology, or to "laws of development" of a Frazerian or Comtean kind, or according to a Malinowskian theory of "needs," or a Functionalist theory of social utility. Religious symbols, rituals, and beliefs could not be so "explained" they could only be "interpreted" in terms of what they meant to the believers. The humanist-Catholics, and their nonreligious humanist bretheren, were, across the board, remarkably undogmatic about it all, even in their most programatic statements such as Evans-Pritchard's *Social Anthropology* of 1951, or his *Theories of Primitive Religion* of 1965. They preferred on the whole to make their points by making superior demonstrations rather than by claiming a superior epsitemological status.

What has happened since is that these movements, which, as I keep insisting, were genuine intellectual resistances initiated by the postwar generation to what appeared to be a barren Functionalist heritage, have been hijacked by ideologically motivated, blatantly political movements of the anti-Vietnam baby-boom generation. The "spirit of '68" infuses them, the women's rights movement in its latest avatar of "feminism" has climbed aboard, the fashionable movements in philosophy of knowledge in Frankfurt and Paris (deconstruction, hermeneutic) lend strength to them, and, following on the genuine achievements of the civil rights movement, various groups claiming "empowerment" have plugged in, with the demands for "multiculturalism" and the overthrow of "Western Civilization" that have become so depressingly familiar and so politically oppressive. The rather bewildered leftover Marxists who have seen their political and intellectual worlds crumble are trying to accomodate, however clumsily. What was a shift in emphasis in the social sciences has become a revolutionary, relativistic, antiscience, political ideology, with a frightening tendency in the U.S. at least, to harness the worst forces of Puritan fanaticism, which seem always so eager to burst out and have their day, in a new wave of campus totalitarianism, which threatens with academic gulags and thought reform those who do not accept the moral absolutes of the cultural relativists. (Logic has been the most obvious loser in the whole sorry history.)

The sadness of this for me—and I write as a humanist, in the broad sense, for humanists—is that the majority of "humanistic anthropologists" seem to feel it necessary to identify with the hijackers, and hence with their antiscientism. There is not only no need for this, but I would argue it is a dangerous and in the end futile road to take.

In reacting against Functionalism in whichever of its versions, we were reacting essentially against a misconceived science. Because the ideas of science most humanists hold are as outdated as the ideas of the functionalists themselves, they see their revolt as a necesary rejection of science as such. I should point out at this juncture that this essay was originally directed at humanist anthropologists in one of their own journals so I did not need to explain to them who they were or too much about their "interpretative community." I can only say here, to the nonanthropological reader, that what I describe is now utterly pervasive in cultural anthropology, and the reader can pick up the catalogues of the university presses and see the hundreds of books that pour out each year based on these assumptions, which, indeed are rarely even argued any more but taken as givens. It has become impossible, for example, to talk to most cultural anthropology graduate students—always desperate to be up-to-date—except in this dreadful sublanguage. I told one student that I didn't think the Wenner-Gren Foundation would like his grant proposal—far too empirical. He explained that the actual proposal he would submit would frequently mention "hegemony" and "patriarchy" as well as "signifiers" and "Others" so it should be OK. For those who want a quick rundown on the "attack on objectivity" in anthropology I strongly recommend Roy D'Andrade's "Moral Models in Anthropology" (D'Andrade 1995b) where he deals with some of the more obvious offenders, as well as Spiro, 1992.

But let me slip into autobiography again. I too revolted against Functionalism as early as the "symbolists"—but I did not throw over science, since I saw that what I was rejecting in the Durkheimian or Boasian versions of social science I was taught was not in itself very good science (although it was in the scientific spirit and I will come back to that.) Remember our earlier point: just to be doing science in some way or another is not good enough; one has to be doing it right. My reaction was to equate Functionalism with "inadequate science" (and cultural anthropology in fact with outworn ideology) and seek for a more adequate scientific approach to human society—one that eschewed the tabula rasa and the Durkheimian separation of individual and social, for example, and proceeded within the framework of a theory (e.g., natural selection) that would produce testable hypotheses about proximate mechanisms in human social behavior (see Fox 1989b, chs. 3, 4, and 5).

I, personally, found it in Ethology, as it was then called. Originally a science of animal behavior based on observation growing out of Darwinian "natural history," it was introduced to experiment by Lorenz, von Frith, and Tinbergen, and expanded to human behavior by a growing group of interested social scientists with varying degrees of scientific usefulness, and indeed a few wild and woolly exercises thrown in. It needs its own history, but now, commonly known as "sociobiology" after a coinage of E. O. Wilson's, is thoroughly established as workable science, (normal science in Kuhn's terms) with its branches and its schools and its infighting—typical of all young sciences, where youngsters out to make a name constantly reinvent the wheel and call it a vehicular motion-facilitation device (Fox 1995).

I do not mean here to defend this "human ethological" approach in detail, that would be out of place. In any case I get tired of having to explain basic processes of natural selection, with which I expect all freshmen to be familiar, to senior colleagues of the humanistic persuasion. It's embarrassing. I simply mean to point out that the route out of Functionalism was not *necessarily* the "symbolic" or "interpretative" one; that one did not have to ditch science and opt for some other mode of knowing in order to escape the trap. For that way leads to the absurdities of epistemological relativism and even more dangerous ideological traps. The way out of bad science is to find good science, not to ditch science altogether and embrace various forms of opinion mongering that masquerade as knowledge while they deny its possibility. (Logic loses again.) Others who were disillusioned with Functionalism did not necessarily go the ethological route; they chose other routes like cognitive anthropology (see the recent excellent history by D'Andrade 1995a), or cultural (historical) ecology (e.g., Crumley, ed., 1994), or a more cybernetic approach (Bohannan, 1995)—all of which stuck to science while rejecting its teleological Functionalist version.

But, again, you might be itching to interject, we *are* humanists. We want to interpret, not explain. We want to look for meaning, not for cause. We do see what we do as "literary" not as "science." And we like it that way. To which I say: bunkum. (Actually I wrote something else, but this is a polite academic occasion so I changed it.) You want to be *believed*. When you insist that something is the case either about human behavior in general or about some local behavior in particular, you want your reader to accept it as "true." You do not in fact say: well, this is just my opinion, this is just a story like *Gulliver's Travels* and you can take it or leave it. If you have asserted that the X do Y about Z, you will be peeved if another observer says no, they do W about Z not Y. You will want to show that you are right in your "interpretation" and that it was not just a whimsical invention. There may be "multivocal" interpretations, but you will be prepared to admit that some are simply off the wall and others "make sense." You must therefore appeal to some criteria of judgment—some things we would all as rational observers agree on—to decide the matter. You would want, in other words, to frame a falsifiable hypothesis and test it at however low a level.

The last phrase is significant since it goes back to what I said and put on one side about "in the spirit of science" and all that. You may mistakenly think that science is what happens in physics or biology classes (a lot of "humanists" seem to think this way) and that it must, for example, always involve quantification and statistics. But this is not the case. Science is a mode of knowing. If we have a disputed line in a French troubador which scholar A insists is genuine and scholar B says was inserted later, we can settle the matter if evidence is available. Say the line refers to an artifact that was not in existence when the troubador wrote, then we can all accept that it must have been inserted later (unless there is some other, nonmetaphysical, hypothesis that is better of course.)

We are here accepting the "spirit of science" as much as if we quantify and use statistics. These are only relevant to certain kinds of hypotheses. If you are indeed interested in the "truth"—and whatever you might think, you really are—then you *must* use the scientific mode, at however low a level, to arrive at it. Evolution would not work otherwise. We would not be here to discuss the matter today. In our everyday thinking we are constantly testing and confirming and falsifying hypotheses; this more than "conditioning" explains how we behave as we do. We are natural natural scientists; we have no other choice. I am here invoking Popper's powerful argument that our perception of the world and our decision making about it, work on the basic principles of hypothesis testing and refutation, and that "scientific method" therefore is simply the extension of basic cognitive principles (see Popper 1979). (I do not mean that this exhausts the principles on which our cognition works—I have written at length on our use of intuition, probability, stereotyping, matching and representability for example [see ch. 14 in Fox 1994, and ch. 8 in Fox 1989b.] I am simply stressing the Popperian component as basic and necessary.)

This is why the current antiscientific relativism makes no sense to humanists. It is simply a kind of throwing in the towel: a confession of intellectual cowardice. The sins of Functionalism lay in the false notion of science as a pursuit of general laws (which were largely teleological truisms.) The virtue of Functionalism lay in a devotion to the idea of rational inquiry at the empirical level; to at least an attempt to adhere to objective standards in fieldwork—the anthropological mode of gathering data.[6] This did not necessarily involve quantification and statistics; it all depended on the kind of question posed and the kind of answer sought. But at the very least there was a commitment to a descriptive objectivity that was in principle "replicable" by other fieldworkers. Truly, when it came to interpretation and judgments there were differences, but it was accepted that somewhere in the conflicting accounts, the different styles of writing and presentation, there was a possibility of truth. Of course there was sloppy work, and sometimes there did seem to be irreconcilable differences. But these were rationally (if not always reasonably) argued, and the source of bias or the nature of the diffferent interpretations examined in an attempt to see just what was bias—what, for example, resulted from incompatible prior assumptions—and what was fact. Anthropologists, in other words, were held accountable in a way that tourists and journalists and novelists were not. And that is how it should be. It's tough, but no one said anthropology was easy. If you want it easy then be honest: join the creative writing program.

There was in fact a pretty good agreement as to what constituted evidence for a statement of "fact" in ethnography, and in teaching fieldwork seminars I always stressed the need for evidence to back up generaliza-

---

6. I am here addressing the humanistic anthropologists and so concentrate on fieldwork which is their metier. Obviously I do not need to address these remarks to physical and biological anthropologists who as a matter of course adhere to the scientific method, as do most archaeologists, although there is some wavering here (see Fox, 1993).

tions. I was always leery of ethnographies that simply stated the "customs" of the so-and-so about, say, land tenure, in the absense of any detailed maps and evidence of inheritances. When I came to do my own fieldwork, inspired by the examples of Malinowski on Kiriwina, the meticulous data gathering of the Manchester school, Firth on Tikopia and Leach on Pul Eliya (among others), I made sure that I documented my "interpretation" of Tory Island land-holding with as rich a data base as possible, and one that was open to objective scrutiny by any other interested anthropologists who might wish to contest my version of the facts (Fox, 1979).

Land tenure is "hard" data, I suppose, but the principle applies just as much to interpretations of religious symbolism or magical rites: if you say the X do Y because of Z, I want to see the data that supports this view as opposed to the view that they do it because of W. If you say that the X "mean" Z when they do Y, then I want a good reason to suppose that this is a fact and not just your fancy. And indeed, as you know very well, fieldwork and interpretation could not proceed and be convincing if this were not the case. After all, in some sense, all studies of cultural rules and customs are studies of "meaning." What did it "mean" for the Tory Islanders to say that all children should be provided for from the land when at least half the children never got any land? One could not answer this question of meaning by writing confessional poetry or deconstructing the concept of land tenure, but only by gathering empirical data to test various hypotheses about what the meaning could possibly be. This is the "spirit of science" at the fairly low observational level at which we practice it. Most of the time we do not notice it because it is, as I have said, the normal human way of processsing and testing knowledge anyway. But when we come to want our interpretations accepted by the community of scientists/scholars, then we have to become self-conscious about them and play by the elementary rules of science whether we like it or not.

In short: *If you wish to be believed you must accept the burden of falsifiability.* You must accept that your statements are hypotheses that are in principle subject to refutation. If you refuse to accept this burden, on any grounds whatsoever, then there is no reason why we should pay any further attention to anything you say, since you could just as well utter complete nonsense or gibberish; it would make no difference. The same goes for so-called "deconstruction" as an intellectual activity. The critical analysis of concepts in order to reconstruct them as better hypotheses is very necessary to science. Again I have done more than my fair share of this critical service. But the deconstruction of concepts as an end in itself, and, if I understand Derrida rightly (and I am convinced that part of his program is that he should not be understood), as a never-ending, self-cancelling activity, while it may satisfy some cloudy demands of Husserl, Heidegger, and the "phenomenologists" (who have as far as I can see no relevance to social science whatsoever) is useless to those of us concerned with the assessment of empirical reality. Of course, you will respond, the existence of empirical reality is what these theories hold to be moot (or at least they question the possibility of our knowing it). To which I can only reply: let me hear you say that when told you need a difficult operation to save your life, or the life of one of your children. Christian Scientists are at least consistent on this issue; academics who hold these ridiculous theories are simply hypocrites.

I have done "science" at all levels from the purely descriptive to the quantifiable and statistical. I also think of myself as a "humanist" in the broad sense: I approach my fellow human creatures as being in a deep sense the "same" as I am, and I "interpret" their differences from me against the measure of this sameness. This is what we do about all other people all the time, starting with the most familiar and working out to the seemingly unfathomable other. The real poet—like any artist—tries all the time to see the general in the particular. In this he is no different from the scientist. They are siblings under the skin. In its original, Renaissance, meaning, "humanist" referred to someone who took man as the measure (as opposed to God or angels). It did not differentiate between scientists and artists in this respect, and the greatest of the humanists was himself the greatest artist and scientist of his day, and saw no conflict between the two ways of knowing. If for Leonardo they were one, why not for us? Later ages which split off "humanities" from "sciences" (beginning, I think, in the seventeenth century with the use of humanist to mean a student of the classics) started a rot of which we are the ultimate heirs. The tragedy of anthropology is that it is the perfect discipline to unite the two again, and thus to be a light to lighten the gentiles and the glory of "humanism." The "science of mankind" is not a science that would or could ignore art and poetry. How would this be possible since these are two of mankind's most distinguishing achievements? But it would try to deal "scientifically" with them in the sense I have outlined above, not just reiterate their own structures, but envelope them in the fold of humane scientific examination, which is its own kind of poetry for those who have the ear.

Let me end by reaffirming that I am indeed committed, as an anthropologist, to the furtherance of humanistic studies as currently understood. I am, after all, a humanist *manqué*, and would have been a composer, guitarist, poet, or playwright in a perfect world. Nothing I have said about the necessity of scientific method in the pursuit of truth need alarm anyone who is devoted to the study of the art, poetry, music, or drama of native peoples (or anyone else). Go ahead with my enthusiastic blessing. All I am asking is that you do not join the fashionable science-bashing that politically and ideologically motivated groups and individuals seem to think is necessary to their positions. It is not necessary to humanistic anthropologists, who, I maintain, if they are doing a good job as such, will not violate the rules or the spirit of science anyway. Let us return "humanism" to its original meaning (the meaning that led Sartre to insist that Existentialism was a humanism), and let anthropology be the shining example. Humanistic insight and scientific objectivity are not and never should be opposed: a devotion to humanistic values will lead to a more insightful science, and an equal devotion to scientific values will lead to a more convincing humanism. We are equal partners in the task of achieving a better understanding of mankind. Let us cease the useless warfare and conclude a fruitful peace. Both anthropology as a discipline and mankind as a species be will the better for it.

References

Argyros, Alexander. 1991. *A Blessed Rage For Order*. Ann Arbor: University of Michigan Press.

Bohannan, Paul. 1995. *How Culture Works*. New York: Free Press .

Carroll, Joseph. 1995. *Evolution and Literary Theory*. Columbia: University of Missouri Press.

Crumley, Carole L. 1994. *Historical Ecology*. Santa Fe, NM: School of American Research Press.

D'Andrade, Roy. 1995a. *The Development of Cognitive Anthropology*. Cambridge: Cambridge University Press.

———. 1995b. "Moral Models in Anthropology." *Current Anthropology* 36:3, pp. 399–408.

Fox, Robin. 1978. *The Tory Islanders*. Cambridge: Cambridge University Press. 2nd ed. Notre Dame University Press, 1995.

———. 1989a. *The Violent Imagination*. New Brunswick, NJ: Rutgers University Press.

————. 1989b. *The Search For Society*. New Brunswick, NJ: Rutgers University Press.

————. 1993. "One World Archaeology: An Appraisal." *Anthropology Today*. 9:5, 6–10.

————. 1994. *The Challenge of Anthropology: Old Encounters and New Excursions*. New Brunswick, NJ: Transaction Publishers.

————. 1996. "Sociobiology" in *The Social Science Encyclopedia*, A. and J. Kuper, eds., London: Routledge.

Popper, Sir Karl, 1979. *Objective Knowledge*. Oxford: Clarendon Press, rev. ed. (first published 1972.).

Schilpp, Paul Arthur, ed. 1974. *The Philosophy of Karl Popper*, 2 vols. La Salle, IL: Open Court Press.

Spiro, Melford E. 1992. *Anthropological Other or Burmese Brother*. (New Brunswick, NJ: Transaction Publishers).

Turner, Frederick. 1995. *The Culture of Hope*. New York: Free Press.

Interview

An Accidental Life II

with Alex Walter

The story continues but doesn't quite conclude. The contingencies and accidents continue to pile up. I never meant to go to Tory Island or to get mixed up in neonate cognition any more than I meant to write a book on kinship or meet a man called Tiger at the London Zoo or run a research foundation. We really do bob like Schopenhauer's corks on an ocean of improbabilities. On the other hand, once launched, the fragile bark does develop, almost organically, a rudder and a direction. At least by this point in the interview I have found a steering oar, and by great good luck again, it turns out to be not only my personal rudder but the great director of life itself: natural selection. While it has no intrinsic goals—it is, like Hardy's "Immanent Will," essentially without purpose—it can, paradoxically, provide a firm telos for the individual searching for clues to the pattern of existence. For even if Life, like a life, is really a series of accidents, the accidents have causes and results, and these results are what we call organisms and species, and we can understand their causes and consequences without ever having to invoke purpose at all. This view was alarming to the Victorians, and provoked Tennyson and Arnold to their poetical philosophizing. Even Huxley, Darwin's "bulldog," could not face the awful consequences of a universe without purpose. Hardy and Nietzsche faced it, and we must face it. Bertrand Russell taught me to face it in "A Free Man's Religion." But we can face it with the weapon of understanding: we may not know why we are here, but we can know how we are here, and why we are how we are. It is this mixture of accident and understanding that caused Darwin's uncharacteristic outburst at the end of the Origin *"There is a grandeur in this view of life..." For look at the wonders, including one's own odd episode on earth, that accident provokes when married to the struggle to survive.*

WALTER: Was it the impossibility of bringing ethology to bear on British social anthropology that drew you to the United States?

FOX: On the intellectual side that was it, but I won't say that there were not other considerations. Material considerations, for example, weighed heavily in my decision. We were underpaid slave laborers at the time. I had three kids and a damp house with a large mortgage, and I didn't see much prospect of getting out from under that situation. Also I was getting very despondent about the educational situation in England. In terms of ideas however, yes, it was. I had had those two years in America, and I had also grown up with the great dream of America, the kind of vision of America that Europeans have. It was an immigrant's dream, if you like, and my few years in America had convinced me that this was right and that ideas in America were treated very differently than they were in England.

WALTER: How would you characterize the difference?

FOX: Let me phrase it this way: A new idea in America was considered to be good simply because it was a *new* idea. In England it was quite the other way around. The old ideas were always the best; the new ideas really had to be proven. There was also an American excitement about ideas. People got fascinated and worked up about ideas. In England that was considered undignified and not done, certainly not in academic circles. The down side of this, I later discovered, was that the obsession with novelty meant that ideas had a short shelf-life.

But the chance to start a new department, to come to America, and for Lionel and me to get together was simply too tempting. All these things came together at one time, like a finger pointing from heaven, but it was something I stumbled into; it was not positively planned for.

WALTER: What did you wish to accomplish when you came to Rutgers?

FOX: Tiger and I set out to do three things: to write a book, to set up a department, and to invent an invisible college of likeminded colleagues who could be pulled together to show that they were not alone. The model we had in mind was similar to that behind the origins of the Royal Society. We started setting up the department at Rutgers, but, of course, we had to set up a genuine anthropology department; we could not set up an ethology department. We tried to set up as many contacts as we could with the natural sciences, but we had to hire archaeologists and other types of anthropologists in order to set up a bona fide anthropology department. The writing of the book was very strange, because we really intended to write a textbook. In fact, we had a contract with Thomas Nelson to write a book called something like *The Evolution of Human Behavior.* We sat down to write this pompous tome and found that we really couldn't do it because there wasn't a subject, and you've got to have a well-established subject to write a textbook about it. We were in fact creating a subject—very much as the culture-and-personality people were doing in the twenties and thirties. It wasn't until the fifties and sixties that textbooks on culture and personality began to appear. In that respect, it was several removes from being a textbook or anything else; it was an idea for an idea of a book. We never expected it to have the kind of impact that it did.

WALTER: Were you surprised at the response of anthropologists and of your other university colleagues to the publication of *The Imperial Animal*?

FOX: Absolutely, and more so by the general public response. We regarded it as a benign little effort. We did not see ourselves as biological reductionists at all. Rather, we saw ourselves as promoting an interactionist view of nature and nurture. Nature provided a program, but this program unfolded during the life cycle and needed releasers in the environment for its completion. These releasers in the environment are what anthropologists call culture, and we therefore saw ourselves as open not only to analyzing culture better but also to a normative and ethical view of being able to say how we should run cultures so that they could in fact act as appropriate releasers for the programs provided by nature. We didn't realize how deeply entrenched was the opposing notion that there was no genetic program. The extreme entrenchment of the Lockean *tabula rasa* view of human nature and the passionate degree to which this was held led many people to react severely and violently to *The Imperial Animal.*

WALTER: The hold of the Lockean view was something you came to analyze later in *The Search for Society* (1989a).

FOX: Exactly. How, during Western history, did this dominant view of human nature, as opposed to the medieval view of human nature as basically evil, come to be? While we knew intellectually that it was there, we were not prepared for the emotionality of the response or for the idea that we had not only proposed a new way of doing social sciences but somehow unleashed the dogs of war. One reviewer compared our book to *Mein Kampf.* We suddenly began to be reviled as neo-Nazis and to be threatened physically, sometimes having rooms cleared because of bomb threats. The Students for a Democratic Society threatened to boycott us, and the feminists came down on us.

WALTER: Did you expect to get such a hard time from the feminists?

FOX: These were *arriviste* feminists; they arose at the same time we did, which was another unfortunate thing. I think if the book had come out five years earlier it would not have generated nearly the same reaction, but it came out at about the same time as that early wave of careerist feminism, promoting the view that there were no differences whatsoever between the sexes but socialization had made them so. So we got roundly jumped on by everybody. Now, this was not part of the plan, but it certainly made for a lot of fun and sold a lot of books.

WALTER: Not everybody was opposed to you. The Guggenheim Foundation made you and Tiger codirectors of its program for research on aggression and violence.

FOX: That was another interesting accident, you see. Mason Gross, who was president of Rutgers and a great pal of ours (and to whom I dedicate my latest book [1994]), had retired from Rutgers. He was made president of the Harry Frank Guggenheim Foundation with the mandate of getting it going. He phoned me one day and said that he thought he could get us some money for our research. He had just read Skinner's *Beyond Freedom and Dignity* (1971) and thought it was a terrible, soul-destroying book. I gave him a copy of *The Imperial Animal,* and he sat up the whole night, read the book, called me up the next day, and said, "This is it; I want a program based on this." Lionel and I went on half-time with Rutgers and half-time with the foundation.

This was before the outcry really started. The foundation, to its immense credit, stood with us throughout all this and didn't bat an eye while continuing to support the research.

WALTER: What would you say were your major achievements with the foundation?

FOX: I would say that we pretty much kept alive the human-ethology enterprise. It hadn't developed a name. I called it biosocial anthropology, and Lionel had called it biosociology.

WALTER: You and Tiger helped get much of the research in sociobiology funded when you were at the Guggenheim.

FOX: We funded most of the names you now read, including Ed Wilson, Richard Dawkins, Napoleon Chagnon, and Daly and Wilson. We were supposed to do research on aggression and dominance, but we took the rather lordly view that research on aggression and dominance should be viewed only in a larger ethological context, so we took it as our mandate to fund anything and everything that might throw light on the evolution of human behavior—which would, in turn, help us to understand aggression and dominance. We included cognitive science, which led to my cooperation with Jacques Mehler on *Neonate Cognition* (1985). We funded these people when the established foundations wouldn't. We couldn't give very large grants, but we were able to give a lot of seed money out to a lot of people, and a lot of people who are now sailing ahead with this type of research got pushed off in our little boat. Also, the foundation backed our personal research. I fulfilled two ambitions: doing my own primate fieldwork and studying the bullfight as a *novillero* in Colombia. So far I have only written poetry about that—something the postmodernists actually commend me for, if not for killing bulls!

WALTER: Some reviewers seem to think you have been relegated to the dust heap of history by the very people you supported.

FOX: Unfortunately, that could well be true. A book of readings came out early on, after Wilson's *Sociobiology* (1975), in which Tiger and Fox were placed among the forerunners of sociobiology along with Darwin, Spencer, Huxley, Kropotkin, and Allee. Considering what young whippersnappers we were at the time, this is really rather hilarious. I think it was George Bernard Shaw who said that you knew you were finished as an intellect when you began appearing as an exam question. I think our appearance as the "forerunners" of something before we were forty years old indicates that we must have been already washed up!

WALTER: You and Tiger eventually left the Guggenheim. Why?

FOX: We parted company after twelve years. It was a long time to be with a foundation. We parted company because we wanted to keep up the very broad approach and go on doing that, while they wanted to narrow it down to aggression-and-violence research. But they are going on. They keep on holding conferences on ethnicity and violence in the Near East and things like that. Good work, but I think it lacks the panache, the bravado, the sense of sailing the ship into new waters that we had when we launched it with Mason Gross.

WALTER: What is the relationship of the program of research that you and Tiger envisioned to sociobiology?

Fox: Lionel and I had recognized the importance of the work of Bill Hamilton way back in the sixties, and we immediately saw the importance of Robert Trivers's. In *Biosocial Anthropology* (1975) Hamilton figures prominently as a contributor. I even brought him to an Oxford conference of social anthropologists in 1973 and had him attempt to educate them. It didn't work.

What we hadn't done was to see inclusive-fitness theory as an overarching theory of the evolution of human behavior. We saw it as explaining certain aspects of human behavior, and we certainly didn't see the maximization of reproductive fitness as describing all human behavior—and I don't think they did either. What Ed Wilson had done was to take Trivers and Hamilton and put this together with the huge amount of material from ethology and call this sociobiology. I think what has happened since is that rather than this being an expansive sort of basis for a theory of human behavior it has been terribly narrowed down into this one little aspect of the maximization of reproductive success. This eventually leads to the misuse of Hamilton and Trivers, who were not propounding a general theory of human behavior at all. Hamilton was talking about how certain hypothetical genes might win out in a competitive situation in a hypothetical population. He was not talking about how to explain ongoing human customs, something better explained by proximate mechanisms. I have been critical of some current trends and some particular modes of explanation in sociobiology, but I am obviously supportive of the general effort if not of its imperial ambitions.

Walter: Even though you don't buy into the reproductive-fitness-maximization mode of explanation and, in fact, much of your work doesn't have anything to do with sociobiological themes at all, you still seem to get classified as a sociobiologist.

Fox: It is a guilt-by-association thing. I am not a sociobiologist, at least not in the sense in which it is currently used by the people who call themselves such. Although I am interested in what they do, and I think they are onto something that is very important, I see it as only one branch, one part of the much larger ongoing enterprise of the evolution of social behavior.

Some of the books I have written, such as the *Tory Islanders* (1978), have nothing to do with ethology at all, at least in the sense of sociobiology. Perhaps in some sense it is ethological: a study of the territorial, kinship, dominance, and aggressive behavior of a group of primates on an island. That these are *Homo sapiens* and that they speak a language are interesting facts about these primates, and so in this sense it is a piece of primatology. I say something whimsical about this in the preface, but in a narrow sense the book is a pure piece of social anthropology.

WALTER: You have said that your research on Tory Island is the best thing you have done—what you are most proud of, in fact. What took you to Tory in the first place? Was it anything to do with your Irish ancestry?

FOX: Very much so. I was always fascinated with the Irish thing. I spent a lot of time there and had quite an Irish identification. At Exeter sociology was administered by the philosophy department, and the head was Dan O'Connor, who, besides being an Irishman, was a good linguistic philosopher. Together we tried to learn Gaelic from those old 78-rpm Linguaphone records. I got the idea of doing fieldwork on bilingualism in the West of Ireland from him. I was still interested in Sapir-Whorf and wondered how it worked out in a community with two different languages. But once I got to Tory I found I had an ethnographic goldmine. Tory was virgin territory, anthropologically speaking. They were not like the Aran Islanders at all. They were a stubborn northern bunch with folkways all their own. We hit it off immediately. It was a singing culture, and I literally sang my way into it.

WALTER: I've heard that you played a trick there on another visiting anthropologist.

FOX: Yes. He was there for a week, and our little joke was to have the islanders present me to him as a monolingual simpleton who had never left the island. Eventually, I broke down and told him the truth. I think that's why he didn't stay on. But he too was fascinated with the differences between these remote islanders and the rest of Ireland. They got away with things that neither church nor state would put up with elsewhere.

WALTER: Like what?

FOX: Like the business of married couples not living together, for example, or the ignoring of land laws in the inheritance of land. Not paying taxes was another widespread custom. They also defied the church in a manner virtually unknown on the mainland. The curates that were sent there sat lightly on the community.

WALTER: How did you come to do a study of kinship and land tenure?

FOX: What interested me initially was the political situation in Donegal and the place of the Tory swing vote in a marginal constituency. They wielded uncommon power by means of it. But I got too involved in knowledge of a dangerous kind involving IRA activities and had to drop it, and so I took up the kinship and land tenure stuff instead. I was pushed by Meyer Fortes to examine the whole living-apart phenomenon as an example of the domestic cycle. In doing so I think I challenged his contention that the consanguineal household was a product of matrilineal descent. Nevertheless, Meyer was pleased. I had kept my credentials straight with him, and this mattered a great deal to me. The book is my pure piece of social anthropology.

WALTER: *The Red Lamp of Incest* (1983), on the other hand, directly addressed the origins of society in the contexts of primate social organization and hominid evolution.

FOX: *The Red Lamp of Incest* is difficult to describe. Nelson Graburn called it my "mini magnum opus." Many actually think from its title that the book must be about incest. This is a little like assuming that *The Golden Bough* must be about arboriculture. In other words, you shouldn't judge a book by its title—which is why, when the paperback came out, I put in the subtitle "A Study of the Origins of Mind and Society." That is really what it is about; incest is only incidental to this. Virgil's golden bough got Frazer into the whole thing about mythology, and the incest taboo gets me into the evolution of inhibition and consequently the origins of thought, specifically totemic-type thought, and consequently the relations between thought and society. The book is about Durkheim's problem concerning the relation of the individual mind to the social mind, but people don't usually get that far.

WALTER: Do you just mean anthropologists or everyone?

FOX: The people who really got it were people in literature. Several have come out with books based on *The Red Lamp of Incest* much as Lionel Trilling took up Freud and T. S. Eliot took up Frazer. Where the anthropologists dumped Freud and Frazer, the literary people took them up. I think the same thing is happening with *The Red Lamp of Incest*. The anthropologists are paying it no attention because they don't get the argument, and the literary people who do are coming up with all sorts of work on drama and myth that draws heavily on this as a source for their ideas.

WALTER: Is there someone in particular who has responded well to the book?

FOX: There is an extraordinary book by Dudley Young, called *Origins of the Sacred* (1991), which is one of the most interesting pieces of work done on myth since Joseph Campbell. He uses the theory I developed in *The Red Lamp of Incest* as the backbone for his notions of the role of myth and drama in human life.

WALTER: What would you say your major contribution to anthropology has been?

FOX: That's always a dangerous one to answer. It's much easier to have people say it about one. It is hard for me to say, because I know the things that have interested me the most, but I don't necessarily know the things that have had the most influence. I know the books that have sold the most. *Kinship and Marriage* has sold the most books in the most languages. It is still selling. I don't know who is buying it, and I don't know what it is being used for. I think it is being used for introductory classes in anthropology, which are always ten or twenty years behind the times. They haven't caught up with the fact that kinship isn't in fashion anymore.

WALTER: But would you agree that your work on kinship has been your most important contribution?

FOX: To anthropology proper, yes. I started by trying to reanalyze the logical basis of kinship systems, moved on to the question of change in kinship systems, then to the derivation of human kinship systems from primate kinship, and finally, most recently, to the issue of conflict between kin organizations and the state in modern history (1993). I even try to reinstate the importance of the avunculate as the most crucial element of human kinship.

WALTER: In fact, you discuss the avunculate in terms of its being a primate pattern of association.

FOX: Well, I find the roots of it there. When we take Lévi-Strauss's atom of kinship to pieces, we don't have the incest taboo as the foundation of society; we don't have the nuclear family as the foundation of society; we don't have exchange as the foundation of society. What we are left with, in fact, is the avunculate. So I take a serious look at what my colleagues will probably find breathtakingly stupid: that the foundation of human culture is based on the relation of the sister and brother and sister's sons.

WALTER: Would you say, then, that your major contribution to the study of human kinship has been to trace its links to primate kinship from an ethological and evolutionary point of view and to derive the differences between the two, thus tracing the emergence of human forms of kinship?

FOX: I guess you could say that.

WALTER: Why do you think the *American Anthropologist* responded so positively to *The Violent Imagination* (1989b)?

FOX: This was fascinating to me, because I never intended *The Violent Imagination* to be seen as a contribution to anthropology; it is something I wrote on the side. I do think it is a contribution to an understanding of the human condition. In that sense it is, very broadly speaking, anthropology—but in that broad sense everything is anthropology. It was verse, historical drama, dialogue, satire—but the *American Anthropologist* did say, "If there was ever a book that showed how there is another way to 'say' anthropology, this is it." In other words, they took it as a sort of paradigm for humanistic anthropology, which is not what I intended at all because I really do not recognize that distinction. I said in the beginning of the book that what we ought to be aiming at is a raised consciousness that simply doesn't see or recognize this distinction between humanism and science. So I was rather taken aback by this sudden acceptance into the bosom of humanistic anthropology, especially since I spend so much time poking fun at it, accusing the humanists of being too lazy to do science.

WALTER: Do you think its reception is due to the popularity of hermeneutics and deconstruction in anthropology today?

FOX: Maybe, but I don't find much of either in there—certainly not consciously. I mean, we have been deconstructing all our lives, all of us; we have all done our share of deconstruction. Goldenweiser's analysis of totemism in 1910 was a brilliant piece of deconstruction. Deconstruction is not a new thing in that sense. It is the uses to which it is being put which are new.

WALTER: How do you feel about the various directions that anthropology is taking today?

FOX: I think the major problem with anthropology today is the fragmentation that has taken such a deadly grip. The career structure is such that you can make it only if you specialize in some area. You cannot be a synthesist. You cannot be a holistic anthropologist. There is simply no way kids can do it these days, the way we could. I think we could in our day when everything was open to you and nothing was politically incorrect and you could go anywhere you pleased. It just doesn't happen that way today. The possibility is there with individuals; some individuals will do this. I think that anthropology as it is taught is very valuable because it may turn up these individuals. It may turn up a systematic kind of approach that would do away with the barrier between humanism and science to produce scientists with humanistic imaginations and humanists with scientific skills. It is like Snow's two cultures, except I don't think teaching poets the second law of thermodynamics is necessarily the way to deal with this. I think anthropology is a better way to go because anthropology deals with both cultures in the same framework: all the sensitivity of the humanities towards things human while at the same time using the power of the scientific approach. It was my hope to develop a scientific humanism in the real sense—a discipline that would consist of scientific and humanistic imaginations, a discipline where this barrier is not recognized. If I tried to do anything positive with my anthropological life, it was to try to show how an anthropologist could be both. These were not considered incompatible virtues in the Renaissance. But we have lost that—partly out of the necessity of specialization, partly out of intellectual laziness. It seemed to me that anthropology was one of the few disciplines where there was the possibility of making some sort of progress along these lines.

WALTER: As the scientific and humanistic subdisciplines within anthropology part ways, the idea of an overarching anthropology that can encompass all the human sciences becomes less feasible. Does the increasing partitioning of anthropology into subdisciplines portend the end of anthropology? Could we parcel anthropology out to the different sciences and humanities and make anthropology disappear?

RW: I think that is what is going to happen. Nevertheless, anthropology as we now know it will stumble on through sheer inertia. There are all those people who still have tenure, and they are going to be there for a long time. What is the university going to do with them? I was recently reading Richard Rorty, who beautifully demonstrates that there is nothing left for philosophy to do but says that there will always be jobs because someone has to stick around and teach the old philosophers and why they are wrong. I think in anthropology it is the same. They are going to be around teaching anthropology through sheer inertia, but as an intellectual force it is disintegrating and will continue to disintegrate. There has been a rather sad attempt by the *Anthropology Newsletter* to promote the four-field approach as still alive and vigorous. The four-field model is still useful as a teaching device, but it is not alive as an intellectual movement as it was in the 1920s and 30s, during the extraordinary golden age of anthropology.

There will always be individuals who will pursue issues across disciplinary boundaries. I have never let the fact that I am an anthropologist put limits on where I would search for answers to the questions that I was interested in. If the questions took me into brain evolution or cognitive science or, for that matter, constitutional law, that's where I've gone. You asked why I left England. What I objected to was the notion of "That's not done"—that your curiosity must stop at this point, that you can be curious about kinship systems but you can't be curious about primate kinship systems, that that's where our discipline draws the line. The world is not divided into realities called sociology, biology, psychology, and anthropology. Those are just convenient labels adopted in the nineteenth century by academic departments in the burgeoning universities, and we are stuck with them. There will always be people who won't accept these boundary distinctions, and this is where the hope lies. It lies in individuals, not in disciplines.

The big mistake of my life has been to assume that the hope lies in the discipline. The more I read current works in anthropology, the more depressed I become with it as a discipline. There is no sense to it as a discipline. Nevertheless, it still seems worthwhile to me to keep it going as a teaching operation, simply because by bringing young minds into contact with things as diverse as brain evolution, on the one hand, and the symbolic qualities of flower arrangements in Japan, on the other, you make students put those things together in their heads and you at least pay lip service to the idea that this is all one discipline. Let us pretend that this is one discipline to students, because some of them may get sparked up and we might produce a humanistic scientist. With enough of these the "science of man" could eventually be realized.

WALTER: What occupies you at present?

FOX: I have developed a fondness for archaeology. I visit the Florida Gulf Coast regularly to study the sites of the Calusa kingdom—one of the most remarkable in North America. The shift from the Paleolithic to the Neolithic fascinates me especially in regard to the question of increasing social complexity. I think the future of scientific anthropology may well be in archaeology.

WALTER: Do you plan to become a full-time archaeologist?

FOX: I'll never be a full-time anything.

References

Ayer, A.J. 1954. *Language, Truth, and Logic*, 2nd edition. London: Gollancz.

Fox, Robin. 1962. "Sibling Incest." *British Journal of Sociology* 13:128–50.

————. 1967a. *Kinship and Marriage*. London: Penguin.

————. 1967b. *The Keresan Bridge*. London: Athlone Press.

————. editor. 1975. *Biosocial Anthropology*. London: Malaby Press.

————. 1978. *The Tory Islanders: A People of the Celtic Fringe*. Cambridge: Cambridge University Press. 2nd ed. Notre Dame University Press, 1995.

————. 1983. *The Red Lamp of Incest: An Inquiry into the Origins of Mind and Society*, 2nd edition. Notre Dame, IN: University of Notre Dame Press.

————. 1989a. *The Search for Society: Quest for a Biosocial Science and Morality*. New Brunswick, NJ: Rutgers University Press.

————. 1989b. *The Violent Imagination*. New Brunswick, NJ: Rutgers University Press.

————. 1993. *Reproduction and Succession: Studies in Anthropology, Law, and Society*. New Brunswick, NJ: Transaction Publishers.

————. 1994. *The Challenge of Anthropology: Old Encounters and New Excursions*. New Brunswick, NJ: Transaction Publishers.

Frazer, James G. 1911–15. *The Golden Bough*, 3rd edition, 12 vols. London: Macmillan.

Mehler, Jacques, and Robin Fox, editors. 1985. *Neonate Cognition*. Hillsdale, NJ: Erlbaum.

Radcliffe-Brown, A. R. 1952. *Structure and Function in Primitive Society*. London: Cohen and West.

Skinner, B.F. 1971. *Beyond Freedom and Dignity*. New York: Alfred A. Knopf.

Tiger, Lionel and Robin Fox. 1971. *The Imperial Animal*. New York: Holt, Rinehart and Wilson.

————. 1966. "The Zoological Perspective in the Social Sciences." *Man* 11:75–81.

Wells, H.G. 1951. *The Outline of History*, revised edition. London: Cassell.

Wilson, E.O. 1975. *Sociobiology*. Cambridge, MA: Harvard University Press.

Young, Dudley. 1991. *Origins of the Sacred*. New York: St. Martin's Press.

Epilogue

What the Shaman Saw

Incident at Lascaux, circa 15,000 B.P.

(To the Memory of Matthew Arnold)

Coolness of the spirit cave
spluttering oil wicks   ochre   soot
        spread and stencil   line and grave
cold wet floor-clay underfoot
        twang of bowstring   bison gut
                dead painted deer
                good hunting year
        a walking protein glut

Song by lamplight   frightened eyes
strobe-like flickers   frescoed bulls
        boys to men through shaman cries
scars and paint and bear-cult skulls
        twittering lads like nervous gulls
                seize the spear
                stab painted deer
        Magnetic manhood pulls

Yet all must make the female sign
and stroke the pregnant bison cow
        leave handprint and a male design
so culture will not disavow
        the natural union   but allow
                cult-making man
                into the plan
        that Nature must endow

Nothing severed   all is joined
boy to man and man to maid
nothing natural purloined
only borrowed   then relayed
through ritual and magic aid
with calm recourse
back to the source
that started the cascade

For what is killed is born again
and what is born again must die
The round of metabolic strain
that shaman seeks to signify
while searching with his inner eye
tracing on walls
of painted halls
that never see the sky

Emerging from the painted dark
savage sunlight sears his eyes
a blazing flash   a sudden spark
a spike of terror and surprise
unfolds the future centuries
in vision sought
now dearly bought
as penalty and prize

He sees the wheel and then the cart
and then the metal cart of war
the stirrup and the lancer's art
the cloven bodies by the score
the thousands and the tens and more
of thousands lying
twisted dying
on his valley floor

He knows that warriors fight and die
for he has fought and he has killed
    but never has he seen the sky
with blackened smoke of bodies filled
        and lime-white pits with corpses spilled
            like reindeer pinned
            but dressed and skinned
        by ranks precision drilled

        He used to hear the drumming feet
of star-drawn herds on summer nights
    but now he sees a crowded street
and human herds and city lights
        that overwhelm the hunting sites
            deny the space
            the ungulate grace
        requires for its delights

        Neon flare blocks out his moon
while spreading towns obscure the grass
        This transformation came too soon
yet he intuits it will pass
        this anti-nature reel en masse
            beneath the need
            of its own speed
        surpassing to surpass

        Fanatics rage and millions die
while millions more are born and scream
        Their birth song is a hunger cry
a lifetime is a pointless dream
        as driven to a mad extreme
            they quicken pace
            reduce the space
        pollute the human stream

The herds are gone   the forest felled
the tribes are scattered   few survive
The trampling billions have expelled
the hunters   and the cities strive
like cancers mindlessly to thrive
consuming that
sustaining fat
they need to stay alive

Yet still they shout the shining hope
(a hope the shaman does not share)
that science will expand its scope
and ingenuity will spare
the victims from that final scare
its bag of tricks
a magic fix
the ultimate repair

They craved the tyranny of things
worshipped the icon of ideas
deified and destroyed their kings
embalmed   entombed   despoiled their fears
and yet could never stop their ears
against the sound
from ancient ground
of faint   forbidden tears

The shaman sees the fabric rent
the contract broken   nothing gained
the treasury of Nature spent
the sacred lake of Nature drained
the seething numbers uncontained
the losing race
the shrieking pace
that cannot be sustained

He turns in sorrow to the cave
the vision gone   the darkness deep
The painted world he cannot save
he leaves to its extended sleep
We of his vision now who peep
with awe and fear
can faintly hear
the phantom of him weep

Index